A Prince of a Boy

ALSO BY BRIAN MCNAUGHT

Books

A Disturbed Peace—Selected Writings of an Irish Catholic Homosexual
On Being Gay—Thoughts on Family, Faith, and Love
Gay Issues in the Workplace
Now That I'm Out, What Do I Do?—Thoughts on Living Deliberately
"Sex Camp"
Are You Guys Brothers?
Brian McNaught's Guide to LGBTQ Issues in the Workplace
Two Guys and a Dog Make a Family
Grogg is a Frog Without Polliwogs
"What's 'Gay'?" Asked Mae
Professor Tuttle's Lesson on Friendship
The Lincoln Chronicles—Puppy Wisdom for Happy Living
The Lincoln Chronicles—A Young Dog's View of Life
On Being Gay and Gray—Our Stories, Gifts, and the Meaning of Our Lives

DVDs

A Conversation with Brian McNaught on Being Gay
Gay Issues in the Workplace
Growing Up Gay and Lesbian
Homophobia in the Workplace
Gay/Straight—Can We Talk?
Understanding and Managing Gay and Transgender Issues in the Workplace
Anyone Can Be an Ally—Speaking Up for an LGBT Inclusive Workplace

Films

"What's 'Gay'?" Asked Mae—Award-winning three-minute animated film by Mark Schoen at Sex Smart Films

Podcasts

"Are You Happy Without the Movie?"

Syndicated Columns

A Disturbed Peace
Two Guys and a Dog
The Wise Snowy Owl

A Prince of a Boy

How One Gay Catholic Helped Change the World

Brian McNaught

CASCADE Books • Eugene, Oregon

A PRINCE OF A BOY
How One Gay Catholic Helped Change the World

Copyright © 2024 Brian McNaught. All rights reserved. Except for brief quotations in critical publications or reviews, no part of this book may be reproduced in any manner without prior written permission from the publisher. Write: Permissions, Wipf and Stock Publishers, 199 W. 8th Ave., Suite 3, Eugene, OR 97401.

Cascade Books
An Imprint of Wipf and Stock Publishers
199 W. 8th Ave., Suite 3
Eugene, OR 97401

www.wipfandstock.com

PAPERBACK ISBN: 979-8-3852-0395-6
HARDCOVER ISBN: 979-8-3852-0396-3
EBOOK ISBN: 979-8-3852-0397-0

Cataloguing-in-Publication data:

Names: McNaught, Brian.

Title: A prince of a boy : how one gay catholic helped change the world / Brian McNaught.

Description: Eugene, OR: Cascade Books, 2024

Identifiers: ISBN 979-8-3852-0395-6 (paperback) | ISBN 979-8-3852-0396-3 (hardcover) | ISBN 979-8-3852-0397-0 (ebook)

Subjects: LCSH: Brian McNaught (1948–) | Gay men—United States—Biography | Catholics—United States—Biography

Classification: HQ75.8.M36 2024 (paperback) | HQ75.8.M36 (ebook)

VERSION NUMBER 12/06/24

I dedicate this book with gratitude to the Spirit that flows through us all, enabling our personal evolutions to the awareness that we are one Divine entity.

It's also dedicated to all the people in my life who have helped bring me to this grand stage the synergy between my relation to the Divine and the celebration of my sexuality.

My stories will naturally be different from theirs, but there are many millions of people today, and throughout history, who found that their spiritual hunger, combined with the truth of their life experiences, put them at odds with the teachings of their church, synagogue, mosque, or other institution of religion. We who have made "the hero's journey" to the serenity of liberation must tell our stories because that is how the Universe manifests itself and the world is healed.

This is one such story with many players.

He's a Prince of a Boy
—Sister Claire Marie, IHM, 1962

Contents

Acknowledgments | ix
Introduction | xiii

Chapter One   "He's a Prince of a Boy" | 1
Chapter Two   Can I Be Both Gay and Catholic? | 8
Chapter Three   I Was One of Five Who Lived | 15
Chapter Four   Learning About Sex from Jokes | 18
Chapter Five   On Stage in Second Grade | 25
Chapter Six   I Want a "Do Over" for My First Sexual Experience | 32
Chapter Seven   Gay and Catholic, Both and Not | 37
Chapter Eight   My First Love Was an Episcopal Priest | 45
Chapter Nine   The First Conference on Homosexuality and the Church | 52
Chapter Ten   "He Came Out of Nowhere" | 57
Chapter Eleven   Creating a Home and a Family | 70
Chapter Twelve   "Dear Anita" | 76
Chapter Thirteen   How and Why My Message Changed | 81
Chapter Fourteen   Five Queers and Me | 89
Chapter Fifteen   The Mayor's Gay Liaison | 102
Chapter Sixteen   Four Great Responses, and a Death Wish | 110
Chapter Seventeen   Are You Cuddling with Me, Malcolm? | 115

Chapter Eighteen   Was Jesus Fully Man? | 118
Chapter Nineteen   "Stop This Shit" | 123
Chapter Twenty   First Workshop on Gay Workplace Issues | 127
Chapter Twenty-One   Use What the Universe Gives You | 136
Chapter Twenty-Two   "I Don't Know What to Do With You." | 141
Chapter Twenty-Three   Me, Maya, and Intimacy | 147
Chapter Twenty-Four   Same Heart Beats in Tokyo and Mumbai | 152
Chapter Twenty-Five   What's Your Music? | 160
Chapter Twenty-Six   Sex In and Out of Camp | 166
Chapter Twenty-Seven   Facing the Fear of Straight Men | 172
Chapter Twenty-Eight   Manifesting the Result of the Work | 176
Chapter Twenty-Nine   Say the Words, Then "Thank You" | 183
Chapter Thirty   Would You Take a Pill to Make You Straight? | 188

Glossary of Terms | 197
About the Author | 201

Acknowledgments

As has been true for every book, magazine article, column, and Facebook post I've written, my husband Ray Struble is the first person to see them, offer suggestions, and give me an enthusiastic "thumbs-up." He is also the rudder in my life who helps keep me sailing smoothly and in the correct direction.

The impetus behind this memoir is my college sweetheart and dear friend, Charlene Gaynor, who knows me as well as anyone, although she admits to learning in this book things about me that she didn't know. But she was the one who kept saying, "You need to write your memoir. I want to know what you were thinking and feeling when you first stood before a college and corporate audience."

My younger brother Tom, whom I'm once again allowed to call "Tommy," has been an invaluable help in prompting me with the correct times, names, and circumstances for our childhood experiences. He also knows many of my stories and has reminded me of those which merit inclusion. As is true with Charlene, Tommy is an excellent writer and editor.

My good friend Bill Konigsberg, a highly successful author, gave me the very best advice to just keep writing, and to go back when I'd run out of storyline to see what I'd written and how I wanted to add to or subtract from it.

My colleague and soulmate Pam Wilson worked tirelessly on superbly copyediting every sentence in every chapter and did her best to prepare and calm me before I saw all the red lines through entire paragraphs. Breathe, Brian.

My new friend, who I wish I could have known sooner, Toby Johnson, is a prophetic author on Gay spirituality and has given me invaluable guidance on this book. His wisdom and maturity are reflected on these pages.

My corps of readers, who were asked to give me feedback on the tone, clarity, and level of interest in this memoir have been a great source of challenge and comfort. They include dear friends Carol Dopp, Lesley Jones, Diane Magnum, Michael Vita, Joe Kort, Steve Moyer, Joseph McCormack, Sheila Landers, Deb Dagit, Jean McGlynn, Bill Baird, Bill and Kathy Stayton, Piet Lammert, Ron Robin, Joseph Sankovich, Ronni Sanlo, Tim Retzloff, David Bouford, Bill Glenn, Tih Penfils, and Hayley Evans. My gratitude to my copy editor at Cascade, Stephanie Hough, for her most helpful guidance.

A Prince of a Boy

Introduction
What Does Your Obit Say?

WITH FRIENDS I'LL OFTEN ask, "What would you like the first line of your obit to say?" The question helps focus what we feel is the most significant thing about our lives.

People in their twenties or thirties often think about an accomplishment in which they take the most pride. "... made a million dollars before he was twenty." "... climbed Mt. Everest at age twenty-five."

Middle-aged people often think of their children, or perhaps something they did that made a difference in the lives of others. "... was a devoted wife and proud mother." "... worked at the Red Cross for thirty years."

Those of us over the age of sixty-five might focus on our lives from a different angle, thinking more about our personal growth. "... a man of faith but few words."

I'd like my obit to say, "... known for being kind." Loving kindness is what enables us to sing the song we were meant to sing and to help others do the same. It manifests itself well in the telling of our stories, and in listening intently to the stories of others, even from those we feel are the most difficult to like. Once they're allowed to express their anger and hatred, perhaps even of us, we find that behind the bluster beats the same heart, and the soul that links us as one.

Many years ago, on the screened porch of our summer home on Tupper Lake, in the six-million-acre Adirondack State Park of New York, an in-law niece who I imagined would be the least interested in my life's work, asked me after dinner, when the plates had been cleared, "You've been around the world. Will you please tell me how you got from being fired for being Gay to being asked to speak in all those countries?" Surprisingly, it was the first time anyone had ever asked for the whole story. Lori Beth sat and listened to me for two hours.

My husband, Ray Struble, loving, devoted, and patient partner of forty-eight years, and I are both Midwestern Irish Catholics from families of seven. Our whole worlds were centered on the church well after college. Ray, whose obit should also begin with the word "kind," went into religious life to be of service to others. I did the same. After college, I did my alternative service for the Selective Service as a conscientious objector to the American war in Vietnam at the Catholic newspaper in Detroit. As a guy who loved to write and who loved the church, I was in heaven.

When I came out, I was fired for being Gay and that started a career path that tapped my best talents and enabled me to practice loving kindness to all others. I told my story to anyone who was interested, and probably to many who weren't, and I have listened to their feelings. That's how I helped change the world. Anyone can do it, and I believe we're all called to be the window of God's light.

I knew I was Catholic before I knew I was Gay, but for not too long a time. I could say I was Catholic and know it was not only safe to say it but welcomed. I couldn't safely do so with my attractions to men. But, once I did, my being Gay was more relevant to college and corporate audiences than my being Catholic. Ray made it possible for me to do the work I did, especially in the beginning when I wasn't paid to speak and was given a pittance to write.

If you've got the time, I'd love for you to sit with me on the screened porch here and learn how I helped change the world and came to fully know and love myself. I hope it helps you sing your song as it did me.

Chapter One

"He's a Prince of a Boy"

When Ray, my roommate and boyfriend, was taking a class in paranormal psychology at Boston College, there was a weekend Psychic Fair. For $15 you got to sit with three psychics, astrologers, or mediums, among others, for five minutes each. It seemed that everyone who attended raved about a guy from New Jersey who told you your future.

When I entered his tent, he said, "Sit with me and give me your hand." I did as instructed without delay. We both closed our eyes.

"I'm not going to tell you about your future," he said after a minute, eyes now open. "I'm going to tell you about your past."

"Okay," I replied, a bit surprised but curious.

"Throughout your past lives you've been a healer—a high priest, a witch doctor, a medicine man, and a shaman, among others."

I was delighted and shocked. I didn't know whether I believed in past lives, but a tingle of recognition went up and down my spine. This stranger was affirming for me my hope and belief not that I was ever a high priest, but that in this life, despite de facto excommunication from the Catholic Church, and rejection by anti-religious elements of the Gay community's leadership, I was nevertheless a channel of God's healing love.

I believe we all are called to be so, but we manifest it differently. My light, I aspired, would shine on both the church and on the Gay community. This has been and is also true for hundreds of thousands of Gay and Lesbian people of all faiths all over the world. "How do I reconcile my faith, my sexuality, and my calling to serve humankind?" At the time I came out in 1974, my friend Bill Johnson became the first minister in any denomination to be ordained in modern times as an openly Gay man. That was in the United Church of Christ. But the Presbyterian Church at the time denied ordination to two Lesbian friends of mine, Sandy Brawders and Selisse Berry. They both went on to do great things. And they weren't the only ones by far.

"Can you see anything about my future?" I asked quickly, knowing my time with him was limited.

"I see you speaking before large audiences, and" as an afterthought, "you're going to write a book and help change the world."

"Wow! Thank you."

At that time in my life, I was regularly speaking to large college audiences around the country about what it is like to grow up as a Gay person. Former congressman and Gay icon Barney Frank said of me, "No one has done a better job of chronicling what it is like to grow up Gay." There was also a collection of my Gay newspaper columns and magazine articles that were to be published under the title, *A Disturbed Peace— Selected Writings of an Irish Catholic Homosexual*. Was the five-minute session with this psychic a coincidence, a fluke? I don't know, but I want to believe he picked up a vibration from me which he recognized.

Since childhood, I've aspired to be like the saints the good sisters told us about in grade school, saints such as Tarcisius and Maria Goretti. Tarcisius was beaten to death by boys his age for not revealing the consecrated bread he hid under his tunic at the priest's instruction. This, of course, supported my caution of being around super macho straight boys. Maria Goretti was murdered for refusing a sexual assault.

As I grew older, I was especially drawn to St. Francis of Assisi, the gentle son of a rich man who left behind everything in order to serve others. Could I not do the same? Would I not do the same? Not long ago, a clairvoyant energy guide, Hayley Evans, with whom I now co-host bimonthly podcasts ("Are You Happy Without the Movie?") told me at the beginning of our first conversation that St. Francis was my spiritual guide and guardian. Where did that come from? How would she know? Was it a coincidence?

Since kindergarten, I've also known that I was drawn to handsome older boys or men, most mesmerized by those who had hair on their chest. The first experience I had of the innocence of my religious beliefs intersecting with the innocence of my physical attractions was when I saw a picture of St. Sebastian. He hung near naked from a pole, pierced with arrows. Was it okay to be both inspired by, and physically drawn to him? Was it a sin to wish his loin cloth would fall? And, if the sister said it was a sin, did that mean God truly disapproved? Who could I ask? My parents? My younger brother, Tommy, with whom I shared a bedroom? It turns out he was a friend of St. Sebastian, too, but was afraid to tell me, or Mom and Dad. St. Sebastian is now unofficially considered "the patron saint of Gay men," not because of his sexual orientation but because he was a magnet for multitudes of other little Gay Catholic boys.

As was true for nearly every Gay boy in every country of the world, I knew throughout my childhood that I was different because of my being drawn to cute boys my age, and to dashing older men. I would tell audiences everywhere that the horror of growing up Gay is having a secret you're afraid to tell anyone for fear they won't love you anymore. That's true in Singapore, Tokyo, and Mumbai.

But I also felt different because I could tell what people were feeling, and I was strongly pulled to help them if I sensed they were in need. I was told that I was an "old soul." Was there a conflict between both my intense drives of sexuality and my spirituality? Did they repel each other's pull, or could they be in sync? While I knew saying that I was attracted to men's bodies and their energy wasn't a safe thing to do, I've never felt these attractions were a sin for which I'd be punished. I trusted three things—that God was always with me, that I liked shirtless, handsome men, and that I wanted to be saintlike. I've also always known not to mention the latter to others either.

Some of my happiest moments as a youngster, and still as an adult, were in church in quiet prayer. Not too long ago, I was transfixed while standing in the extraordinary back chapel of St. Mary's Basilica at the University of Notre Dame. The unique beauty of the nineteenth-century stained glass and French-style painting on the walls and ceiling touched my heart deeply. The whispers I have welcomed in my soul since early childhood I heard quite clearly there, encouraging me to continue to be of service to others, to be nice and to be kind. My siblings would tell you that I often failed miserably at that. But mostly, it was true, and it made me stand out.

In seventh grade, Fr. Bush, the pastor of Holy Family Church, drove me from Grand Blanc, Michigan to St. John's Seminary in Detroit. He thought that I would be a good priest. I also felt that priesthood was my vocation, but how did I tell Fr. Bush that I was attracted to him and to the seminarians? "Ah, Father, do you like watching wrestling?" "Hey, Father, did you think that seminarian named Buck was handsome?" Are there priests who are attracted to men, I wondered?

In eighth grade, in Birmingham, Michigan, Sr. Claire Marie, IHM (Sisters of the Immaculate Heart of Mary) pulled my mother aside to tell her that she felt I was "a prince of a boy." While it was nice to hear that from Mom, I didn't know exactly what it meant. Did Sister Claire Marie say that because I was well-behaved? Nice? Funny? Or did she see in me a vibration as the empathetic soul I aspired and imagined myself to be?

In high school, we were given the Kuder Career Preference Test. When the results were tabulated, I was pulled aside by the guidance counselor and told that I got the highest score recorded for social work. The Christian Brothers of Ireland, my teachers at Brother Rice, gave me a tour of their living quarters when I verbalized my interest in religious life, and when I graduated, they unanimously selected me to receive the Christian Leadership Award. I was both grateful and anxious, with good reason. My name was taken off the plaque when I publicly came out as a Gay man eight years later. It has since been reinstated because of the insistence of one Straight guy, the track coach, Bob Stark, who was two years ahead of me. Not once but twice he had new name plates made up and kept replacing them when removed. But could Brian McNaught be both a homosexual and a Catholic "saint" in his desires? Even more basically, could I even be a Gay Irish Catholic? At the end of one of my corporate presentations on Gay issues in the workplace, a woman came up to me and sternly said, "I don't like you saying that you're Irish Catholic. I'm Irish Catholic and you don't represent me." "I could tell them I'm Jewish," I replied with a smile. She was unappeased.

When I left the tent of the psychic back in Boston in 1979, as short as my stay with him was, I felt understood and affirmed as a healer. It was a message I kept getting from others in my life. Ray was the first person I talked to about the words of the psychic, and he didn't laugh. He also saw my work as an educator and counselor on Gay, Lesbian, Bisexual, and Transgender issues as a ministry of healing.

Ray aspired to be a minister, too, and had studied to be a priest of the Holy Cross Congregation. He majored in psychology when he was in the seminary. He wanted to be a therapist, helping others, and he was that and more when he ended up on Wall Street with a rainbow flag in the pencil holder on his desk, the first openly Gay man on any bank's trading floor. Ray was a minister in investment banking as a role model and as an educator of his peers.

In 1979, I was a very nice, polite, thoughtful, but "notorious" thirty-one-year-old Gay man who had moved three years before from Detroit to Boston after being very publicly fired by the Catholic newspaper there for affirming in *The Detroit News* that I was Gay. By the time of the psychic fair, I had a syndicated column in the Gay press, had won the award for "Best Magazine Article of the Year" from the Catholic Press Association for "The Sad Dilemma of the Gay Catholic," and my open letter to Anita Bryant had just been published by the Syracuse University Institute for Family Research and Education in their annual magazine, *Impact*.

At that time in the church, John Paul II was preparing for his October 1979 pilgrimage to the United States, visiting six cities, including Boston. Gay, Lesbian, and Bisexual Americans had our first national March on Washington. I was on the big outdoor stage representing Dignity, the national organization, with local chapters, of Gay, Lesbian, Bisexual, and Transgender Catholics. Each Gay faith group had a representative, and we were each allotted a short time to speak.

A minister from the Metropolitan Community Church (MCC) went first. MCC, founded by the Rev. Troy Perry in 1968, is an international denomination with its focus on the spiritual lives of LGBTQ Christians. This minister felt inspired to speak about racism, with the hope of healing rifts in the community. She ended up taking all the time allotted for us, so no one else from the other religious caucuses got to speak. Two years earlier, I was inspired to say something that I hoped would help heal and inspire others, and I had no time limit.

"Dear Anita—Late Night Thoughts of an Irish Catholic Homosexual," I wrote in the evening of June 7, 1977, the day the voters in Dade County, Florida, rescinded the protections against discrimination of Gay people. The very personal letter, which I typed clickety-clack with two fingers on my old Underwood, described in intimate detail what it was like to grow up as a Gay man, and how Anita Bryant's campaign had negatively impacted me, and every Gay person I knew. In the letter, I asked Anita to imagine the possibility that her son Bob Jr. was Gay. (We now know that Bob Jr. is the father of Anita's Lesbian granddaughter who invited Anita to her Gay wedding.)

In part I wrote: "I knew we were going to lose in Dade County because people don't understand what 'Gay pride' is about. They mistakenly see it as one more threat to stable American life. But if you and your family experienced the real psychological terror that Bob Jr. would go through as a homosexual you would understand what this 'Gay civil rights movement' is all about.

"It's a primal scream, Anita, by millions of people who want to live. It's an angry denunciation of all the lies which have been heaped upon us for as long as we can remember. It is a pleading to Straight society to refrain from forcing us to live in shadows of self-hate. What could be more inhumane?

"Gay civil rights are human civil rights . . ."

The New York Times Magazine had said they were going to publish the piece in 1977, but I suspect my father, through his connections with the press from his job as a General Motors public relations executive, when GM was the largest corporation in the world, had something to do with the article never getting seen in the *Times*. But when it did get printed by *Impact*, it got a lot of attention, including a call from the executive director of Anita Bryant Ministries. Anita wanted me to know that she had read the article, liked it, and wished to respond.

Shortly thereafter, I was flown down to Miami to debate on a popular local television show the head of Anita Bryant Ministries' conversion therapy program. The man's name was John Hansen, who proudly pointed out his two sons in the studio audience. John acknowledged his homosexual attractions, but said it was a very lonely lifestyle that he would never succumb to again. Not long ago, I heard from John's Transgender granddaughter that despite his assurances he would never again act on his sexual impulses, he finally accepted himself, and affirmed his homosexuality later in life. Today, I usually expect that to happen to others who live in fear or denial.

A good deal of my time was, and still is, spent responding to those who write or call for help. When I came out in 1974, there weren't a lot of openly Gay people of faith whose name was known nationally. The press coverage on my civil rights battle with the church in Detroit started a flow of letters and calls that have never ended. My address and phone number were easily secured. One Catholic bishop called, as did many priests. I heard from people in the Salvation Army, Southern Baptists, Seventh-day Adventists, Mormons, and from people unaffiliated with any denomination.

One young man wrote me a thirteen-page letter filled with questions. I answered every one, and stayed on the phone with others for as long as it took to have them feel heard and supported. Listening was the key, as was empathy, compassion, and the promise of confidentiality.

At the end of every presentation I made, whether to college students or to a public or corporate audience, I encouraged people to write or call me if they wanted to talk. I did so because I didn't want anyone, Gay or Straight, to feel lost. Some people needed to write and call over a long period of time. I sought to calm their fears and to give them wings with which to fly.

One woman who called and wrote me many years ago, and who insists I saved her life, recently sent me a copy of the first letter I two-finger typed to her following our first phone call after she learned her husband was Gay.

It read in part, "I wish I could be with you in a more personal way . . . but I'm with you and I won't leave you until you are ready to let go. You are right, the story you told me I have heard a hundred times. The details vary from person to person but the frustration, anger, fear is always a constant . . . You're feeling naked and vulnerable right now, and I'm sure very alone . . . But everybody has a story to tell, and if nothing else, this jolting experience will put you in touch with that. The world will not fall apart when your truth is shared . . . Allow yourself to be angry, sad, relieved, shocked, and even happy. The future seems worse than awful, but the same heat that melts butter strengthens steel . . . I want so to hit the key phrase that opens the door you stand before . . . We'll continue to talk and grow. That's a promise."

There were many more phone calls and letters with this person who is now very happily married to the perfect guy and has two adoring children and grandchildren.

All the letters I received are now among my papers in the Cornell University Human Sexuality Archives.

Chapter Two

Can I Be Both Gay and Catholic?

I WAS THE ONE IN the family who used to tie a towel around my neck and pass out Necco wafers to my younger brother and sister. I've never stopped feeling that I was called to be a priest, although my concept of priesthood has become quite fluid. I entered the order of the Christian Brothers of Ireland in the summer between my sophomore and junior year at Marquette University. I stayed for only two months, realizing it wasn't a good fit for me, or for them. Not only was I not well suited for the promise of obedience, but I had also developed a very secret crush on another Christian brother.

Years later, after I came out publicly, I applied to join the Jesuits, but they turned me down. I never applied again to another religious order. I accepted that the official church didn't consider me worthy of ordination, so for less than $100 I became one of 20 million people throughout the world who have been ordained by the Universal Life Church, and I have the laminated minister card to prove it. Feeling that it was silly, I knew nevertheless that I had studied theology as much as any seminarian, and I had a more sophisticated education on sexuality as a certified sexuality educator and counselor. My nephew and niece asked me to baptize their three children, and I performed two marriages. Katie Couric attended one of them on Fire Island, and afterwards punched me lightly in the shoulder and said, "Good job, guy."

It took me nearly fifty years of writing, speaking, and counseling on LGBTQ issues before I truly understood and fully accepted that I am a priest, or at least a minister, as is true for so many, many others like me, consistently in an intimate relationship with God, using every gift I've been given to affirm and celebrate that Lesbian, Gay, Bisexual, Transgender, and Queer people are important parts of God's plan. I also have grown to understand that Gay men, such as myself, have talents and insights to share, based not just on our experiences of dealing with oppression, but also our genetic makeup. This ministry of mine as a window of God's light, I'm often told, has made a big difference in the lives of Gay and Straight people around the world. Helping others in loving kindness is something each of us is called and able to do.

Many individuals, particularly Gay men, have told me how helpful it was for them to have read my first, or second book, *On Being Gay— Thoughts on Family, Faith, and Love*. As Ray will tell you, I don't accept personal credit for the positive influence of my writing or speaking. I deflect. While I'm delighted that something I wrote or said helped others to love themselves, to accept and celebrate the goodness of their sexual orientation or their gender identity, or that of their children, their gratitude was never taken to heart by me as something special that I did. I love to write and to speak to audiences, but whatever brilliance, whatever wisdom that came out of me was totally due to the Spirit, or the Universe, whatever word recognizes a wisdom beyond ourselves.

You don't have to believe in God to identify with my journey. There were moments in my life when I questioned the existence of a higher power. I thought the concept of God being a Holy Trinity was pointless. But I ended up choosing to believe because of my many experiences with the God of my youth, with Jesus, and with the Holy Spirit. Even if you can't prove it, you can't deny the ongoing lessons of your life experiences. For some, that may support their atheism, but not for me.

I heard a great story when I was a closeted Gay Catholic columnist at *The Michigan Catholic*. The priest asked the first graders, "Who can tell me what a 'saint' is?" The little boy in the back row raised his hand, stood, and said confidently, "It's that thing in the church that the light shines through." A minister of the Metropolitan Community Church in Boston once told me that he saw himself as the conscience of the Gay community. That was never my aspiration. I've always hoped to be just the window through which the Light would shine. My full-time job has always been simply to keep the window clean of the dust and smudges of my ego.

If my ego was in charge, it would have spent a lot of time promoting myself, competing with others, and being frustrated as hell that I wasn't getting the recognition I deserved in Gay history books. I've welcomed the thought of obscurity. Yet, all the courageous and steadfast prophetic service of those Gay and Lesbian people who have stayed in their denominations to impact their church's understanding of sexuality is normally ignored by Gay historians. Who and what do these writers imagine made allies out of Straight people around the world?

I've often been asked how I was able to speak to banking executives in Mumbai, Tokyo, and Singapore where no one had spoken before about Lesbian, Gay, Bisexual, and Transgender issues in the workplace. I used to speak for one or two hours without notes and usually had members of the audience laugh and cry and stand and applaud at the end, including the senior leaders at the National Security Agency (NSA). "How were you able to do that? Did you have lessons in public speaking?" "Weren't you afraid?"

No lessons in public speaking but, yes, I was afraid, terrified even, and sick to my stomach, especially in the beginning of this unintended and unchartered career. But, when I finally got on stage, I surrendered to the magic that flowed between me and every audience member. I never felt that I was the source of the tears and smiles in the audience. I have been fortunate enough to be the right Gay man, at the right time in history, in the right place. I feel that God has used me as a balm of healing, and a source of enlightenment for the church, universities, corporations, and others about the injustices and indignities experienced by Lesbian, Gay, Bisexual, Transgender, and Queer people daily and globally.

Being used as an instrument of the Spirit doesn't mean that I didn't get an upset stomach and need to use the restroom just before I spoke, nor that I didn't go back to the hotel and fall exhausted onto the bed, with only Ray to call for comfort. The instrument of God's love is itself very human. The ego comes in as a cheerleader telling me that I can do this. But I prepared for each speaking engagement over these many years not by reflecting on what had been accomplished to date, but rather by reading to myself the Prayer of St. Francis, and by thanking God for using me in such an effective way.

"Lord, make me an instrument of Your peace," reads the Prayer of St. Francis. "Where there is hatred, let me sow love; where there is injury, pardon; where there is doubt, faith, where there is despair, hope; where there is darkness, light, and where there is sadness, joy.

"O Divine Master, grant that I may not so much seek to be consoled, as to console; to be understood as to understand; to be loved, as to love; for it is in giving that we receive, it is in pardoning that we are pardoned, and it is in dying that we are born to eternal life."

Wow! There was my road map, my guidance for the day. It still is.

Ray and I, as part of our morning meditation, read the Prayer of St. Francis that's printed on my mother's funeral card from 1991. We begin each morning meditation after forty-eight years together, with the intention, "Today I'm going to work to be the person I aspire to be." We then read an affirmation, such as, "I easily and joyfully listen to my inner wisdom, always following its guidance," and selections from the *Tao te Ching* and the *Wu We*. We say the Serenity Prayer, and end with words of gratitude for our lives, both the challenges and the opportunities. We also light a candle and a cone of incense daily in honor of a person in need. On Sunday mornings, we often listen to Gregorian chant. You can take the boys out of the church but not the church out of the boys.

One huge challenge that I, and legions of others, faced in the first several years after coming out was "Where do I belong?" Where would I find my community, my family of genuine loving support?

Would I find such loving support in the Catholic Church? I certainly felt at home with renegade Catholics, such as the members of Dignity, Fr. Paul Shanley, Fr. Matthew Flynn, Sister Jeannine Gramick, Msgr. Clement Kern, Fr. Sam Campbell, Fr. Tom Hinsberg, Fr. Norb Brockman, Fr. John McNeill, and Fr. Bob Nugent, among many others. I hoped that I might get indications of support from those in authority. But, even the most liberal bishop in the church in the US couldn't be there for me when I asked for his understanding in 1974. My alma mater, Marquette University, as well as the University of Notre Dame, each disinvited me to speak on their campuses. I was scheduled to speak at a conference of Catholic priests in Miami but was disinvited with the explanation that "Brian McNaught makes priests leave the priesthood."

When I came out and challenged the teachings of the Vatican on homosexuality, one national columnist referred to me as a heretic, and Detroit's progressive Cardinal John Dearden had the priests read from the pulpit a letter saying that I was wrong about the goodness of the love found among Gay people. Was I still a member of the Catholic Church? In my mind I was, and always have been despite my nonacceptance of church dogma, but the official church would say, "No. I excommunicated myself by my actions of defiance and by my beliefs about sexual morality."

Once, when I was invited to speak at the University of Vermont, the Catholic chaplain asked me to also address the faculty, staff, and students who normally gathered in the chapel for services. The chapel was packed, as the priest and I sat in an adjoining lounge, waiting to begin. The phone rang, and I said to him, "That's the bishop saying I can't speak tonight." When the priest hung up the phone, he said, "That was the bishop saying you can't speak tonight. What do you want to do?" he asked. "I want to speak," I answered. "What do you want me to do?" I asked. "I want you to speak," he replied. And so, I did, and was enthusiastically received. The next day, at Sunday Mass, the chaplain announced he was leaving the priesthood, as he found the lack of compassion in the church intolerable. Soon thereafter was when my invitation to speak to priests in Miami was rescinded.

Did I belong in the Gay community? Was that where I'd find my community of loving support? Most of the leadership of the Gay community hated the Catholic Church. Fr. Malcolm Boyd, the Episcopal priest author of *Are You Running with Me, Jesus?* and *Take Off the Masks*, among his twenty books, wrote me the same observation. "We are caught between anti-religious Gays, on the one hand, and homophobic religionists on the other."

The first time I met with and spoke to a Gay audience was at the University of Michigan during my civil rights battle with *The Michigan Catholic* newspaper. I got a chilly reception when I arrived, and it was explained to me by Jim Toy, a faithful Gay Episcopalian and the longest serving Gay liaison in a university, that it was because I came in a sport coat and khakis. The Gay students were all in jeans. I apparently appeared to them as a representative of the Catholic Church, rather than as a Gay man who had just had his column dropped by the Catholic newspaper. My clothing and association with Dignity singled me out as a Straight-looking "papist." Their blue jeans, in their minds, in this situation, declared them as rebels. From the very beginning, I have felt like an outsider in the Gay community. I think I'm not alone in that feeling.

Just as I was starting to speak at what for me was my baptism as a Gay educator, the double doors to the room flew open, and in marched a bearded man in a wedding gown and veil, followed by three bearded guys in matching bridesmaid dresses, all of them challenging gender roles in their "skag drag." They came up and sat down on the floor directly in front of me. One of the bridesmaids elbowed another, nodded his head at me, and said, "Get a load of her." I nervously thought to myself, "This is my new family? Jeans? Check. I've got those. Wedding dress? Did Mom keep hers?"

When I was selected to be the mayor of Boston's liaison to the Gay community, the first such full-time position in the country in 1982, members of the *Fag Rag* newspaper collective created and pasted posters on the trees in the Boston Garden that read, "Brian McNaught, the mayor's new liaison, invites you to a public orgy in the Boston Common. Bring toys and boys, slings and things. Co-sponsored by Dignity and Integrity." Dignity is the LGBTQ Catholic organization, and Integrity serves the same purpose in the Episcopal Church. I was considered dangerous because it was believed I was an apologist and a Catholic assimilationist.

One Gay man who bought several copies of my books told me that he was asked by the far-left Gay bookstore owner, John Mitzel, "Why are you buying his stuff? Read something else."

At one Gay Pride celebration in Boston, at the time of our fight with Anita Bryant in Miami, radical academic Charley Shively was the main speaker. He had a burning cauldron on the stage and dramatically threw things into the fire as he spoke, all things that he said oppressed us, such as a copy of his college degree, and a dollar bill. Finally, he held up the Bible, and the whole crowd knew where he was going. The radicals cheered and the people of faith booed.

My friend, Elaine Noble, the extraordinarily brave and super-savvy woman who was elected the first openly Gay person to a statehouse the same year I was fired, sought me out in the crowd and told me that the organizers of the event wanted me to come up on the stage and say something about what Charley did. I anxiously took the microphone and said, "The Nazis burned books. We don't burn books. Burning the Bible is an affront to anyone who, like me, came out as Gay because of what is in the Bible." Those in the crowd who cheered Charley booed me, and those who booed Charley cheered me. No one likes to be booed, including Charlie and me, especially when you've given up so much to feel at home in the community.

What I've come to understand from these and other experiences is that the light that shines through me, as it does through every other person who allows it to do so, is a manifestation of an aspect of God for which we were chosen. Yes, of course, I belong in the Catholic Church, and in any community of faith, just as I belong in the Gay community. I may not be liked or welcomed by everyone in both communities, but the differences between me and other people of faith, and between me and some LGBTQ people are natural and understandable given our different backgrounds, life experiences, and perspectives. Working hard to find peace in each group is what has helped make me the person I aspire to be. It helped knowing that there would always be a place for me at the table in my family's home, and in that of my grandmother. Even more important, though, was knowing that Ray had my back, and still does after forty-eight years.

Chapter Three

I Was One of Five Who Lived

I WAS BORN AT DINNERTIME on the east side of Detroit on January 28, 1948. The pope was Pius XII. Harry Truman was president. The Soviet Army removed $170 million in art from a museum in Dresden, Germany. Five days of frigid weather forced Detroit to lay off 200,000 workers. *Gentleman's Agreement,* based on the book about antisemitism by Laura Hobson, was praised by critics as the best movie of the year. (My younger brother Tommy likes to remind me that the Challenger exploded on the anniversary of my birth.) The Mattachine Society, one of the earliest Gay organizations, was founded two years later.

Just three years before I was born, the Holocaust ended, but when the concentration camps were liberated, some prisoners were expected to complete their sentence for violating Paragraph 175, a provision of the German Criminal Code that made sexual relations between men a crime. Between 3,000 and 9,000 homosexuals died in the camps. Between 2,000 and 6,000 were required to finish their sentence in a German prison.

Mom said there weren't many nurses available when she went into labor. I was her fourth child, after two boys and one girl. The third child died at thirteen months in a manner we weren't to discuss. Michael, Kathy, Terry, Brian, Tom, Maureen, and Patricia Ann (Pam). Of the seven, two didn't celebrate a second birthday, Terry and Pam. Pam was almost two when she died of multiple birth defects, despite Mother's prayers, relics, and many novenas. Now there are just three of us, with me as the oldest. I guess that makes me in charge. No, thank you.

We weren't supposed to talk about Terry's death because it made Mother cry, which, in turn, got a train-stopping glare from my father at whoever brought it up. Apparently, Terry was bitten by the family dog, Cheeky, or he was scratched by a rusty toy truck in his playpen. He got sick, was taken to the hospital, and died a couple of weeks later. My sister, Kathy, who was not yet four years old at the time, apparently lifted Cheeky into Terry's crib. Her entire life she felt guilty for his death, despite all our protestations. Yet, I wondered, where was Mom? She, too, undoubtedly felt unbearable guilt throughout her life.

When I was two, I got pneumonia. Mom and Dad had me bundled up for the ride to the hospital but were stopped in their tracks when eight-year-old Michael blocked the door. "You're not taking my brother to the hospital," he said. "The last one you took there didn't come home."

When I was born, Dad was the photo and Sunday editor at *The Detroit Times*, a Hearst publication that's no longer in print. He was the oldest of seven children, and a journalism graduate of Marquette University, one of the few universities to offer a degree in journalism. Dad served in the Navy during World War II, and was assigned as a personal aide to Edward Steichen, one of the most prominent photographers of the time. Steichen was the cousin of Carl Sandberg and the father of Mary Calderone, the founder of SIECUS, the Sex Information and Education Council of the United States.

While a lieutenant at Steichen's side, Dad had the job of disseminating photographs from the war in the Pacific Theater to news services across the country. Joe Rosenthal was one photographer whose work Dad released to the press. He signed one of his original photos to my father, which hung in our home for many years. It was Rosenthal's most famous picture, that of the Raising of the Flag on Iwo Jima.

My parents met at *The Detroit Times*. Mother worked in the Fashion section, reporting on weddings, and special events of interest to women. She was born and raised in Detroit to James and Elizabeth Day. Her dad was an electrician. Her mother was one of eight Branigans who lived together in their parents' house if they weren't married or had become a priest. Their home was initially on the west side of Detroit, but my mother and her siblings moved them away after a man walked into the house and held a knife to the wrinkled neck of my Great Uncle Frank. Every Thanksgiving, Tom or I was sent down to pick up Grandma Day, Great Aunt Florence, and/or Great Uncle Frank, who were widowed or unmarried.

Mom was the only girl in a family of four boys. My middle name is Robert in honor of Mom's brother, Bobby, a pilot shot down during World War II. Mom was a physically beautiful but very humble woman of deep faith, a kind, generous, and thoughtful heart, a person who wouldn't swear or gossip, and was always the lady she was raised to be. She was the quiet balance to my father's bravado. He was a center-stage storyteller, a clever and critical thinker, a hardworking family man who hated his name, "Waldo," and who could write but not say "I love you." Dad went by "Mac," which is what my mother called him, or "W. E." for Waldo Everett by most others. Only his parents and siblings called him "Waldo."

In the early 1950s, the folks moved us from Yorkshire Street in Detroit to 802 Blanchard in Flint, so that Dad could live near his new job as the director of public relations for Buick. The city thrived because of the GM car company Buick, and Dad glowed as the funny, inventive, and dedicated PR director, the first full-time PR position in the country. He was known for the deft manner with which he handled the press after the accidental shooting of a friend by GM's retired president, Harlow Curtice. Dad once created a trout pond in the lobby of the fancy Durant Hotel and had the press catch their fish for dinner. One year, Tommy and I as youngsters accompanied Dad and the University of Michigan's marching band on a train to Minnesota where the televised halftime program featured the band spelling out "Buick" and playing the automobile's well-known jingle.

I recall going with Dad to the recording of the song for Buick commercials. There were two guys and two women standing tightly around a big, round microphone singing, "How I love to drive my Buick, with my love sitting by my side. Pretty girl and shiny Buick fill a fella with so much pride. Riding down the road on Sunday, with my car and my heart riding high. Oh, I know that very soon, we'll take a honeymoon, my Buick, my love, and I."

I secretly found the men attractive and imagined myself sitting by their side in the shiny Buick.

Chapter Four

Learning About Sex from Jokes

FLINT WAS A GREAT place for a kid to grow up. The 1950s were a decade of prosperity in Flint, due in no small part to the presence of the Buick automobile offices and factories. It was safe, clean, and loaded with children my age. We had tons of lightning bugs, could safely play kick the can in the street, and walk alone several blocks to kindergarten, always followed by our dog, Tippy. Tippy would bark so much outside the classroom that I'd get sent home with him.

My best friends were Alan Goldstein, who lived directly behind us, Martha Halligan, who lived on Court Street around the corner from us, and Todd Crocker, who lived at the end of the block on Maxine. Alan and I splashed in his plastic pool. His mother had thoughtfully made a tuna fish sandwich for me at a Friday celebration of Alan's birthday. At that time, it was a sin for Catholics to eat meat on Friday. Alan's younger brother, David, was a playmate of my younger brother, Tommy. Alan taught me about Hanukkah, and how he got double the presents because they also celebrated Christmas. The clothing store in Flint, "David Alan," was owned by their father, and was very successful.

Martha and I played hopscotch on the sidewalk in front of her house, and jacks on her front porch. We had coloring and handwriting contests. Her father owned a bowling alley and brought home warm salted cashews that Martha and I secretly got into. It was always assumed that when we grew up, Martha and I would get married. I saw her not long ago at my sister Kathy's celebration of life, and she looked as beautiful as ever. She had married a dentist, and happily raised a family in Ohio.

When people learn that I had a girlfriend since kindergarten, they sometimes get confused as to how I knew I was attracted to boys, and how I reconciled my feelings, especially as a Catholic. While walking the short distance to Martha's house to spend time with this kind, fun person who I really liked, I'd pass the driveway basketball court where Eric Warren might be shooting hoops. Looking like Troy Donahue in a sleeveless T-shirt, Eric was another one with whom I would have run away if he had asked. I was just six or seven years old, and I had the same fantasy about running away with the handsome male friends of my father. Later, I'd have crushes on grade school and high school coaches, and male TV stars such as Robert Conrad. I just wanted to be by their side with their arm around me in whatever car they drove.

I was very lucky as a youngster to grow up with lots of diversity that positively impacted my view of what was normal. Alan was Jewish, Chucky Livesey was Protestant and rich, Joey Witherow was a dwarf, and Vernon Paine was Black. If these good friends were different, then maybe it was okay for me to be too. I was submerged in a traditionally White Catholic culture, but my life wasn't without its colors and flavors.

The night before I was to make my First Communion, Flint was hit hard by a tornado. We stayed in the basement most of the night. The next day, Vernon Paine missed making his First Communion because his house was left with a lot of damage.

While I loved to go to confession and Holy Communion, I also liked to put my hand on the arm of the haircut chair so that when the barber leaned over, I got the very exciting feeling of touching him. Once on vacation to Key Biscayne, Florida, a friend of my father's, Mr. Strong (I'm not kidding), changed into his bathing suit in front of Tommy and me. He had a hairy chest and I saw his penis. That afternoon, we were all out on a boat, and I, at age eight, felt compelled to sit on Mr. Strong's lap, to the chagrin of his son and the confusion of my father.

Alan Goldstein and I lost touch when my family moved to Grand Blanc in 1958. Years later, I learned that he had been killed in 1985 trying to rescue the super athlete, Kari Swenson, from the clutches of the father and son mountain men, Don and Dan Nichols, who had kidnapped her. They shot and killed Alan as he tried to sneak into their campsite.

My exposure to difference didn't mean that I was aware of my own racism or sexism. I went back to Flint for Halloween when I was in the fourth grade. A year earlier we moved from Flint to Grand Blanc, where Dad was soon to be hired by General Motors in Detroit to do for them the same public relations work he did for Buick. The houses in Flint were close together and I figured it would be easier to fill our bags with candy. I stayed overnight with the Halligans, which meant kneeling around the bed to say the rosary, which Martha and I giggled through. I brought with me a homemade clown costume. But Martha's parents the night before had gone to a party as cannibals and won the prize for best costume, so Martha and I decided to use their outfits instead of our own.

Our costumes were made up of black long johns with red crepe paper grass skirts, blackface, and a white dog biscuit necklace hanging around our necks. It's one of those events you recall from childhood with horror, even though at the time it felt very innocent. We were just ten years old, and we had no idea that what we were doing would be offensive to others. However, I'll never forget the looks on the faces of a group of Black children who crossed our paths while trick-or-treating. There was bewilderment, and confusion as to how they should respond. We and they said nothing, but I felt embarrassed.

When we moved from Flint to Grand Blanc, it was a huge change. We went from living in a modest house with one and a half bathrooms, to the biggest house in town with three and a half baths and five bedrooms. Dad spearheaded the creation of Warwick Hills, an eighteen-hole golf course and subdivision. The property and living quarters had been a significant estate. In fact, when we moved into our home, there were still horses boarded in what is now a very elite pro shop and bar. The mansion was converted into the clubhouse, with a dining room.

I remember feeling giddy as a ten-year-old running through the big home my parents had built. Tommy and I would still share a bedroom, but it was more than twice the size of the one in Flint. One of the sisters at school had talked to my class about the Red Chinese Communists and how they would torture us by pulling off our fingernails and shoving chopsticks in our ears if we wouldn't give up our faith. I woke Tommy up to tell him what I heard. We happened to have big shoe drawers in our bedroom so Tommy and I felt comfortable knowing we had a place to hide. We never figured out who was going to let us out of the shoe drawers once the Red Chinese Communists left.

It was great sharing a room with your little brother until it wasn't. Tommy liked to dress up the statue of the Infant of Prague, which showed great flair and talent, but after I received the sacrament of Confirmation, I looked over in the night to see the statue of the Blessed Mother I'd received as a gift. She glowed in the dark. It was cool until Tommy put lipstick on her mouth. What I saw in the dark was a big gaping hole in the bottom half of her glowing face.

We lived in the first house on the first fairway at 9196 Idle Hour Court, the only home on the cul-de-sac at the time. We lived at the top of a hill that was challenging to navigate in a car when the road and driveway were covered with ice and snow, but great fun for tobogganing down, which we did regularly.

There were very few other homes in the subdivision. We had great freedom to ride our bikes, and to play on the golf course or in the farmer's fields across the street where there were goats and cows. I'd ride my bike to a wooded lot where I'd find lots of garter snakes and bring them home, along with an armful of trillium for Mom. (I now know that if you pick a trillium, it won't come back.) I made my first friend in Warwick Hills while doing so, a boy a little younger than me named Jeff Sexsmith. He and I became inseparable. After school, I'd toss a golf ball on to the fairway and with one wood, a putter, and two irons in my hands, I'd play to the third hole where Jeff would join me. We'd swim together at the club's pool, and both sought the attention of the hunky male lifeguard. I didn't start thinking that Jeff might have been Gay until I began writing this book. Jeff had a very nice sister who I later learned was a Lesbian.

My dad started the Buick Open, which at the time had the highest cash prize of fifty-two thousand dollars. During the first year of the open, our collie, named O'Lassie, chased and picked up a golf ball that had been hit down the fairway next to our backyard. The announcer said over the microphone, "Will somebody please get that dog off of the fairway?" In the early days, a lot of the big-name golfers would come to the house to pay their respects to my father, including Sam Snead and Billy Casper. Movie stars like Bob Hope also came to Warwick Hills as part of Buick's promotion. I remember when Dale Robertson, star of the TV program *Tales of Wells Fargo*, came to our home. He was a handsome man.

There were two people with whom my mother didn't want me to spend time. One was Don Ellis, an older, more mature boy than me who lived across the golf course in a much humbler home. We met when I was looking for frogs at one of the golf course's ponds, called "water hazards" by the golfers. Mom feared he wasn't a good influence. I didn't understand why she was concerned, but I think she knew he and I might sexually explore together. The other person I was told to stay away from was Tom, the young adult son of a neighbor. He was known to be homosexual, which was never explained to me. I wish I had known and understood all of this at that time, as I think Tom might have helped me navigate my feelings and confusion. It was Jeff Sexsmith who was the first to stick his hand down my underwear during a sleepover. I didn't let it go further than that, which I also regret.

Catholic school kids rode with public school kids on the buses, as our schools were next door. Ralph Buttz was our driver, and when his apple trees produced, he'd bring big bags of apples and give us each one. At one time, a girl by the name of Pauline Rabideau threw up in the bus, and from then on no one was ever supposed to sit where Pauline once threw up. I remember making it a point to sit in that seat. I broke the silly curse.

I went to Holy Family School in Grand Blanc from fourth through seventh grade. I was an altar boy who memorized the Latin responses to the priest at Mass, a patrol boy, and a Boy Scout. Our scout troop got to sell programs at the Buick Open. The patrol boys were treated once a year to a bus trip to Tiger Stadium in Detroit for a ballgame, and on the way home we'd stop at the Elias Brother's Big Boy for dinner. I always ordered a Slim Jim, melted cheese over ham.

My brother Tom and I, and our friends, loved living in Grand Blanc. I had a girlfriend, Collette Schulte, who had horses, and I rode one in a horse show. On Mondays, when the country club was closed, we'd sneak through the small door in the living room wall where they'd pass through and store firewood from outside. The smallest of us would squeeze in and unlock the entrance door. There was always the sound of a typewriter clickety-clacking upstairs, so we had to be careful as we ate ice cream out of the big cartons in the freezer.

In 1960, Senator John F. Kennedy ran for president against Vice President Richard Nixon. Kennedy would be the first Catholic president. My father was a Republican, and I ended up representing Nixon in a grade school debate at age twelve. I didn't want to represent Nixon, but I wasn't bold enough yet to stand up to my father.

In 1957, the word "Transsexual" was coined by Dr. Harry Benjamin. The Wolfenden Committee recommended decriminalizing homosexual relations in the UK, and psychologist Evelyn Hooker released her study that showed that homosexual men were as well adjusted as heterosexual men. In 1960, Executive Order 10450 was applied to ban Transgender people from serving in the military.

You won't be surprised that my homosexual feelings grew in intensity as I entered puberty. My dad would have one of us boys shower with him each morning to scrub his back. Each time it was my turn, I'd have an erection from start to finish, and I'd explore Dad's body with my soapy hands, but we'd never talk about it. ("What boner? I don't see a boner. Do you see a boner?") I know that Dad sensed that I might be at the very least Bisexual, as did my mother. We never had the "sex talk," which was too bad, but not all that unusual in Irish Catholic homes. In retrospect, I think my father was probably Bisexual, and chose the option to marry and have kids because of his attractions to my mother. I believe he thought that I had the same option. But I didn't.

Mothers of Gay boys always know, even if they don't want to admit it. And how could my parents not know? When my brother Mike ran away with his pregnant girlfriend the night of the senior prom, I got my own room, and the walls were soon filled with Scotch-taped pictures of wrestlers, and not just any wrestler. I didn't have pictures of big Happy Humphrey or Haystack Calhoun, both of whom easily weighed over 300 pounds. No, my photos were of handsome, muscular, hairy chested wrestlers, like Leaping Larry Shane.

There were some boys in my class that I found to be handsome, boys with whom I'd cultivate a friendship. But I was too sexually shy and scared to pursue my feelings, and too intent on being a caretaker and guardian. I gravitated toward the students who no one else played with, like Jim Thornton, a Hispanic boy who wore the same badly stained tie to school every day, and whose nose always seemed to be running. When I drew his name for Christmas gift exchanges, I asked Mom to buy him some ties. I didn't want him made fun of because of how he dressed.

I learned a lot about sex and about homosexuals from jokes other kids told. One was about a naked man and a naked woman looking at each other's bodies. "What's that?" the man asked. "Those are my headlights," the woman responded, "and this is my grass," she said as she pointed toward her hairy hole. "What's that?" she asked, pointing to the man. "That's my snake," he said. In the middle of the night, the man wakes up the woman and says, "You better turn on your headlights. My snake got lost in your grass." That was my first clue about sex and what Straight people do.

In the other joke, Percy and Clarence were standing on a bridge. Percy points and asks, in an exaggerated lisp, "What's that?" Clarence, with an equally exaggerated lisp responds, "That's a ferry boat," to which Percy responds, "Gosh, I knew we were organized but I didn't know we had a Navy." Cleary the message was that homos had names like Percy and Clarence, they lisped, and accepted they were fairies. The secret got buried deeper.

I remember the day well when Dad walked in the house after his one-and-a-half-hour commute from Detroit back to Grand Blanc and said, "Virginia, find us a house closer to work." We were all very upset that we had to move. We loved our free, fun lifestyle there. I think Tom, Maureen, and I cried when once again we left our friends, and we enrolled in a new school. We moved into our home at 1419 Sandringham Way in Bloomfield Village, which was part of Birmingham. Dad now had to drive just forty minutes to work. I learned with time that the General Motors executives lived in Birmingham and the Ford executives lived in Grosse Pointe.

What we kids didn't know when our folks bought our new home, was that Bloomfield Village didn't sell homes to Blacks or Jews. Jewish people lived on Ardmore, the next street up Big Beaver, where the houses were made much grander. I don't know where upper-middle-class Black people lived, but I know they weren't next-door neighbors because of institutional racism. My parents were quite friendly with one Jewish family, and my dad served on the board of the United Negro College Fund. There were no Black children in Holy Name School, which I attended for one year, nor in Brother Rice High School. I truly don't understand the hearts and minds of people who are knowingly racist and antisemitic. Some of the most influential people in my life, including Jesus, were Jews or Black. Jesus was both.

Birmingham turned out to be a great place to live. I could ride my bike or walk to and from school. My best friend in eighth grade was Will O'Sullivan, with whom I'd play basketball in the driveway, and have sleepovers to watch scary movies. Will entered the seminary after that year, and I went on to Brother Rice.

I made friends with a neighbor, Ken Weber, with whom I'd play ping-pong, driveway basketball, and pinochle if we could get his mom to stop what she was doing and play with us. There were only a handful of houses that had been built when we moved in the summer of 1961. It was with Ken that I first got drunk. I recall standing up watching my mother strip the bed of my sheets, with me shakily saying "I have the flu. That's why I threw up," and my dad saying, "I'm going to kill him." Ken and I also smoked together in his basement. My father smoked L&M, and I'd sneak a pack out of the carton Mom bought for him.

Chapter Five

On Stage in Second Grade

IN FLINT, AT ST. Matthew's grade school, I had Sister Marie Anita as my first-grade teacher. She moved in her full habit with such grace and silence that it was as if she floated around the room with only her face and hands visible. It was in first grade that we learned about the seven sacraments, and we were taught how to confess our sins to the priest. "Bless me, Father, for I have sinned. My last confession was a week ago." You had to know how to admit your failings before you could welcome Jesus, in the form of the Holy Communion wafer, into your body, your sacred temple.

One area of concern to me were the "sins of impure thoughts, words, and deeds." I learned then how to just say "impure thoughts" and "impure deeds" for years without having to give details about my attractions to male TV stars and my self-pleasuring. It was very fortunate that Fr. Powers, Fr. Bush, and subsequent priests didn't ask for details, as some priests did and do. "Tell me about these impure thoughts. Who were you thinking about? Were you touching yourself?"

In second grade, Dad took the family to Key Biscayne, Florida, for vacation. He always brought with us my maternal grandmother, "Bessie," who we all adored. Our vacation went beyond the time allotted by the school for Christmas break, so when I returned, I had missed the casting of the second graders' school play. It was the story of a king and golden pears.

"What's my part?" I asked my second-grade nun.

"You'll be a stagehand," she said. "When the king's servant comes to the curtain to get the pears, you'll be out of sight holding the tray, and you'll give them to him to present to the king." I was so disappointed that everyone else would be in costume, and I would be in my school uniform of blue pants, blue shirt, and a blue tie.

When the day arrived for the performance, with my mom and her friends in the audience, I stood behind the curtain as I was told. But when my classmate came in costume to get the platter of pears from me, I walked around him, brought the golden pears to the king, bowed, and went back behind the curtain. My mother said that she and her friends all laughed, and the sister didn't reprimand me. In my mind, I was called to be on stage in second grade.

In third grade, Todd Crocker started talking to me and I answered him. The nun, who claimed to have eyes in the back of her head, called out our names and told us to go stand in the hallway until class was over. I was mortified. This isn't the behavior of a good boy. At the end of the day, I went to sister and asked, "Sister, does this mean I'm going to get a bad mark in conduct?" She replied, "If you're good as gold every day for the rest of the year, you'll get a good grade." Then, every single day, at the end of class, I'd go up to her and ask, "Sister, was I good as gold today?" "Yes, Brian, you were good as gold." Later in life, I wondered if I might have driven her to a nervous breakdown with my persistent yearlong daily questioning.

Some Catholics have horrifying stories to tell about the nuns they had as teachers in grade school and high school. Those stories usually include mention of the ruler or stick. I have no such stories, and was, in fact, inspired by the spiritual aura of the sisters. Except perhaps that of Mother Genovefa, SSJ (Sisters of St. Joseph). She was the principal at Holy Family grade school in Grand Blanc. At the end of one day when I was in seventh grade, she stepped into the room as we were putting on our coats and gathering our things, and said in a loud, commanding voice, "Brian McNaught, you don't create quite the impression you think you do." Some kids laughed, but I naturally was embarrassed, and perplexed. I had no idea to what she was referring.

This was the same sister who one year before pulled me behind a hanging map in a classroom as others my age looked on, and she encouraged me to pull down my pants and point to that part of my body that had kept me out of school for a few days. She knew very well that my younger brother, Tommy, had kneed me in the balls, and my testicles were so swollen and black and blue that I had to lie on the sofa with an ice pack between my legs for a couple of days. "Point to where you were hurt," she said smiling as we hid behind the map. But one bad experience with one nun doesn't spoil my good memories of the women and men of religious orders who dedicated their lives to teaching.

In eighth grade, at Holy Name school in Birmingham, Michigan, I had the best teacher I had in sixteen years of Catholic education. Sr. Claire Marie, IHM, a sister of the Immaculate Heart of Mary, taught our homeroom class about opera and symphonies, how to pick and follow a Wall Street stock, and how to say the "Hail Mary" prayer in French, which we did every morning. She also told us to read *Lorna Doone* by R. D. Blackmore. It was the thickest book I'd ever seen, thicker even more so when it fell into the bathtub as I was reading.

Sister Claire Marie required that every day, we turn in three international news items and three national news items. She wanted us to follow world and local events. We also had to memorize and give a well-known speech to our classmates. One by one we walked alone up the stairs to the stage. We were allowed to have a prompter, but I didn't need one. I got very high marks for reciting the speech given by King Edward VIII when he abdicated the throne of England to marry an American divorced woman, Wallis Simpson. A+. What's funny to me today is that I can forget the names of my friends, or how a conversation started, but I can still recite the Latin from Mass, and King Edward's abdication speech. "At long last, I am able to say a few words of my own . . ."

A few of my friends and I went to the convent one night, rang the bell, and asked to see Sr. Claire Marie. We were so crazy about her that we bought her the latest album by Chubby Checker, which included, "Do the Twist." She was surprised and delighted.

It was Sr. Claire Marie who told my mother that I was "a prince of a boy." I was a good fourteen-year-old, who gladly participated in everything Sr. Claire Marie had us do, such as quickly add numbers and correctly spell words. She had a system that rewarded you for good behavior. It was a SCM (Sr. Claire Marie) yellow slip of paper that could be used to excuse you for not turning in a homework assignment. I gave mine away to a very smart but friendless girl in our class who cried when she didn't have her homework. "I'll give you a nickel after class," she said, drying her tears. I didn't want her nickel. She was in distress, and I instinctively wanted to do what I could for her. But a nickel?

It can take a lifetime to really know yourself. It's certainly not something that happens by eighth grade. I knew that I got tingles up and down my spine when I was in church, praying intently to God. My parents had taught me to be very polite. My older sister, Kathy, had helped me become a very good dancer, swimmer, and ice skater. I didn't say "hell" or "damn" until high school. I was a good student, an amateur artist, and respectful of authority. It was only through Facebook messaging that I learned from former classmates many years later that I was thought to be a leader and a protector of weaker students from harm when I was in the eighth grade.

In high school, I was taught by the Christian Brothers of Ireland. I loved the lack of haughtiness I saw in the brothers. Sometimes, I felt put off by the assumed authority and the seemingly inauthentic piety of some priests and bishops. But I also met some amazing priests, such as Dan Berrigan, Tom Hinsberg, and James Groppi, and bishops, such as Tom Gumbleton and Bob DeWitt, who I felt walked the talk humbly.

In 1961, John F. Kennedy was sworn in as president, the Soviet Cosmonaut Yuri Gagarin was the first human to orbit the earth, the wall was built between East and West Berlin, and Fr. Gustavo Gutierrez of Peru introduced the theology of liberation that took Latin America by storm. Its basis is that the Gospels were written for humans and if the Bible didn't speak to the lives of humans, the biblical passages weren't relevant. In Rome, despite the leadership of Pope John XXIII, the Vatican declared that anyone who is "affected by the perverse inclination" toward homosexuality should not be allowed to take religious vows or be ordained.

My best friend in high school was Henry Grix. Starting in sophomore year, we were always together, so much so that my father called Henry's home during the dinner hour to suggest that our friendship might be homosexual. Mrs. Grix hung up on my father, which very few people got away with doing. I didn't learn of the phone call until many years later.

Henry and I, my girlfriend Jody, and other high school friends went to France for six weeks the summer between our junior and senior year as part of a Catholic family exchange. My French family was wonderful, but I was much more interested in my exchange student Dominique's younger brother, Jean, than I was in him. While I was there, my French family also hosted a very handsome boy from England named Alister Peebles. (Truly.) At the end of the six weeks, Dominique came to live with us in Birmingham for a month and a half. I so wanted it to be Jean.

It was in high school that my focus on God shifted from the Father to the Son. I totally resonated with not just the words of Jesus, but the spirit behind them. The words of Jesus guided everything I said or did. "Feed the hungry, give drink to the thirsty, clothe the naked, give shelter to travelers, visit the sick, visit those in prison, and bury the dead." I experienced everything that Jesus said as a calling for all of us to serve and protect others. "I tell you, whenever you refused to help one of these least important ones, you refused to help me" (Matt 25 31–40). How much clearer can that be?

> Blessed are the poor in spirit for theirs is the kingdom of Heaven. Blessed are those who mourn, for they will be comforted. Blessed are the meek, for they will inherit the earth. Blessed are those who hunger and thirst for righteousness, for they will be satisfied. Blessed are the merciful, for they will receive mercy. Blessed are the pure of heart, for they will see God. Blessed are the peacemakers, for they shall be called sons of God. Blessed are those who are persecuted for righteousness' sake, for theirs is the kingdom of Heaven. Blessed are you when others revile you and persecute you, and utter all kinds of evil against you, falsely in my account, rejoice and be glad for your reward is great in Heaven, for so they persecuted the prophets who were before you. (Matt 1:11)

Those are the words that guided the rest of my life, words made clear not just in books, in church, in school, but also in the news of the world. I identified with these words. I saw in them the affirmation of what I had felt since early childhood, but also my refuge. Jesus was my very best friend, and he was talking about me doing good deeds, and having good deeds done to me.

What I struggled with as a Catholic was that it felt as if everyone was focused on the death of Jesus on the cross, suffering for our salvation, to wash away our sins. There were crucifixes everywhere, in every classroom and in every house of worship, some with Jesus hanging, and others with the crosses empty. But that was not what I focused on in my relationship with Jesus. Instead, I embraced his words as they related to my daily experiences, to my daily challenges. And yet, I lived in the real world, and I didn't have such clear guidance about my sexuality.

One day, in senior year, our English teacher, Brother Markert, brought our attention to a Gay pictorial magazine that he said he received erroneously in the mail. Nevertheless, he wanted us to know about such things, so he raised the magazine high, the cover of which was a naked man in a stream, his foot up on a rock, with a star, like a fig leaf, covering his penis. Of course, the guys in my honors class went crazy with jokes and accusations. I sat very still, looking away, and hoping my name wouldn't be brought up as someone who was interested.

I couldn't shake the intense desire to see that magazine. Something told me that it was published for people like me, even though I hadn't yet totally gotten my arms around the fact that I was a homosexual. How could a "prince of a boy" be a homo? It was a frightening label. That night, I called the brothers' residence and asked to speak with Brother Markert. When he took the call, I told him that I was disturbed by the magazine, and asked if we might meet after classes the next day.

The brother allowed me to smoke in the empty classroom, which was very kind, as it was against school rules, but I was addicted to nicotine, having started smoking my freshman year. I told Brother Markert that I wondered if I wasn't Bisexual. There are a lot of Gay people who when they hear someone say that they're Bisexual they suspect that they just aren't ready to come out as Gay, which was true for me. I'd dare say though that most people are Bisexual to some degree, which is what Brother Markert said, as would my dad when I came out to my parents many years later. He even offered that several of the brothers were probably Bisexual.

I will never forget his kindness that day and said so in a letter I wrote to him from college. But not all the brothers were so understanding and supportive. That same year, Brother Duffy, a man with his master's degree in guidance and counseling, and who was the person to whom we were told to go to if we seniors had any problems, stood before my class, and said, "If any of you guys come into my office and tell me that you've screwed a chick, I'll talk to you. You tell me you're queer and I'll kick you out of my office."

I suspect that it was Brother Duffy who took my name off the Christian Leadership Award plaque, and I also believe that he was probably wrestling with his own sexual orientation. Often, the most vocal critics are those men who fear they are Gay, and those women who fear that their husbands are Gay.

As is true with many closeted Gay high school students, I dated a girl from Marian High School who was fun and funny, and who thought I was the same. Jody and I took over the dance floor at school sock hops and entertained our friends with wit. When our friends headed home, I know they did a lot more kissing than Jody and I did. I'd walk her to the door, kiss her "good night," and head home.

Closeted Gay men subconsciously are often attracted to women they suspect have very low sex drives, and often women with low sex drives, or who have the desire to remain chaste, are attracted to closeted Gay men. It makes sense, just as it does that closeted Gay men often choose religious life over marriage, or over years of being asked by their parents and friends, "When are you going to get married?" And it's also true that many Gay men are drawn to professions in which they can help others, such as nursing, teaching, therapy, and the priesthood.

When I applied to enter the Christian Brothers after my sophomore year at Marquette, I was required to see a therapist as part of their screening process. When I told the therapist that I might be Bisexual, he said that it was not something I should be concerned about, because I "had the sexual experiences of a twelve-year-old." I didn't know how to react. Proud? Embarrassed?

When I entered the novitiate of the Christian Brothers, I immediately attached myself to a guy a year or two ahead of me. In religious life, they discourage "PFs," particular friendships, with good reason. With so much repressed sexuality in such a homoerotic setting, having a special friend can lead to the very same feelings I had for an older brother, Jim, and I hoped he had for me. Each time we gathered in chapel, I would kneel next to him.

We took summer courses at DePaul University in Chicago, and I'd sometimes sneak out to see a movie. One that changed my life was Federico Fellini's *Juliet of the Spirits*. The story, as I recall, was about a prim housewife whose husband was having an affair. They lived next door to a pleasure palace where a handsome, hunky, young, blond man waited for Juliet to choose sexual bliss. She knew her husband was cheating on her, but nevertheless she wanted to stay faithful to him, and chaste at home. But she also wanted to break out of that role and allow herself to experience sexual pleasure by just visiting next door, which she eventually did. I saw myself as the chaste housewife, with the sexual experiences of a twelve-year-old. I wanted to go next door, but I was afraid. Would I get caught? What would happen to me? Would I like it so much that I'd never want to leave? Would God still be with me if I sought out the handsome blond man?

It disturbed me that I was so inexperienced, and it frightened me that I was attracted to Jim. He probably saw me as a nice new friend and was flattered by my attention. I left the Christian Brothers about four weeks later, in time to reenroll as a junior at Marquette. I was required to live in a dorm, or "student housing," because I hadn't made other arrangements earlier. It was there that I finally lost my virginity.

Chapter Six

I Want a "Do-Over" for My First Sexual Experience

After Christmas break, while waiting for my plane back to Milwaukee, I picked up the book *Eustace Chisholm and the Works* by James Purdy. I did so nervously because it looked to have a homosexual theme, and I was afraid of the judgment of the airport news center cashier. I read the book voraciously.

Every night, many of the guys on my dorm floor would gather in the TV room, some just waiting for Stan Freberg's creative Jino's Pizza Roll commercial, and the next episode of *Star Trek*. I noticed that there was one guy who stayed in the room until the national anthem came up on the screen at midnight. I watched way too much television and wish that I could have a "mulligan" for my college education. But the truth is, I spent a lot of time in the TV lounge waiting for people to leave. As time passed, he and I were the only ones in the darkened room. He sat up front in a gray silk bathrobe. I sat in the back, fully clothed, but there was a strong sexual energy in the room, though neither of us ever spoke to the other. This went on night after night for weeks.

One night, I worked up the courage to walk over to him and offer him the book by James Purdy. "I think you might like this," I said. He took the book from me and asked, "When do you want it back?" I took that as code for "When could we get together?" I replied, "How about tomorrow morning at 8:30?" I knew my roommate Chuck would have gone to class.

I WANT A "DO-OVER" FOR MY FIRST SEXUAL EXPERIENCE

At 8:30 the next morning, there was a gentle knock, and in walked a very handsome freshman that I had not really focused on before. He was ready to climb into my single bed, but I hemmed and hawed so long that he headed for the door. "Where are you going?" I asked. "You don't seem to want to do anything," he replied. I then pulled back my sheet and blanket to expose my erection. He dropped his robe exposing his erection and he climbed on top of me.

You know how some people say, "I wish I could do that over"? I so wish that I could do that over. I have thought about it for decades since. I've even tried to track him down, but his name was so common, Jim Clark, that I had no luck. I wasn't looking for a do-over, but rather the opportunity to tell him how much I regretted the way I responded to him.

Knowing he was coming to the room, I should have brushed my teeth, gargled away the smell of my cigarettes, and shaved. In my memory, he was stunningly handsome with a well-muscled body and large, hard penis. We kissed awkwardly, and reached orgasm quickly by body rubbing, called "frotting." When we were finished, we jumped up and I said, "Thank you. You've just proven to me that I'm not a homosexual." What nonsense! What a desperate need to be "normal." Please can I try again?

For the next couple of weeks, Jim would follow me in his beautiful gray robe into the bathroom. I avoided him. One time, though, when I came out of the stall, he stood in front of me with a huge hard-on poking out of his robe.

"I can't," I said. "I need to have sex with a girl to know what I am." He and I stayed in the large bathroom leaning on sinks and talking. He told me that his dad was a postman. Jim, too, was high school senior class president. Eventually, I said "good night" and returned to my room. He kept his eye on me for several weeks. The second semester of my junior year, I moved with my roommate Chuck into a fancy apartment a few blocks from campus. Chuck's parents were wealthy, and I didn't need to pay more than I did for my dorm room.

I used to walk by Jim and his friends in the student union as I headed to play bridge with my friends the rest of the year. In my senior year, I was rarely in the union because I was co-editor of the university's yearbook. I never saw Jim after that.

What do I wish had happened? I wish I had prepared myself properly for my first Gay sexual experience. I wish I had said, "Thank you. This was my first sexual experience with a guy, and I loved it." I wish I had hooked up with Jim as often as possible. I wish he and I had gotten an apartment and had a full, happy, sexual life the rest of my time at Marquette. This has been a fantasy of mine.

Then, I remind myself that I would never have met Ray, the wonderful, handsome, attentive, protective, thoughtful, generous, and forgiving love of my life. I wouldn't have been fired by the Catholic newspaper in Detroit, thus not helping to raise the issue of homosexuality throughout the church. I wouldn't have done the work on LGBTQ issues with college, corporate, and government audiences, and I wouldn't have been a window of healing for the multitude of people who struggled with their sexual desires and their faith. Things happened as the Universe directed, but that doesn't stop me from wondering, "What if?"

Somewhere in this timeframe, I did have sex with a woman. I was asked that on a national talk show. She didn't go to Marquette. I bought some beer and a massage book and knocked on her door, as I had seen others do. We took a bath together, we kissed, I performed cunnilingus, and then penile-vaginal sex. The young woman said she couldn't believe it was my first time. I felt no erotic excitement, and it took a lot of work to keep my penis firm enough to enter her vagina. As awkward as my first Gay sex was, I knew it was my home.

Sex, or wanting to have sex with other students or professors, was not something I thought much about at Marquette. I fantasized at night about frotting with Robert Conrad from the TV program *The Wild Wild West,* and I self-pleasured regularly. However, during the day, my focus was on issues of civil rights, as that is what was called for in the Sermon on the Mount, and in my soul. Freshmen year, I picketed for free speech after the university disinvited Alan Ginsburg because he was a homosexual. I also walked with Fr. James Groppi, an activist in the civil rights movement in Milwaukee. As a sophomore, I stayed with others past closing time in the student union to deliberately provoke the administration to address racist behaviors of some faculty members. Junior and senior year, I passionately demonstrated against the American war in Vietnam. This behavior infuriated my father. When I called to tell him that I might be taken to jail for a "sit-in" past closing at the student union, he said, "Don't waste your dime on me," and hung up.

The Stonewall Rebellion occurred on Christopher Street on June 28, 1969, the summer before my senior year. It got little to no press in the Detroit newspapers, and only a couple paragraphs in *The New York Times,* but the Gay, Lesbian, Bisexual, Transgender, and Queer patrons, and those who lived in the neighborhood, created an event that rocked the world. It launched the feverish response of Gay Pride, which prompted many US Gay organizations to start up that year, including Dignity.

In the Catholic Church, Paul VI was pope. The summer before, he issued the encyclical *Humanae Vitae,* which outlawed the use of birth control. It showed the world how out of touch the Church in Rome was with everyday life. Subsequently, a fifth of American priests left the priesthood, as did seminarians, and nuns and brothers from their religious orders. Church attendance dropped.

Woodstock attracted more than 350,000 music fans in 1969. Neil Armstrong was the first human to step foot on the moon, PBS was founded, the American war in Vietnam escalated, as did the anti-war movement,

The 1970 yearbook that I, my co-editor, and the dedicated staff created was extraordinary, reflecting the mood of change and challenge that swept the country. One hundred thousand people gathered in Washington to protest the war, and the Ohio National Guard opened fire on unarmed students who were peacefully demonstrating against the war, killing four and wounding nine. The massacre at Kent State University triggered outrage across the country.

The yearbook, called the *Hilltop,* was explosively political, rejecting the old, boring yearbook photo format of the administration, and of the graduates of the various schools, such as law, medicine, or journalism. Instead, we attempted to capture the environment and life that students, faculty, and staff experienced living in the center of a large urban area. We started with the photo of the university president, but the next photo was that of Samson, the very popular gorilla at the Milwaukee Zoo. Interspersed with pictures of deans were photos of the homeless people we'd pass daily on our way to class. We worked hard to be a yearbook that manifested values. Regrettably, on the night of our big gala where we'd unveil the yearbook, there was a bomb threat, as was happening at universities across the country, and the dinner in the student union was cancelled. Every student, though, eventually received a copy of the book. That night, at a yearbook staff pity party, I got so drunk and sick on Scotch that I never drank it again.

W. H. Auden, poet laureate of the U.K., was invited to Marquette to speak. I went to the dean of the school of journalism and asked, "Dean, why wouldn't the university allow Alan Ginsberg to speak, but they will W. H. Auden?" The dean replied, "I believe it's because Auden is a poet who happens to be a homosexual, and Ginsberg is a homosexual who happens to be a poet."

I learned from him that my sexuality would be excused if it wasn't my identity. However, it would be my identity, and I was invited to speak around the world because I was Gay, not despite it. When we lived in Atlanta, the executor of the Margaret Mitchell (*Gone with the Wind*) estate, Hal Clark, lived two doors down, and being Southern was very cordial to Ray and to me, but other neighbors reported that he referred to me as "the Professional Homosexual."

Chapter Seven

Gay and Catholic, Both and Not

THE WHOLE YEARBOOK STAFF sat around the radio in 1969 to listen to the drawing of draft numbers. If your number was above 200, as I recall, it wasn't likely you'd be drafted. I was number seventy-seven, which meant I would soon be notified of where to report for duty. But I knew that I could never take another person's life. I also knew that aggression was completely opposite of what Jesus asked of us. So, I formally filed as a conscientious objector. Doing so was so upsetting to my father that he angrily said to me, "I'm so embarrassed by you that I'm either going to reenlist in the Navy or kill myself." He did neither. My father had a flair for the dramatic, which made him a good person for public relations, but a challenging one as a father. Nevertheless, I know he loved his family dearly, and that he did the best he could for us. Ultimately, he was very proud of me, and I of him.

My draft board in Pontiac, Michigan, was known to be the most difficult one in the state. I was required to write a thorough explanation on why I couldn't serve, and then face fierce questioning by members of the board. I could have told them that I was a homosexual and immediately been discharged, but I wasn't ready to come out then, and I wanted to go on record as someone who objected to combat service because of my conscience.

Even the most casual observer of my life would understand why I couldn't fight. The message I got from the nuns and brothers, my parents and neighbors, my pastors and those whom I so admired was nonviolence. Jesus didn't take another person's life, nor did Francis of Assisi, Gandhi, Buddha, Martin Buber, Martin Luther King Jr., or any of my other spiritual teachers. The books that we were assigned to read in high school included *Hiroshima*, *Mr. Blue*, and *Animal Farm*. I read on my own the books *Siddhartha* by Hermann Hesse, and *I-Thou* by Martin Buber.

There wasn't violence in my home, and I'd never been in a fistfight. I'd step in to stop violence when I saw it, like the day I spotted a large circle of students making noises about whatever was going on in the center of the ring. My friend John Sullivan was playing slap hand with Bob Rininger. John was a big guy who agreed to paint himself green when as juniors we chose the theme of "The Jolly Green Giant" for Field Day. John's hands were beet red, but he kept smiling as he got slapped, pretending it didn't hurt because he wanted to belong. I stepped in, told John "That's enough," and took his place in slap hand. Bob Rininger's hands were pink when we heard the bell for the start of afternoon classes. Not long ago, I learned that John took his own life, and that he was thought to have been Gay.

I couldn't understand how any Catholic could participate in this ridiculously unjustifiable violent war of aggression. Americans called it the war in Vietnam. The Vietnamese called it the American war in Vietnam. "Blessed are the peacemakers." Those people in the administration that were pushing for more napalm, and bombs, and young recruits who would lose their lives had no idea what they were doing and had been doing for years. By the end of the senseless war, 58,200 Americans had died, which doesn't take into account those who were maimed for life physically or psychologically. Had I agreed to go and receive training on how to kill another person, my life commitment to serve others, and to maintain my relationship with Jesus would have been shattered. The men who engineered the war had an energy around them that was dark, and untrustworthy, as was revealed by the Pentagon Papers, secret documents released to the press by Daniel Ellsberg. The people with whom I marched and protested the war had an energy that was warm, bright, loving, and inviting. There was no question where I belonged.

I had no support from my parents in my fight to reject induction. I had heard of other moms and dads driving their sons to Canada, or using their influence to ensure their child didn't die in a jungle on the other side of the world. But I felt support from my brother, Tommy, and from my friends, as well as from my paternal grandparents and Aunt Joan, my father's youngest sibling. My grandfather set up a job for me in a Veterans Administration hospital, should I need it, and for Christmas, they sent me a painting of a dove, the sign of peace.

I spent a great deal of time in reflection and wrote passionately in defense of my position as a conscientious objector. I then received notice of the day and time at which I was to appear before the draft board and respond to their interrogation. I recall four or five men glaring at me from the other side of the table across from where I stood. No smiles.

"Would you stop someone from raping your mother?" I was asked.

"Yes, I'd stop them, but I wouldn't kill them," I replied.

I took such questions for what felt like a half hour. When I finished, one of the men came over to me, shook my hand, and said, "You ought to be a lawyer." It was through the mail that I learned that my conscientious objector status had been approved, as it had for one hundred and seventy thousand other men my age. I was relieved and felt affirmed. The next challenge was finding work that satisfied the requirement of two years of alternative service, making no more than $100 a week.

While I waited, I was hired by *The Michigan Catholic* newspaper to be a reporter and copy editor. My degree in journalism from Marquette helped me, as did the news editor knowing my father from the old days of *The Detroit Times*. My job at the paper was to copyedit stories to make sure there weren't misspellings, and to handle raw copy, editing it down to the basic questions of who, what, when, where, and why in the first paragraph. I was also a reporter who went out to interview individuals about their work in the church of Detroit.

One person I interviewed was Fr. Tom Lumpkin who was engaging in a hunger fast in protest of the American war in Vietnam. He explained to me that hunger fasts had to be about something tangible that could be achieved. Otherwise, you'd just die. Dick Gregory, the Black comedian and civil rights activist, created a means to fast that minimized the damage to your body. You began by drinking fruit juice, preferably grape juice, for seven days. You then drank a gallon of water each day, with a teaspoon of honey and lemon juice to coat your intestines. You had to give yourself a daily Epsom salts bath to clean out your pores of the toxins in your body, and regular enemas.

The Michigan Catholic was one of the most liberal diocesan newspapers in the country, and Detroit was led by some of the most progressive clerics, including Cardinal John Dearden, Bishop Tom Gumbleton, and Bishop Joseph Imesch. The minor seminary, Sacred Heart, was in

Detroit. It was at Sacred Heart during the race riots of 1967 that the face and hands of the statue of Jesus were painted black. The head of the seminary insisted that they be left that way. The college seminary, St. John's, was home to a couple of the most forward-thinking theologians in the country, Fr. Tony Koznik and Fr. Ron Modras. These men and other theologians wrote the groundbreaking book, *Human Sexuality—New Directions in American Catholic Thought* for the Catholic Theological Society of America.

The editor of *The Michigan Catholic* was Fr. Bill Kienzle, one of the most liberal priests in the diocese, who regularly wrote provocative editorials. He encouraged us to be a cutting-edge newspaper. Fr. Kienzle wrote to the Selective Service in Michigan asking that they allow my work at the newspaper to satisfy the required two years of service. At the very last minute, the draft board approved. If they hadn't, I would have headed the next week to work in the mental ward of a Veterans Administration hospital in Massachusetts, the job my grandfather had secured for me. Looking back, I clearly see the influence of a higher power.

Shortly after I began working at the paper, I was encouraged to write a weekly column aimed at people my age who wanted their voice to be heard, and who needed reasons to stay in the church. The title of my column was "Write On," playing with the popular saying of my generation, "right on." My column developed a following which grew with time. I was subsequently asked to lead a group of young people in a catechism class, and to speak at father-daughter communion breakfasts and at senior citizen luncheons.

During the lunch hour, my good friend, Margaret Cronyn, the women's editor, and I would go to Holy Rosary Church for Mass and to receive Holy Communion. We'd then come back and split a sandwich. Margaret and I sat across from one another at work, passing notes back and forth about what was going on in the office and at home.

Look magazine, in an issue in 1971, focused on "The American Family." Among the people featured were the Gay couple Mike McConnell and Jack Baker in Minneapolis, Minnesota. They were the first male couple to get a license and be married in the United States, long before it was sanctioned by the Supreme Court. The photo essay had these handsome men standing in front of a bathroom mirror shaving together, and other domestic shots. I was so excited to see it, as it portrayed exactly what I wanted in my life. The guys are not that much older than me, but I fantasized about them adopting me. Still, though, I wasn't yet out to anyone.

Not long after I started writing my column, a seminarian from St. John's asked if I might like to spend some time together. His name was Dennis, and unbeknownst to me, his plan was to seduce me into bed in the rectory of a friend. Since my junior year one-time experience with Jim Clark, I hadn't had sex. Once Denny and I did have sex, I latched onto him like a barnacle to a sea wall. I'm one of those romantics who wants sex to take place in the framework of a relationship. Denny was on-again, off-again, uncertain about whether to stay in the seminary, and not wanting any emotional attachments. He'd come on to me and back away from me. This lack of consistency and honesty drove me crazy, and we stopped seeing each other. I got an apartment, which I shared with another seminarian who was taking time off to think about his vocation.

John was a Bisexual and was having sex with me and with a close woman friend of ours, Cathy, who had a big job in the diocesan offices of the church. John and I were having sex that consisted of kissing, exploring each other's bodies with our hands, oral sex, and frotting. I found this to be heavenly. But John was also too erratic. Like Denny, he was on-again, off-again, finding his way through his sexual identity, and whether he wanted to pursue being a priest. His intimacy with me felt very real, but unreliable.

What the psychologist who I saw years ago, before joining the Christian Brothers, failed to tell me was that not only did I have the sexual experiences of a twelve-year-old, but also the emotional maturity about sex of a preteen. Between the "yes" and "no" physical and emotional behavior of both Dennis and John, I was an emotional mess.

What made it worse was that I didn't have anyone to talk to about it. In my mind, I would find a male partner with whom I'd build a family life and home to match that in which I grew up. Both men were struggling with their religious vocation and had no desire to have a life partner. I didn't think of that at the time, and looking back I must have scared them both with the intensity of my feelings. I was a clinging, needy, emotionally volatile twenty-three-year-old. Gay people my age went through puberty with only the irrelevant guidance offered to Straight teenagers. "Don't get pregnant!" The only sex education we got in my high school was a half-hour movie from the Navy on gonorrhea.

While seeing Dennis and needing a supportive ear, I found a therapist and made an appointment. On my first visit to his office/home, I saw equipment that intrigued me. Years later, I learned it was to measure biorhythms. In our first session, I talked him through my life and current emotional struggle. On my second visit, he asked me to first allow him to say something.

"I had a dream about you last night," he said. "At the base of Mount Fuji, there were many lights where people lived, but the mountain also glowed with the fires set by those who had left the security of the city to seek awareness. There were campfires at different levels, with fewer and fewer as the height of the mountain increased. People would climb to a certain level and join those who sat around a fire. But their desire to know more about themselves and their reason for living prompted them to leave and climb until they found another fire at which they could sit. You, Brian, were at the highest level."

Okay, I was initially startled that he was dreaming about me, but I loved, and have used many times since, the imagery of climbing the mountain of consciousness, of awareness from one height to the next when we feel called to do so. What perplexed me was how he knew so quickly and clearly that my lifetime aspiration was to know and serve God. And what did the mountain have to do with Dennis? I came back to therapy with him only a couple more times, feeling affirmed, but unguided. At the end, he thanked me for teaching him so much about homosexuality. That is what I heard from every Straight therapist I would see over the years. "You've taught me so much I didn't know."

It was Valentine's Day, and I drew and colored for John a wonderful, large picture of Winnie the Pooh trying to catch a butterfly. I don't remember exactly what I wrote beneath it, but it was about love and how hard it was to catch and hold. I waited and waited for John to come home so I could celebrate with him and give him my gift. Finally, at around eight o'clock, I called Cathy, the woman with whom he was also having sex.

"Yes, he's here," she replied. "Do you want to talk with him?"

"No, thanks," I said, and hung up.

What I wanted to do was kill myself. It wasn't a very serious thought, but it reflected that I had hit what was my twelve-year-old emotional bottom. But, instead of trying to take my own life, I drove downtown and parked behind what I had been told by either Denny or John was a Gay bar. It was called "The Woodward," and it was totally nondescript, one that only the informed knew how to find.

I was very nervous. This was the first Gay bar I had ever been to. I didn't know what to expect. I had no contact with Gay men beyond the two seminarians and Jim Clark. The bar was dimly lit and smoky. Neil

Diamond was singing "I Am I Said." There was a strong scent of cologne, mixed with the smoke and distinctive smell of beer.

I sat down at the bar, asked for a beer, lit a cigarette, and started mildly flirting with the bartender. "Would you please give everyone here a drink and say, 'Happy Valentine's Day from Brian?'" I asked. There were only a handful of people there at that hour. How would I know that Gay bars didn't get busy until 11 PM? It was a good thing for me, because I wouldn't have been able to afford to buy drinks for everyone there at eleven. I left the bar a little high, but knowing I had to go to work the next day.

I had been baptized by Neil Diamond, and in the incense of Aramis. I didn't meet anyone I liked, except maybe the bartender. I was too scared to look around the room, or to make eye contact with anyone. But I now knew where I could go to find people like me.

I had laid out on the dining room table the drawing of Pooh and it was gone when I got home. John was in his bed, a mattress on the floor. I quietly got undressed and got into my bed. That's the last thing I remember of John, although I have the suspicion that he got up, walked over, sat on my bed, smelled beer, and asked where I had been. We might have even had sex. Having an awareness of The Woodward, and knowing I could go back at any time, gave me a ticket out of my dramas. I didn't need Dennis or John. I could survive without them.

On my second and third visit to The Woodward I sat at the bar still too afraid to look around. I'd drink a couple of beers, smoke a couple of cigarettes, and go home. On my fourth visit, I got the courage to look around the room and I made eye contact with a nice-looking guy in a black-and-white–striped sailor shirt. He came over and sat next to me. We chatted for a short while, and he asked me if I'd like to come home with him. I did, and I followed his car. We went straight to his bed, had an orgasm from frotting, and then started talking.

"I'm surprised you came home with me," he said. "You have the reputation of being aloof."

"Huh," I thought. I didn't think people were aware of me. "I'm just new to all of this, and a little scared."

"I understand," he said. "I was like that too when I first came out. Are you out to your family?"

"Not yet," I said, "but I suspect they know."

I don't think it came as a surprise to my mom and dad when I asked to meet with them to tell them that I was Gay. My father said he thought

I had a hormone imbalance and that I'd outgrow it. He suggested that everyone was Bisexual. As Dad and I talked, Mom excused herself and went to the kitchen to cry. She told my older sister, Kathy, that the world was going to be awful to me and there was nothing she could do to protect me. Shortly after I came out, my mother's cousin and best friend, Sr. Marcella Gardner, an Adrian Dominican nun, said, "Virginia, he's the same fine boy he was yesterday." That made a difference.

I gave my parents a couple of books to read. The one they found most helpful was by a well-known author whose son was Gay. Laura Hobson, who wrote *Gentleman's Agreement,* also penned *Consenting Adult.*

Mom and Dad had met Dennis and John. Everyone was welcome in my family home. It had always been so. With Dad's job at GM, we entertained a lot, and had people at all economic and social levels over. All our friends from grade school, high school, and college were welcome. Though I had brought home a couple of girlfriends, Mom and Dad knew in their heart that I was Gay.

In the years that followed, despite all the national awareness of me being Gay and fighting the Catholic Church in Detroit, my boyfriends were still always welcome.

Chapter Eight

My First Love Was an Episcopal Priest

After John moved out, I went to The Woodward, with its familiar smell of cologne and beer. It welcomed me as did the smell of incense and candles in church. Neil Diamond's "I Am I Said" felt the same as God's answer to Moses, "I am who I am." (Break out the chorus from *La Cage aux Folles*.) The freedom described in Janis Joplin's song *Me and Bobby McGee* mirrored for me the freedom found by St. Francis when he stripped off his expensive clothes, returned them to his father, and lived in a cave. He had nothing left to lose. I had come to accept that I had three homes—the bar, the church, and where my family lived.

It was in The Woodward that I eventually met my first real love, Dan, an Episcopal priest with a congregation about an hour's drive from downtown Detroit. He came up to me at the bar and put his hand on my thigh. He was handsome with dark hair and he wore a black leather jacket. I followed him home in my car like a puppy. He had a nice apartment, and there were twinkle lights in a hanging branch on the ceiling above his bed. Was this it? He's my type and a priest. He, too, had to reconcile his sexual orientation with his faith and with his job.

My initial visit with Dan was the first time I experienced penetration. Knowing that I was a virgin in that regard, he was slow and attentive. I don't recall if he invited me back for the weekend, or if I looked to hook up with him again in the bar, but my sights were clearly set on this dashing man who I assumed shared my beliefs and values.

The obvious pattern of all my sexual experiences after college were with men who were "holy," or seemingly so. It was the same with my first girlfriend at Marquette. Freshman year, I went to Mass every day at 5:30 PM, and often served as the lector, the person who stood on the side of the altar and led the singing and some of the prayers. My girlfriend, Charlene, would often come, along with my best friend, Dave. On my residence hall floor, I was referred to as "the dorm Catholic" or "the saint" because I went to Mass so frequently.

Dan was fifteen years older than me, something he tried to hide until he was in the hospital with signs of a heart attack after a vacation, and I looked at his driver's license. What I realized later was that because I was attracted to older men, I probably wouldn't have allowed a younger man to penetrate me. I submitted to Dan, at least in bed.

Having run away from home when he was young, Dan was fiercely independent. It's a marvel that he let me into his life, but I can be persistent. We ended up purchasing a house together. My dream came true. I had my man, and my home with him, with the knowledge and support of my parents. Dan was always welcome not only in the home of my parents but also of my grandparents who lived outside of Boston. He came with me to my grandparents' home to celebrate Christmas one year.

I became active in Dan's parish life, training the acolytes (altar boys) and typing the congregation's newsletter. I didn't attend services, as I continued to go to Roman Catholic services during the week. We teased back and forth about our Christian denominations, with me referring to Episcopalians as "Catholic-lite." One back-and-forth ended with me saying, "My religion was started by a man who died on a cross. How did the man who started your religion die?"

I've painted a rosy picture of my life at that time. The truth is that I could be intensely attached and jealous, and Dan could be emotionally abusive. When we'd fight, I'd go home to my parents and stay there until I felt up to facing him again. Once when we were having sex, Dan put Vicks VapoRub in my anus as a joke, and it hurt like hell. One time I was helping him cook, and I evidently sliced the cabbage incorrectly. "You did it the wrong way, and you've ruined it," he yelled as he threw the cabbage on the floor. I used to cook breakfast for him and have it ready when he got home from church services. One morning, he looked at it, pushed it away, and continued reading the newspaper. I'm painting him as the villain in my drama, but I know he was doing his best, and that he could tell you as many stories about me. I, also, was doing my best.

The more Gay friends I made, usually through Dan, and the more self-confident I became, the more difficult things became with Dan. I was no longer the submissive, starry-eyed "twink" who Dan liked to show off. We had a second bedroom into which I'd move if I was upset with him. However, breaking up with him was out of the question. Though not legally married, which wouldn't be possible for forty years, I felt very strongly that if I left him, I would be divorced. If I was a divorced Catholic, I couldn't remarry. That's how "faithfully Catholic" I was at the time.

Keeping in mind that my emotional maturity around sex and relationships was still stuck in my teens, I got angry and hurt more often than I would today. I didn't have the skills to cope with Dan's behavior and immaturity. I remember the day I wanted to watch myself on television doing an interview on the church's cable program. Our only television was in the bedroom. As I intently watched myself as the host, Dan was behind me playing with his Siamese cat, Sam. When I asked Dan to please be quiet, he said, "Come on Sam. We're not wanted here." At that time, I was twenty-five and he was forty.

As the relationship continued to deteriorate, I became more and more unhappy and desperate. I couldn't stand being in the relationship any longer, and I couldn't leave it. I was trapped and terrified of what the future held for me, especially if I ended up coming out at work to explain my up-and-down moods. So, one Saturday, after yet another argument which ended when Dan got into his car and drove away, I walked over to the utility closet, grabbed the bottle of turpentine, and drank some. I also went to the bathroom and took what pills I could find.

I sat on the floor in desperation, asking myself, "What are you doing?" Subsequently, I jumped up and took a carton of milk out the refrigerator and drank from it, thinking it would neutralize what I was putting in my stomach. And then, I thought, "No, you can't stay, and you can't leave, and no one at work, and none of your readers know that you're Gay. You're going to lose everything." So, I went back to the utility closet, grabbed the bottle of turpentine, and drank as much as I could handle, given the horrible smell.

"If you die, you're going to hell," I thought.

"No, I wouldn't. God is a loving parent who understands."

"But Mom and Dad won't understand, and they've already lost two of their seven children. You're supposed to be 'a prince of a boy.' What is this going to do to them?"

I got up off the floor, got out of my bathrobe and into some clothes, and desperately drove myself to the Catholic hospital. I risked being recognized, as my picture was in the Catholic newspaper every week with my column, but what was I to do? I told the person in the emergency room what I did, they took me directly inside, sat me on a gurney, and then put a tube down into my stomach. I reeked of turpentine.

I felt so, so tired. I cried. I started worrying about Dan finding out. And then I stopped and promised myself that I was never again going to live my life to meet other people's images or expectations of me. When they finished pumping my stomach, I was told to wait until I was checked out by the hospital's psychologist or psychiatrist. After explaining to them my life situation, and my resolve to change it, they gave me the "okay" to go home. I never told Dan what I did, but I planned on coming out to everyone at work, one day at a time.

Fr. Kienzle, Margaret, and the rest of the staff were all great. I asked Fr. Kienzle to lunch on Monday, Margaret Cronyn on Tuesday, Jim, the news editor, on Wednesday, Tom, a young reporter, on Thursday, and Catherine, a young reporter and copy editor, on Friday. Everyone was supportive. Everyone told me being Gay didn't make a difference in how they felt about me. Everyone said the right thing. Tom, especially, was very hip. Yet, weeks later, two days after my column was dropped by the paper, there was a picket line in front of the building, with Gay students from the University of Michigan carrying signs that said, "Give Back Brian's Column." Tom went to the door, opened it, and yelled out, "Which one of you fairies owes me a quarter for my tooth?"

The person I was closest to at work was a Black woman named Mildred McIver. She was a typesetter. Since I first started at the paper, Mildred was the one I wanted most to hang out with. She knew I was Gay long before anyone else, and she was fully supportive. After my column was dropped, and the picketing started, Mildred called me back to talk. She was crying. She said, "They made every employee sign a statement. I signed it because I didn't have a choice." The statement said that the employees resented me using the newspaper as a platform to promote homosexuality. I told Mildred, "Don't worry about it. I know how you really feel." A couple of years ago, I got a call from Mildred's son. "You won't remember me, but I used to come to see my mom at work, and I had the biggest crush on you."

I can't remember where I first heard about it, perhaps from Fr. Kienzle, but shortly after I came out to the staff, I met with a priest who apparently was talking with a small group of other Gay Catholic men. He was very nice and asked me to stay and meet the group he was seeing that night. Not long afterwards, a small group of guys my age appeared at the door. There was Ed, Frank, Skip, and Jerry. After introductions, I told them that I knew about an organization called Dignity, which was for Gay Catholics. There was a national office and chapters around the country. I asked if they might like me to make contact to initiate creating a Detroit chapter. They were all amenable.

At *The Michigan Catholic*, we had access to every story about Catholics from the Catholic News Service. Prior to me coming out, we never ran a story in the paper about homosexuality. After I came out, the news editor was sensitive to the subject, and open to running stories. It was through the news service that I found out about Dignity. I got contact information for the organization's national office in Boston, and I wrote to them, introducing myself, and asking how to start a chapter. Paul Diederich, the president, wrote right back, and I talked on the phone with him and the vice-president, Fr. Tom Oddo, CSC. (Tom eventually became president of the University of Portland, a Holy Cross college.) My ongoing pen pal at Dignity was Jack Hart, who was the secretary.

I met again with the small group of Gay men and told them what was required to be affiliated with Dignity. The priest with whom we met suggested that I go see Fr. Sam Campbell, an assistant pastor at Holy Trinity Church in Corktown, a downtrodden area of central Detroit. The pastor was Monsignor Clement Kern, an older priest who was revered by most everyone in Detroit. He was a compassionate, action-oriented, elderly "saint" who once joined the Playboy bunnies when they picketed the Playboy Club for fair wages. On St. Patrick's Day, every automotive executive who was Catholic, and some who were not, and every politician went to Holy Trinity for Mass, and they filled the collection basket with enough money for Msgr. Kern to run the parish for another year.

Fr. Campbell, who I eventually called "Sam," was a very tall, lean man whose face reflected years of hard drinking. He was clean and sober when we met, and he enthusiastically offered his support for Dignity/Detroit. Like many priests, Sam was a closeted Gay man. The first thing he planned to do was to get a truck and some volunteers to pack me up and move me out of the house I shared with Dan. I needed to first tell Dan and my editor what I was doing.

By that time, Dan and I had pulled apart physically and emotionally. I slept in the guest room every night. At dinner, I told him about Dignity and my intention to start a chapter in Detroit. "If you do that," Dan said, "I want two weeks notice."

"You've got it," I replied. "I'll be moving out in two weeks." Dan was stunned. He finally understood that I had found my own footing and was leaving him. The day the volunteer movers arrived, Dan gave me thirty dimes. "What's this for?" I asked. "Thirty pieces of silver," he replied.

Fr. Kienzle was very supportive of my plans for Dignity, as was Margaret, and the rest of the staff. In my mind, I'd start Dignity to serve the needs of Gay Catholics in the area, and I'd continue to write my column, and be a reporter and copy editor at *The Michigan Catholic*. The two endeavors never needed to cross paths unless the news editor decided he wanted a feature story on it.

Fr. Campbell set up a meeting for me to meet Msgr. Kern, as it was under his wings that we would be protected. Msgr. Kern was very welcoming. I explained to him that Gay and Lesbian Catholics often didn't feel comfortable in the church. Since the Stonewall Rebellion in 1969, a lot of Gay Catholics had come out to themselves and to their families. But, given the teachings of the Vatican about homosexuality, sometimes they'd be in church and hear sermons that condemned people like them. They wanted to be able to have a Mass where they could be open and honest at the Kiss of Peace, and trust that the homily would always be welcoming and affirming.

Msgr. Kern made clear that we were very welcome in Holy Trinity Church, and that Fr. Campbell had permission to be our chaplain.

Sam had found us a big apartment on a seedy street near Tiger Stadium. It was in a huge, classic Victorian house that was painted bright pink. The owner was a short dynamo of an older woman named Gracie who lived in one half of the house and rented out the two apartments in the other half. The street-level apartment was occupied by nuns. I moved my bed and dresser into the second bedroom upstairs, and we made the first bedroom into a library and the back bedroom into a chapel.

My apartment was the Dignity/Detroit Center, the only chapter, to my knowledge, that had a space to call their own. We called it "The Pink Palace." Organizations like Dignity were created in most every other denomination. Our purpose was not only to be a place where people could go to Mass, but also a place where we could meet with potential allies and plan efforts to change the church's teaching on homosexuality. That dual purpose was given equal attention in some chapters, and in others the members only wanted to attend Mass. They were afraid of calling attention to themselves by working as Catholic activists.

On the first Sunday of our existence, eleven men parked their cars on the street, walked into the Pink Palace, and up the steep flight of stairs to our big, sparsely furnished living room. We sat on chairs or on the floor as Fr. Sam said Mass. Afterwards, we had coffee and doughnuts, shared stories, and thought about who else might like to come join us. I felt that I had found my home, a place to be both Gay and Catholic in the presence of other people who were Gay and Catholic. It was truly an exhilarating, liberating experience.

I didn't need Dignity to assure me that homosexual behavior wasn't a sin. I never believed it was. Nor did I need Dignity to have a personal relationship with God. I'd always had that. What Dignity was for me was a way to feel that I was part of a tribe through which I could, as deceased Congressman John Lewis said, "make good trouble."

In 1974, the Watergate scandal forced Richard Nixon out of office, and Gerald Ford was sworn in as president of the United States. In the Gay community, besides Elaine Noble's historic win in Massachusetts, Minnesota State Senator Allan Spear came out of the closet. I remember going to an event at the University of Michigan where both Allan Spear and Elaine Noble were speaking. Spear was not a charismatic speaker. For whatever reason, he was booed by some of the Gay men in the small audience. He passed the microphone to Elaine, who was charismatic and strong-willed. She said as she raised the microphone, "If you boo me, you're getting this up your ass." The Gay men cheered. Many Gay men are drawn to strong, sassy women, which explains the fascination many have with drag queens. We initially didn't have any strong, sassy women in Dignity/Detroit, nor drag queens that I knew of.

It was either through Dignity or through work that I learned of the first conference to be held on homosexuality and the church. My inner voice, the whispers of the Spirit, said very strongly, "You must go to this." It was sponsored by the Marianist priests and brothers at their Bergamo Conference Center in Dayton, Ohio. I got permission from my editor, but I had to come back with a story. I also asked for the blessing of the Dignity/National office. Jack Hart and Fr. Tom Oddo would attend the conference as Dignity's representatives. It was going to be an extraordinarily exciting, historic, and meaningful gathering of Gay activists, theologians, priests, a nun, and many Gay Catholic seminarians, brothers, and laypeople.

Chapter Nine

The First Conference on Homosexuality and the Church

Before I continue to tell you my story about the individuals and events that helped me change the attitudes and behaviors of people around the world toward Gay people and to become "the prince of a man" that I hope to be, I need to acknowledge a conundrum. I can't tell my story without possibly causing some of you great distress.

I have a friend, and you may have one too, whose siblings are evenly divided between those who want to share stories with affection and admiration about their deceased father, and those who don't want him mentioned at all. Three of them grew up with a physically and emotionally abusive alcoholic who terrorized their childhood, and the other three grew up with a man who was a good dad who displayed no such horrifying behavior. Neither of them knew the other's father, though he was the same man. When he died, one sibling reached out to another to say, "I recognize the loss you feel."

In my life, Fr. Paul Shanley, of the Catholic Archdiocese of Boston, was a central character who had a profoundly positive influence on me. He was a charismatic, authority-defying superstar who inspired in me the vision and the strength I needed to continually move forward as a Gay man of faith. Paul came to Ray's and my home for holiday meals, we talked frequently on the phone, and many years later I wrote him regularly. We visited him twice a year in prison, as we felt called by our faith to do.

In the lives of others, unbeknownst to me, Paul was a sexual predator who was eventually charged, found guilty, and sent to prison for molesting a child. I didn't ever know that Paul Shanley, and I understand that some readers didn't know the man both Ray and I loved. To those who have been badly damaged, I say I recognize the anger and pain you feel. However, I can't tell you my life story without writing about the Paul I knew, and the intersection of our lives. I have, however, edited out any unnecessary references to Paul, which I've done with some difficulty but with the purpose of making this story as welcoming to everyone as possible.

The first conference on homosexuality and the Catholic Church, held at the Bergamo center, had a huge impact on my life. It was there that I met Paul, a Boston priest officially designated to work with runaway kids, including those who were Gay. He was a "street priest," who knew where the hustlers hung out, where drugs were dealt, and where homeless kids slept.

I was immediately mesmerized by Paul at the opening cocktail reception. He was very handsome and glowed with self-confidence. He was the first priest in Boston to celebrate Mass for Gay people. Ray was one of the handful of people who helped him start "Interfaith" in 1972, a place where the weekly Sunday service was open to everyone. Before I met Ray, he played the guitar at that Mass. Interfaith preceded Dignity in Boston by more than a year.

I also got to meet Sr. Jeannine Gramick, of the School Sisters of Notre Dame, an order that eventually asked her to leave because of the Vatican pressure they were experiencing due to Sr. Jeannine's ministry to Lesbian, Gay, Bisexual, Transgender, and Queer people, and their families. You didn't use all those words back then, not even an acronym. Sister Jeannine, in her studded jeans, and Fr. Shanley, had ministries to Gay people, a term that at the time took in every sexual and gender minority.

Three years later, Sr. Jeannine and Fr. Bob Nugent started New Ways Ministry as an effort to build bridges between Gay Catholics and their Church, working closely with bishops, priests, brothers, nuns, and the laity. Unlike Dignity, New Ways doesn't have members, or chapters across the country. They don't have a regularly scheduled Mass for Gay people. Instead, they gather information to present to the Catholic cardinals and bishops. They publish the words of progressive theologians and bishops in their newsletter, pamphlets, and books, and they run workshops around the country that attract other nuns, priests and bishops who want to be supportive, as well as Gay people, and their families.

At the time I assumed Sr. Jeannine was a Lesbian, not just because of her dedicated, passionate ministry (she used to teach math at the college level) but also because of her outfit. She now assures me that if she was wearing such studded jeans as I claimed, it was the only thing at Goodwill that would fit.

One of the earliest groups of Gay and Straight members of a Catholic religious order was the Salvatorian Gay Ministry Task Force. Paris Baldacci was a member who I knew from Marquette who walked around campus in a long wool cape. I so wanted to introduce myself to him at that time, but I knew that if I was spotted talking to him, it would confirm that I was Gay too. Instead, I wore my father's Navy swamp coat everywhere, possibly protecting me from speculation I wasn't ready to confirm.

At the opening reception, I met Fr. Tom Oddo, CSC, the very bright, articulate, clear-thinking, and handsome then-secretary of Dignity/National, and Fr. John Harvey, a theologian who at one time was thought to be progressive because he brought into the conversation the word "homosexual," but he never moved forward, and continued to feel that all Gay and Lesbian Catholics needed to be celibate. I also met two revered pioneers of the Gay movement, Jim Kepner, the archivist for One, Inc., one of the earliest Gay organizations in the country, and Dr. Frank Kameny, the astronomer who was fired by the US government for being Gay. He fought his case all the way to the Supreme Court, and eventually received in his old age an apology from the Office of the President. I'm told that at one late night gathering of some of the participants, Kameny threw his shoe at Fr. Harvey. He missed.

All weekend long I was surrounded by people making the same journey as me, who helped give me confidence that I was not alone, that I was on the right path. I made new friends, such as Bill Baird, a future founder of Dignity/Denver with whom I'm still in touch, as I am with Sr. Jeannine, and was for many years with Paul. I introduced myself to Paris and told him my Marquette story, and I met a Gay monk who left the order and years later would be working in the mayor's office in Boston at the same time I did, but not as an openly Gay man.

This historic conference sought to bring under one roof everyone who was doing something around homosexuality and Catholicism. It consisted of presentations, workshops, Mass, shared meals, and perhaps a shared bed.

As the evening of introductions was winding down, I made my way through the crowd to introduce myself to Paul. We went for a long, rambling walk together during which we both smoked and talked about our jobs in Boston and in Detroit. We were equally irreverent about conservative bishops and cardinals in the church.

I spoke to the group at Bergamo in one workshop as a Gay Catholic diocesan columnist who had the support of his priest editor, and as the founder of Dignity/Detroit. The group laughed and loved the stories of the Pink Palace. Paul spoke too, as the official representative of Cardinal Humberto Medeiros who he said had blessed his ministry. *People* magazine did a profile on Paul, showing him roller skating with Gay and Transgender youth. When Paul spoke at the conference, he began with "Gay is good for Gays. Bi is good for Bisexuals, and Straight is good for Straights."

As you might imagine, celebrating Mass with Gay priests at the altar and being surrounded in the pews by other Gay Catholics who were making the same journey, who were as committed to the teachings of Jesus, and who longed to be agents of change in the church they loved, it was impossible not to cry.

It was difficult leaving this very special place where my two worlds of being Gay and Catholic finally fit together so easily and comfortably. I was pumped and primed for the challenges we all faced in changing the beliefs and practices of the church to which we were so devoted. The conference in Bergamo not only inspired me, but it also gave me wings. Jesus was with me; I had no doubt. The Spirit was eager to express itself, and I was more than ready to be used.

The first thing I did when I got back to Detroit, after reporting to Dignity/National, to the members of Dignity/Detroit, and to Fr. Kienzle was to write my weekly column with the heading "Gay or Straight, Love is the Goal." I quoted Fr. Paul Shanley and wrote about the challenges faced by Gay Catholics. I didn't come out in the column, but I got word that every Gay seminarian in Detroit had read it. Normally, the news editor would just send my column to the typesetters, but this one he walked into Father's office. After a while, I was called in, prepared to hear that they weren't going to publish what I wrote. Instead, Fr. Kienzle gave me some suggestions on how to improve it and to tighten it up.

The paper came out on Thursday, and between then and Monday all hell broke loose. It was made clear to me in no uncertain terms that I wasn't to use my column again to promote homosexuality as normal, and Cardinal Dearden asked every priest to read a letter during Mass that explained the church's teachings on homosexuality. Soon after, Fr. Kienzle left as editor of *The Michigan Catholic* not because of me but because of the church's rule that priests could never marry. Bill Kienzle eventually did marry and became a well-liked writer of church-related mysteries. In his place, Margaret Cronyn was made the editor-in-chief.

Chapter Ten

"He Came Out of Nowhere"

"WHY DID YOU SAY 'yes'?" I was asked a few years ago by a Gay historian. "You could have said 'No,' and kept your job and Dignity too."

"I never say 'No' when God or the Universe calls to me," I replied. When things happen, I trust I'm guided by the Spirit, and I say, "Yes."

We were talking about a call I got at home, a telephone number I shared with Dignity/Detroit. Dignity didn't have any money, so I paid the phone and electric bills. The person calling me was a friend with whom I had yet to come out. Nancy Manser was the religion editor of *The Detroit News*, and she was writing a story about homosexuality and religion. She had called the Archdiocese to see if there was a Dignity chapter in town, and she was given my number.

It was only awkward for a minute. Everything was moving so fast in my life that I didn't have the chance to come out to everyone I cared about, including Nancy.

"Can I interview you for my article?" she asked.

"Yes," I replied. How were any Gay Catholics going to know about the Mass we had every Sunday if I didn't tell her about Dignity, our goals, and where we met?

Nancy interviewed me and the minister of the Metropolitan Community Church, Rev. Tony. Soon after our interview, MCC made clear to every minister that they had to give their first and last names in any interviews. It's so long ago that I don't recall if I was identified as a reporter and columnist for *The Michigan Catholic*. It doesn't matter. I was well-known enough that people made the connection.

I gave Mom and Dad a heads up about the article that was going to appear the next day. My only regret about my public coming out was the impact it had on the privacy of my family and of Dan. I was so caught up in being an instrument of the Spirit, and in the growth and success of Dignity/ Detroit, that I didn't think about how my coming out publicly affected the lives of others. Malcolm Boyd once said that he had been involved in every civil rights movement but his own. The same was true for me. Nothing felt more important than the cause of Gay civil rights, not friends, family, or my career.

Nancy's article ran on a Saturday. I was excited, scared, and proud. On Monday when I went to work, the building was eerily quiet, and Margaret called me into her office. "We're dropping your column," she said.

"Why?" I asked, seriously incredulous because I naively didn't expect my being Gay would change things at work, and since the City of Detroit the week before had added "sexual orientation" to the city charter's nondiscrimination protections.

"We'll say it's because of space limitations," Margaret said. "But the real reason is that we've had calls coming in all weekend from advertisers who threatened to pull their ads, and from priests who buy copies for every parishioner but who said they were going to stop doing so if we didn't address this issue."

Margaret wasn't my enemy, but she was now my boss, and I knew she didn't do anything without the approval of the bishops. I'm sure she also got a lot of pressure from the paper's business manager, John Howell, who never tried to get to know the staff. One great loss of my battle with the newspaper was my good friendship with Margaret. She was a gem of a person.

I went back to my desk and did the copyediting of articles placed on my desk by the news editor, and then got a call from Nancy Manser. "Has there been any reaction to my article?" she asked.

"Yes, they just dropped my column," I whispered.

"Let me get a pencil."

The next day, *The Detroit News* had an eight-column headline that read, "Catholic Newspaper Drops Column by Homosexual." I was accused by management of creating the controversy, and some coworkers quit talking to me. But I never called a single newspaper, radio station, or television station to give them information. They came to me in rapid succession.

At the end of the day, as we walked to our cars, a former employee of *The Michigan Catholic*, a guy who used to show up late every morning reeking of alcohol, and who I knew was a closeted older homosexual, yelled at the top of his lungs, "Faggot. Faggot. Faggot." Mildred walked across the street to calm him down.

Everything changed for me and for many others in that week. I received death threats, and Margaret was sent pornographic pictures of men having sex. There was enormous tension in the newsroom. One morning I spotted an anti-Gay news article taped to the office wall. John Howell asked me for a list of the radio and television programs that I'd be on. There were several. The next day, there were announcements posted throughout the building of what programs I'd be on, on what day, and at what time.

I was both scared and excited that I was now part of the Gay community's civil rights movement. The two early leaders of Detroit's Gay liberation movement, when asked by a historian to describe what they felt at the time, they both responded that "Brian McNaught came out of nowhere." That wasn't true. I was groomed by my family and my faith to step up, speak up, and not to be afraid. I respected and appreciated the past hard work of the early Gay activists in Detroit, and they, in turn, were very appreciative of Dignity's growing size of middle-class Gay men. They had never assembled a group as large as could Dignity/Detroit.

I made an appointment to meet with Bishop Tom Gumbleton. He was the most progressive auxiliary bishop in the country, and because of his ongoing involvement in every major civil rights issue, everyone knew he would never be a bishop who headed up his own diocese. I recall Bishop Gumbleton being quite uncomfortable with the conversation. I was asking for his help with Dignity, and with all the attention my case was getting. He couldn't do that, and I was very disappointed. Several years later, I received a letter from Tom that said "I now have a sense of how very, very difficult it must have been for you. Truly, you were ahead of your time in calling for understanding for the Gay community. I'm sure those days were filled with frustration and loneliness. I'm personally grateful that you persevered . . . Know that I will continue to do all I can to work for justice and understanding for the homosexual community." You must know how affirming those words were for me.

I also met with the head of the Episcopal Diocese of Michigan, Bishop Coleman McGehee to ask for his support. He, in turn, sent a letter to Cardinal Dearden on my behalf. That inter-denominational effort to influence a change in attitude was unprecedented.

As a union member in the Detroit Newspaper Guild, I asked my steward, who was the news editor, to bring a complaint against *The Michigan Catholic* for discriminating against me because I was a homosexual. Doing so ended all conversations with Margaret or John Howell. It didn't stop the letters to the editor that poured into the office, with some, but not many of them supporting me. It was hard to get up every morning and head into the office. All the "good mornings" ended. The coffee and donuts morning ritual ended. I continued to work but felt isolated and hated by some.

In that time, Lou Gordon, a local television host whose program was aired in different parts of the country, asked me to be on his show. It was a great opportunity to get the word out about Dignity and the discrimination experienced by Gay people. I kept my folks informed of what interviews I was doing. Dad hated Lou Gordon I believe because of Gordon's support of Ralph Nader, who said that Chevrolet's Corvair was "unsafe at any speed." My father said, "If you go on his program, you can't come back into our house."

Appearing on *The Lou Gordon Show* jettisoned me into a level of public attention, and gave me a national platform I never otherwise would have had. There was a lot of press coverage of me and of my case with the newspapers both in Detroit and in the national Catholic press. *The New York Times* carried a short article. But, in Syracuse University, a teaching assistant of Dr. Sol Gordon, Michael Crinnin, saw me on *Lou Gordon* and suggested that Sol have me speak to his human sexuality class of 500 students. Once that happened, Sol took me under his wing and gave me the national spotlight. He was my mentor and sponsor, ensuring that I was invited to conferences and recommended as a speaker.

I appeared on *The Lou Gordon Show* twice, once alone and the second time with Sr. Jeannine Gramick. The second interview was after my hunger fast.

There was a lot of activity taking place at that time. Dozens of phone calls came in at all hours of the day and night. I'd hang up immediately if the person was threatening. Most of the calls, though, were from people who wanted to come to Mass, or people across the country who just wanted to talk. Dignity became more structured when it became too much for me to manage by myself. We elected officers and delegated responsibilities.

The atmosphere at work became intolerable, and the response from the Archdiocese was to ignore what was going on. Monsignor Kern was getting pressured to kick us out of Holy Trinity, and Fr. Sam Campbell also got some negative feedback. The Catholic press was filled with reports on Dignity and on my case with the Archdiocese. One columnist, as previously mentioned, called me a heretic, but another called me a saint.

It got to the point where I felt that the only way to quiet the noise and to bring serious attention to the plight of the Gay Catholic was to go on a hunger fast. I first talked about it with the officers of Dignity/National and with the members of Dignity/Detroit. I'd need the support of both groups for it to have any effect. There was concern for me, and good questions about when the fast would end. We agreed that the bishops in Detroit needed to address the issue, so that became our goal. The fast would end when the bishops pledged to educate the clergy. We knew that education was the only means of transforming beliefs and behaviors. That formula has not never and will never change. Educating others with loving kindness enables them to understand.

Both Dignity/National and Dignity/Detroit created press releases. We got a doctor to call *The Michigan Catholic* every day to say I wouldn't be able to come into work that day because of ill health. I needed a doctor's order to miss work for any period of time.

The hunger fast I earlier described for Fr. Tom Lumpkin was, again, created by Dick Gregory. I drank the grape juice for seven days, and then began to drink just water. I did the Epsom salt baths and the enemas. For most of the time, I was alone. Initially, I didn't feel any effects, but then the headaches and insomnia hit me. I would lie awake at night and listen to the rats run up and down the hallway outside of my room. The house and the neighborhood were infested but normally you'd only see them at night. So, nighttime wasn't my favorite time during the twenty-four days. But in the morning, I'd often find a vase of flowers from Gracie, my landlady. She knew what I was doing, and she wanted me to feel her private, loving support.

For me, the fast was deeply spiritual, and I found my strength in passages from the Bible, such as "Is not this the kind of fasting I have chosen: to loose the chains of injustice and untie the cords of the yoke, to set the oppressed free and break every yoke?" (Isa 58: 3–7)

Who are the oppressed laborers? Lesbian, Gay, Bisexual, Transgender, and Queer people come to mind. "When you fast, do not look somber as the hypocrites do, for they disfigure their faces to show others they are fasting. Truly I tell you, they have received their reward in full." (Matt 6:16)

The hardest part of the fast was when Mom called in tears and begged me to stop. "We can't take anymore." My mother rarely cried, and never asked anything of me. It broke my heart to explain to her that I couldn't end the fast. We might take pride in the sacrifices we make for a cause, but there are always innocent victims of our actions, and my family members were among mine.

On the twenty-fourth day of the fast, I received a letter signed by Auxiliary Bishops Tom Gumbleton and Joseph Imesch. Cardinal Dearden and the other auxiliary bishops were in Rome. The two bishops, who I was told fasted on water for one day, wrote, "From the outset, let us say that we respect the motives, and the sincerity of your efforts. We have a serious obligation to root out structures and attitudes that discriminate against the homosexual as a person. We will exert our leadership on behalf of this effort."

Fr. Campbell, who delivered the letter to me, hoped it was enough. I called the Dignity/National office, as well as the members of the local group to get their feedback. They decided that it was enough of a promise for me to end the fast.

Two things happened during the fast that had major significance. I got a call from someone associated with the upcoming Catholic Press Association conference in Chicago. He told me that because of my case with *The Michigan Catholic* they were going to have a panel discussion on homosexuality and the Catholic Church. "We can't officially invite you," he said, "but we also won't stop you from attending." It was obvious to me that they wanted me to attend. Why else would they call?

By that time, I was down to about 126 pounds, losing a pound a day. I asked a friend to drive me to Chicago. I looked quite spent, with clothes hanging off me, and I sat in a seat two rows ahead of Margaret Cronyn. I remained silent through most of the discussion, but then raised my hand. I stood when called upon, identified myself, and said, "All that we're asking is that you tell the truth. Have someone write an article about the American Psychiatric Association removing homosexuality from its list of disorders. Tell us what the Dutch Bishops said about homosexuality in their catechism."

The host of the event, and editor of the *U.S. Catholic*, a national magazine held in high esteem, was on stage. "Will you write the story for us?" he asked. "I'd be very glad to," I responded, and quietly kept a low profile until the session was over. I then came directly home. After my fast ended, I wrote an essay called "The Sad Dilemma of the Gay Catholic." It was about the challenges Gay Catholics face between abiding by church teaching and being true to their nature, and their romantic love of another person. Once again, the article was very personal, with me putting a face on the issue. It was published that year by the *U.S. Catholic* and to my astonished delight was subsequently awarded "Best Magazine Article of the Year" by the Catholic Press Association. This was an astounding affirmation for Gay Catholics at a time when many people still refused to talk about it. It had become an issue that would not go quietly into the night.

The other thing that happened during my water fast was a "Mass of Solidarity," to which every priest in the diocese was invited. Msgr. Kern was asked by Cardinal Dearden to cancel the event, but he politely replied, "Cardinal, I just can't do that." The Monsignor celebrated the Mass at Holy Trinity, opening with the statement, "All of us, Gay and Straight alike, have come here today to affirm ourselves before God in faith, to accept ourselves without regret or self-pity, and to seek a good and full life in keeping with our potential for growth and God's call." Those were extraordinary words of welcome by the most revered priest in the Archdiocese.

Fr. Paul Shanley flew in from Boston to give the homily, and Sr. Jeannine from Baltimore. A group of Gay Episcopalians came to sing in the choir loft. Dignity members were there in force, but only a few priests and nuns showed up. I felt a little isolated as I sat alone in my pew until my best friend, Henry Grix, walked down the aisle and sat next to me. He wasn't out yet, but his presence was very comforting.

One of the things that usually happens when you come out is that every relationship in your life changes. I was very close to my many cousins but only heard from one of them. I know now that the others weren't rejecting me. They just didn't know how to express their feelings. It was nevertheless disappointing. I also felt very alienated from my high school and college friends. It was understandable. Ignorance is the parent of fear, and most people in 1974 had very little awareness or understanding of homosexuality. They thought it was a choice, and usually the result of an absent father or a domineering mother. It became my life mission to educate heterosexuals on the truths of being Gay and to affirm homosexuals on their journey to self-acceptance and celebration in any way that I could.

When Paul Shanley walked over to the lectern to speak at the Mass, a small group from the ultraconservative organization Catholics United for the Faith stepped forth on the altar steps and unfurled a banner that proclaimed, "A Moral Wrong Can Never Be a Civil Right." They were escorted out of the church by Dignity members while the choir and participants began singing, "They Will Know We Are Christians by Our Love." Paul cleverly played off the words of their banner, soothing the nerves of everyone in the church, and inspiring us to believe that we were doing the work Jesus called us to do.

At the end of Mass, all the Dignity members, as well as Paul and Jeannine, went down to the nearby Chancery (Diocesan offices) and walked in a picket line singing and chanting affirmations of being Gay. I was too weak to walk but learned that an old usher standing in front of the Chancery had told a police officer, "Arrest them." The officer explained that they had the right to be there, to which the old Catholic man said in astonishment, "I didn't know cocksuckers had civil rights." I don't think he was trying to be offensive. He just grew up in a very different world, a world that was changing in astonishing and rapid ways, and it threatened him.

After my fast ended, I got fired. Then a Gay newspaper asked me to write a regular column for them as I did for *The Michigan Catholic*. Soon, the column, "A Disturbed Peace," appeared in ten Gay newspapers. My columns were pieces you could have your parents read. I was a different voice than many Gay people were used to. Mine was a moderating, bridge-building voice that appeared in these columns for twelve years. Dignity/National published a collection of those columns and essays under the title *A Disturbed Peace: Selected Writings of an Irish Catholic Homosexual*. The book sold 11,000 copies before Dignity decided they no longer wanted to be in the distribution business, but before that happened, one independently wealthy priest in Chicago paid to have a copy of the book sent to every bishop in the country.

Money wasn't very important to me at that time. In fact, I think I took pride in being impoverished. But, a friend of my parents, a man named Bob Taylor, called and asked me to lunch. After learning how I was doing, he slid a $500 check across the table. I was astounded and speechless. He did that a couple more times in the weeks that followed, realizing I had no source of income, and correctly suspecting that my father wasn't giving me any money. Despite that fact, my family expected me to be home on Thanksgiving, as was my oldest brother, Michael, who had just divorced his wife. My father lifted his glass of champagne at the beginning of the meal and said, "This has not been a vintage year." It was his way of saying, "And we shall move on as a family."

Throughout my life, there have been a multitude of people, Gay and Straight, who made sure I felt supported, be it by the check from Bob, the flowers from Gracie, or the tears of my *Michigan Catholic* buddy, Mildred. That loving kindness expressed by others over these many years, kindness with no expectation of reward, is truly, along with my faith, family, and friends, what guided and supported me through this labyrinth of changing hearts and behaviors.

My most faithful initial supporter, one of the four guys I first met before I started Dignity/Detroit, was Ed Tawyea. I was taken with him from the beginning. He loved what I was saying on the radio and television programs, and in the press, and he admired and was proud of me. Often, he was sitting on the front steps of the Pink Palace waiting for me to return from a radio interview. I could feel his affection, but it felt that he wasn't as attracted to me physically as I was to him.

I was worn down from living in the Dignity/Detroit center. There was little privacy or downtime. Ed was looking for a place to live that was closer to work, so we decided to live together as roommates. Fr. Campbell, who had an enormous number of connections in Detroit, secured for us a furnished two-bedroom apartment on Twelfth and Clairmount where the 1967 riots began. The rats I fled by moving out of the Pink Palace were replaced by an army of cockroaches, but we were very happy to be living there.

After my fast, Ed and I went to see one of the earliest-released, positive Gay feature films called *A Very Natural Thing*. It was about a Gay seminarian who leaves and falls in love with a man. We noticed sitting in front of us a whole row of guys from St. John's Seminary. Coincidentally, I was scheduled to speak at the seminary the next day. A large group of faculty and students sat in a huge circle, with Ed at my side, and I began talking about my life struggle between my sexual orientation and my love for the church to which I was so committed. When I stopped speaking and opened it up to the floor for questions or comments there was utter silence.

"I don't get it," I said. "Ed and I went to see the Gay film, *A Very Natural Thing*, last night and eight of you sat a few rows in front of us. Why aren't you saying anything?" There was a nervous silence, and then members of the faculty got up to leave so that the seminarians might feel the freedom to talk openly.

"It just never comes up," one guy said. "We don't get much instruction in sexuality at all." That comment opened the discussion more, but I sensed a great fear of people being seen by the others as Gay.

Also, after the fast, Lou Gordon invited me back on his program with Jeannine Gramick. Sr. Jeannine stayed with me in the Pink Palace and slept on the bed in what we used as our chapel. "Jeannine," I said, as I headed to bed, "I want you to be prepared for Lou Gordon to ask you about your sexual orientation."

"I know, Brian," she replied.

"What will you say?" I asked.

"Are you asking me whether I'm Gay or Straight?" my dear friend queried.

"Well, I think that good friends should be able to talk honestly about their sexuality, and I want you to know that I'm Gay."

"I'm Straight," she said.

It was all that I could do not to show an expression of shock and great disappointment on my face. I was certain she was a Lesbian because of the great comfort she had in talking about Gay issues.

"Does that disappoint you?" she asked.

"No, I just assumed you were a Lesbian," I lied.

"I don't normally answer the question," she said, "because if I say I'm a Lesbian, people think my ministry is self-serving, and if I say that I'm Straight they don't trust that I really get it." As expected, the next day, Lou Gordon asked Sr. Jeannine about her sexual orientation. As I recall, she declined to say, with the same explanation she gave me.

In the late 1970s, there were so few openly Gay people that the invitation to attend a leadership conference in Denver was a family affair, with most everyone familiar with one another through news items in *The Advocate*, a national Gay newspaper, *Gay Community News*, or their local Gay newspaper. It was very exciting to be a part of the known Gay leadership, although those of us who were working in the trenches of our religious denominations were less interesting to the movement's political leadership. Some saw us as collaborating with the enemy.

There was at that conference at least one well-known person from every denomination who was working hard to change the attitudes of their congregations. We met in reunion not long ago in St. Louis. The sacrifices of those brave and persistent martyrs and prophets have never been adequately acknowledged in Gay history books. What most Gay chroniclers of our story miss is that the shift in cultural attitudes toward

Lesbian, Gay, Bisexual, and Transgender people was due in large part to the discussions that took place in every denomination about homosexuality, all generated by the LGBTQ people who stayed to fight.

At the time of the conference, I was known not just for my role in Dignity, but also because of my syndicated column, which carried more weight than I knew. But I was one of the least sexually aware or sexually driven Gay men I knew. Perhaps it was my Irish Catholic background, but more likely it was the result of hormones and brain structure. Sex was never, or rarely was a motivating factor for me. I loved having sex, although I was always self-conscious that my way of reaching orgasm through frotting would be a turnoff for someone expecting anal sex. I wasn't crazy about being penetrated, but I enjoyed giving oral sex.

Looking back, I was immune to flirtation or sexual come-ons. Dave Kopay, the first out NFL player, came up to me at the leadership conference and said, "I could fuck anyone in this room that I wanted." I thought to myself, "Why is he telling me this?" The same thing happened when two very good-looking, presumably Straight AT&T managers took me to dinner after a day of corporate diversity training. One of the guys gave me a ride back to the hotel. As we approached, he said, "I've been told I have a very fuckable body." "Hmm," I thought. "He must be Bisexual, but why is he telling me this?"

Sometimes I think I'd like to come back as a very sexualized Gay man. I'd carry myself in a sexy way, flirt, go to the bars and bathhouses, especially those described as being over the top. I fantasize about being sexually dominant (a top) and having a great body. I've thought about what it would be like to be desired, and to have sex with every man that interested me. But that just isn't me in this life. I've been in a relationship since leaving college. Dennis, John, Dan, Ed, and Ray. I don't feel cheated in the amount of sex I've had, and I've had sex with a few more people than those mentioned.

Eric Rofes, a Gay leader at the time, said that you're not a real Gay man until you've been fucked. It surprised me that he would say such a silly thing because I thought I knew him well. One night, we sat in my car, and he talked in tears about not fitting in. He was a nice Jewish boy who got into the leather community and took the big step into the sexual life I've fantasized. It was then, I believe, when he lost his perspective that there is nothing special you must do to be truly Gay, Lesbian, Bisexual, or Transgender except to love yourself.

My life's work has been about exactly that. I write and say that you don't have to do anything to be a "real" Gay man, Lesbian woman, Bisexual or Transgender person, or one who calls themselves Queer or Non-Binary. Just be yourself. If you like going to your synagogue, go to your synagogue. If you're happier being single, be single. If you want to experience joy, embrace yourself as being perfect the way you are, and acknowledge that you'll grow and change, just as nature does around us.

When I die, I imagine God will say to me, "Brian, did you sing the song I taught you?" My song, this time around, is that I'm a proud, healthy, and happy Gay man whose heart is filled with gratitude for the many blessings in my life, most especially a husband with whom I've been most joyfully together since 1976.

I ended up settling out of court with the Archdiocese of Detroit. I got $2,500 and was instructed not to talk about the settlement. My Gay lawyer told me there wasn't a jury in the world that would award me money from the church. Okay, "So now that I'm out, what do I do?" (The title of my fourth book). There wasn't a person in my life who didn't know I was Gay, including my nieces and nephews. You've heard the expression, "Love me, love my dog." In my life it was "Love me, love my homosexuality."

My first speaking engagement, after my talks at the University of Michigan and St. John's seminary, was in a private home where friends conducted Bible study. The homeowner answered the door and said, "We're very glad you came, but the lady in the green blazer has said she's going to throw up when you walk into the room." Throw up when "a prince of a boy" walks into the room? It was a startling example of the fear average people had of homosexuals then.

At that time, my presentation included information on the writings of theologians who said that homosexuality was not disordered, as well as the decision of the American Psychiatric Association that homosexuality was not a disorder. I offered the corrected interpretation of the passages in the Bible, talked about the Ford and Beach study that homosexuality exists in every species of mammal, Evelyn Hooker's study of Gay male vs. Straight male emotional health, and Margaret Mead's suggestion that Gay people are in the world to be of service as teachers, nurses, and therapists. I also told my story of growing up with a secret I was afraid to share.

When I finished, someone asked the question every Straight person in the world wanted to have answered and that is, "How did your parents react?" I spent the next twenty minutes talking about my family, and how they wanted me home for Thanksgiving dinner. Once I got into the personal with the Bible study group, I got the attention of the lady in the green blazer, and I watched the expressions on her face change. She laughed with the others when I told them a funny story. At the end of the night, the lady in the green blazer was the last person to leave.

I learned that night a very important lesson. To help people get their arms around someone being Gay, you must tell them your story. You must put a face on the issue. Additionally, at that time, you had to emphasize that being Gay was not a choice, and that if their children were Gay that they, the parents, didn't do anything wrong.

Chapter Eleven

Creating a Home and a Family

My ability to tap both the masculine and feminine in me is perhaps why I'm good at creating a feeling of warmth and welcome in the places I've lived, both inside and out. I also have a gift for cooking, so those were my jobs in our new home. They have continued to be my jobs for the past fifty years.

The first antique I bought a couple years before meeting Ed was a hobnail cranberry glass chandelier. We had moved our landlord Mr. Stevenson's furniture around and pulled up rugs. Ed hung the chandelier, and we began inviting people for dinner. Mom and Dad came, which was a wonderful thing for them to do as the neighborhood was very different than theirs. I remember that Dad kept looking out the window to see if his car was still there.

Ed and I had separate bedrooms, and I made the third bedroom into an office. He was a college librarian, and I worked at home, trying to make a living by writing my column and freelance news stories. I spent the bulk of my time responding to requests for guidance. I answered every letter I received, and returned every call that came in. I also did the grocery shopping, laundry, and took care of Jeremy, the Irish setter puppy I gave Ed for Christmas.

My small settlement with the Archdiocese of Detroit, the $1,500 Bob Taylor gave me, and the $200 a month I received for my columns was what I had to contribute to our rent and household expenses.

Ed and I became more than roommates but not yet a couple. I'm not sure why his feelings for me changed. I did know that I would do anything for him, including move.

We traveled around the country, using my settlement money and my car, looking for a place that would be easier for Ed's asthma. We stopped along the way to see people I had met, or with whom I had corresponded after I was fired. On one occasion, we were having lunch in a restaurant in Galveston, Texas, and the waiter, hearing that we were talking about Dignity, asked, "Can you tell me how Brian McNaught is doing?" My priest friend responded, "Ask him yourself."

It took Ed a long time to decide that I was boyfriend material. He was very proud of me, my courage, and my work, but his primary focus was on his work and his family. As the only son, he felt a commitment to his widowed mother, and enjoyed spending time with his sister, niece, and nephew who lived outside of Detroit.

My family liked Ed very much. He was warm, smart, had a good sense of humor, and was fun to be with. It would be hard not to be taken in by his beautiful smile and wonderful laugh.

As time passed, Ed decided he liked very much the love he experienced from me, as well as the new feelings he was developing for me. He told me that I had taught him how to love. But by the time his focus turned to me, my enchantment had waned, and we found ourselves struggling with different feelings, goals, and needs.

Our sex was infrequent and not very satisfying. We loved one another but our hearts and lives never really connected. In the early part of 1976, I told Ed I wanted to move to Boston to work in Dignity's national office as director of social action. That didn't interest Ed. He loved his work and wanted to stay close to his family. So, after a few understandably difficult weeks he moved out, and left Jeremy with me. "He's more your dog than he is mine," he said. And he was right.

My grandmother and favorite aunt, Joan, lived in Bedford, not far from Boston. After spending summer vacations with them on Pleasant Pond in Epsom, New Hampshire, I had a very special place in my heart for New England. The Dignity/National officers were open to me taking on the job as director of social action but said I'd have to raise the money for my salary. Then, two members of Dignity/Boston who had found an amazing apartment on Beacon Street in Brookline, told me they were looking for a third roommate. They had heard that I was considering the move from Detroit. After a couple of phone calls, I made the commitment to come east.

Patrick Keefe, born and raised Irish Catholic south of Boston, was the Dignity/National treasurer, and Ray Struble, one of seven boys from Wichita, Kansas, was vice-president of the Dignity/Boston chapter. These very kind, thoughtful, and generous men were to be my new roommates.

On May 4, 1976, at age twenty-eight, I arrived in Boston in my red Opel wagon, pulling a small 5 x 8 U-Haul trailer, with Jeremy in the back seat. Hearing from me that I was geographically challenged, Patrick and Ray said they would drive out to look for me so that I could easily make my way home. They spotted me and waved wildly on the Massachusetts Ave. overpass of the turnpike because I had exited and was heading in the wrong direction. I pulled over, and this very handsome, strawberry blond guy, Ray, jumped into my car. Welcomed initially with barking from Jeremy, Ray guided me to my new home where I would live for eight very remarkable and treasured years.

Our beautiful, rent-controlled apartment had a working fireplace in the huge living room, a formal dining room with wainscoting and a beamed ceiling (from which Ray hung my antique cranberry glass chandelier,) a pantry, large kitchen, three large and one small bedrooms, and two updated bathrooms, all for $425 per month, including heat and water. An enclosed back staircase took us up one flight to the roof where we watched the Boston Marathon pass by every year on Patriots' Day, the third Monday of April.

On the day of my arrival, the guys helped me unload my few furnishings and larger number of boxes. They were excited about having a dog and use of a second car. As I unpacked my boxes, I asked if they'd like me to make dinner that night. They did! I searched my boxes and pulled out the electric frying pan I got from the Salvation Army, a bag of egg noodles, and cans of mushroom soup, tuna fish, and dried onions. My being able to cook was a bonus for them. Having two guys to help me take care of Jeremy was a bonus for me.

When we talked on the phone in advance of my move, we each said that we wanted to create our own family together, with no plans of dating others. Patrick was a handsome, tall, bearded, often moody man, far more sexually active than Ray or me. He was very easygoing, and up for hosting parties, going to the movies, and taking drives two hours up to New Hampshire after work to swim in Pleasant Pond. I often played tricks on Patrick. One time, hearing him in the shower, I pulled back the curtain wearing this great gorilla mask and loved hearing him scream.

The guys had been in the apartment a month before I arrived, and Patrick had already done some serious decorating in the living room. He had the biggest bedroom with its own bath. Ray and I had the back two bedrooms, connected by a glassed-in porch. We shared a bathroom.

Ray and I became fast friends, bonding initially over how horrible Patrick's aesthetic taste was. We very gently, and not all at once, convinced Patrick that such-and-such item he'd placed in the living room would look great in his bedroom. He was always amenable and left decorating the rest of the apartment to Ray and me.

Ray and I laughed a lot, especially during an early paint fight in the kitchen. We'd have feet fights as we both stretched out in different directions on the living room sofa, our toes discreetly covered with an afghan. We weren't strictly each other's type. Ray would describe his type as a blond and his age. My type was an older, Mediterranean man with hair on his chest. I was dark-haired, and Ray was younger than me by three years without a single hair on his chest. Despite that, we were drawn to each other by factors such as shared values, a spiritual hunger, a good sense of humor, a love of antiques, valuing the home as sacred space, dancing, loving kindness, polite behavior, a sense of shared responsibility, love for Jeremy, holiday traditions, and big families. We became increasingly attracted to each other.

Tickling one another beneath the afghan eventually led to occasional nighttime visits to each other's bedrooms. It didn't feel serious at the time. We were young, it was fun, and neither of us wanted to start a new relationship with anyone. It's funny how quickly people you don't think are your type become your type, and all that you could want, and how quickly the resolve not to enter another relationship dissolves when you realize you're in love.

Ray hadn't finished his college degree because Boston State wouldn't accept his theology credits from the seminary. I encouraged him to get his degree, which he did at Boston College, as well as to get braces. He has thanked me many times for both encouragements. Ray was a very sharp dresser and a hard worker. When Boston had its major snowstorm in 1978, Ray walked two miles through seven-foot walls of plowed snow to his office in downtown Boston. He and his boss were the only two people in the building all day.

Across from me now is a picture of my Grandpa McNaught holding me as a toddler on his knee. I worshiped the man because of his wisdom, sense of humor, and his ability to do anything, from plumbing to electricity. Before he retired, he was the nonmedical head of the nearby Veterans Administration hospital. I never imagined I'd meet anyone like my grandfather, but I did in Ray. He's wise, has a good sense of humor and there's nothing he can't do. If he doesn't know how to do something, he learns it. Within months of my moving in, he stripped the paint off all the wood on our fireplace and in the pantry.

Our third-floor walk-up apartment became home not just to those of us who lived there and those who stayed with us for long periods of time, but for everyone who visited. It was a very warm, stable, loving, welcoming place to be with fires in the fireplace, the smell of roast chicken on Sundays, and big, wonderful parties. Patrick's friend Ennio moved into the small fourth bedroom for a few months; then my younger brother Tom for six months; and then Ray's younger brother David for six months.

Patrick and Ray drove to Michigan with me for a summer vacation with my folks in August, and the three of us enjoyed the activities that usually I'd plan. However, our initial unwritten commitment to become a core family and not to date had begun to erode quite quickly. Ray and I had kept our growing relationship secret for fear of hurting Patrick's feelings, but we began to acknowledge that we liked each other more than just as roommates. Initially, we'd sneak back and forth into each other's rooms through the glass porch we shared. By Christmastime, it became more obvious, and Patrick realized that Ray and I were in a developing relationship. Even though we never excluded him from outings, he decided to move out. We'd see him at Mass on Sunday, and he visited us once when we moved to Gloucester in 1983. But as Ray and I pulled away from Dignity/Boston's Mass, we lost touch with Patrick, and were deeply saddened to learn that he was one of our first friends to die of AIDS.

To raise my share of the rent and expenses, I continued to write my syndicated column, speak on college campuses, worked part-time in the Dignity/National office, and once a month pull an all-nighter to do the layout for the Gay paper in Detroit, *Metro Gay News*. Paul Shanley had the dream of opening the Exodus Center, a retreat facility for Gay Catholics. He hired me and my friend, Donna Taylor, to try to make it happen but we weren't very successful in raising money.

I applied for full-time work and was almost hired to be the editor of *The Witness*, the liberal magazine of the Episcopal Church, and as director of social action for the Unitarian Universalists, whose headquarters was in Boston. Bishop Bob DeWitt, the publisher of *The Witness*, flew me in for an interview, and I stayed in his home and met his wonderful wife. In both job-seeking instances, the choices from many applicants came down to me and a woman, and in both instances the woman was chosen. When Bishop DeWitt called to let me know, I got so disappointed and flustered that I said, "Please give your regards to my wife." When I hung up the phone, I asked myself, "What did you just say?" It was like the night of our Christmas party at which I was so excited to see so many Dignity friends, I said, "Now, don't say 'good-bye' without leaving."

Bishop DeWitt did ask me to take over *The Witness* as editor when the full-time editor went on vacation. The two editions that I worked on with my very talented artist friend, Dave Woodford, were focused on whether there was a place for Gay people in the Episcopal Church.

Ray loved my grandmother and Aunt Joan, who lived nearby, as well as my younger brother, Tom. Ray shared my desire to make our apartment as wonderful as it could be on our limited budgets. It was a spectacular space, but it was greatly enhanced by the antiques we'd find in shops in New Hampshire. During Christmas, we'd use greenery to make our own roping and wreaths, and string cranberries and popcorn as we watched *The Waltons* and *Little House on the Prairie*. Both Ray's parents and my parents stayed with us in the apartment, though, quite remarkably, they never met.

In the eight years we lived in this wonderful home we had many events, some historic, that included parties for Dignity and others for Christmas. The first Massachusetts safe sex brochure was written in our living room. Congressman Gerry Studds, Elaine Noble, Lisa Myers, Lily Tomlin, Gregory Maguire, Ariadne Kane, Tomie dePaola, Neil Miller, and Stephen McCauley, among others, all spent time in the apartment. It's where we held a huge fundraiser to help Gerry Studds pay his legal bills when he was being censured by the House of Representatives for a transgression with a page ten years earlier, and it was where he hid out when the international press was cornering him for a story. Gerry also spent intimate time there with the now-adult former page, as they were trying out a relationship. He was very grateful for the private space we gave them when Ray and I spent the weekend at the small but charming cabin we bought on Pierce Lake in Hillsborough, New Hampshire. I loved our rich lives in the Brookline apartment, and what we were able to do in that very special space.

Chapter Twelve

"Dear Anita"

In October 1976, Cardinal John Dearden, as head of the National Conference of Catholic Bishops, issued a "Call to Action," where 1,300 bishops, priests, nuns, brothers, and laypeople would work together to create a social action agenda for future church endeavors. Dignity received one invitation and decided that I would be the right person to lobby for Gay Catholics.

From October 21 to 23, we delegates worked in separate sessions on specific topics. Bernard Law, Bishop of Springfield–Cape Girardeau, Missouri, was in my group. Every time I stood to recommend ways to make the church a more welcoming place for Gay and Lesbian people, Bishop Law stood to oppose me. Our group had about fifty people, broken into smaller groups of ten. No one knew each other and very little about homosexuality. I made it a point to spend time with individual people, to ask them questions, to listen to their responses, and to tell them about my priorities. I love meeting new people, listening to their stories, and telling them mine; so, this came easily to me. I do it in the grocery store, on planes, in cabs, and on vacation. I love people, and it's easy for me to focus, listen, and experience empathy.

"Why do you have to use the word 'Gay' all the time?" a Black woman asked me in front of a group. "The word 'Gay' is to 'homosexual' what 'African American' is to 'Negro,'" I replied. "That's all I need to know," she said. "Gay it is." In the end of our large group's work sessions, every proposal I made about the church working hard to protect Gay Catholics from discrimination was approved by the group, except for Bishop Bernard Law and a handful of other conservatives.

There was a great deal of excitement on the final day in Detroit's convention center, Cobo Hall. It was there that the 1,300 delegates would vote on the recommendations from the small groups. I stood to speak in favor of each measure about homosexuality, and the delegates passed each one. Sometime after the conference, I heard from a friend about an older male delegate who had come home from the conference and reported: "It was the strangest thing. Every time this young man got up to speak in favor of homosexuality, I voted 'yes.' I wouldn't have believed you if you told me before I went there that would happen." For me, it was one of the most significant manifestations of the Holy Spirit in my life.

Ultimately, the US bishops rejected the recommendations of the Call to Action conference, just as they did the book, *Human Sexuality, New Directions in American Catholic Thought* by the Catholic Theological Society of America. Having this happen after all the work that had gone into developing the recommendations took me back to a similar experience that happened before I moved out of the Pink Palace. Dignity/Detroit had hosted a historic meeting between Fr. Tony Kosnik and Fr. Ron Modras, authors of the book on human sexuality with representatives from Dignity/National, New Ways Ministry, the Salvatorian Gay Ministry Task Force, and individuals such as Paul Shanley.

Some sat in chairs but the rest of us sat on the floor. Dignity/Detroit members provided food and lodging to out-of-town guests, as well as meals for the group while we met. They also picked people up at the airport and delivered them to the home in which they'd stay. No press was allowed to cover the event. Frs. Kosnik and Modras asked questions but mostly listened to the stories shared by the leadership of the Gay Catholic movement. The theologians concluded that sexual expression was not just for procreation and pleasure. It was also a means of manifesting love. Their description of the purpose of sex was a beautifully crafted definition that included the expressions of love and life in Gay lovemaking. Though the book represented the thoughts of some of the most respected theologians in the United States, it was condemned by the Vatican.

These reactions by the US bishops and the Church in Rome were very disheartening, and they reflected the kind of judgment Gay people were also getting from Jerry Falwell and his so-called Moral Majority, Pat Robertson, Phyllis Schlafly, Lou Sheldon and his Traditional Values Coalition, and James Dobson of Focus on the Family. The 1970s was a decade of protest and of sexual exploration. But it was also a decade of backlash that culminated in Anita Bryant's 1977 "Save Our Children" campaign. Dade County (Miami) Florida had put civil rights protections in place for Gay people, and Anita's campaign was framed as a religious crusade to reverse the law. Anita was presented in the media as the Joan of Arc, and we Gay people were presented as heathen groomers of children, predators, and pedophiles.

June 7, 1977, was a very emotional day for every Gay person in the United States, and beyond. On that day, most people in Miami voted to rescind our civil rights protections. We were angry and felt defeated. The whole campaign impacted my relationship with religion. Some people sobbed because the protections in Miami were among our first legislative successes, and we feared, accurately, that like dominoes, all the other city and county protections against discrimination based on sexual orientation would fall across the country. Ironically, Anita's crusade ensured that every person in the Western world now knew the word "Gay," and she unintentionally created a Gay community that hadn't coalesced before. Because Anita was the spokesperson on television for the Florida orange juice industry, Gay bars across the country poured orange juice into the sewers. Ray, Patrick, and I, like thousands of people, Gay and Straight, quit drinking orange juice. It wasn't long before Anita Bryant was no longer the face of the Florida orange growers.

At age twenty-nine I typed my letter to Anita. I felt compelled to have her understand how her crusade had personally impacted me, another Christian and family-oriented person. I needed to put a face on the issue, so I slowly and patiently created a clear picture of who I was and of what we shared in common. Although I felt angry and hurt, I kept the tone of my letter warm and welcoming. By doing so I brought down the wrath from some Gay leaders who saw my article as too accommodating. However, I knew that expressed anger creates walls built by others that you'll never scale.

When I was finished, I went to bed, and the next morning I asked Ray and Patrick to read it. They liked it a lot, so I sent it to John Ware, a literary agent.

"*The New York Times* Sunday magazine wants to publish your letter to Anita, Brian. Congratulations. This is huge," John told me. That's the same feedback I got from everyone I knew. I told my mom and dad about the article, too. Everyone said that after the piece appeared, I would get book offers, national TV interviews, etc. We didn't get *The New York*

Times in our house, so the first Sunday, I excitedly hurried to the drugstore across the street and bought a copy. It wasn't on the front cover of the magazine, but that was all right. I paged through quickly and couldn't find it. I took the newspaper home and asked Ray and Patrick to look through it.

On Monday, I called John Ware and asked him about it. He said he didn't know, but he'd check on it. He got back to me and said, "Next week." I told more and more people about it, assuring them it would be in the magazine on Sunday. It wasn't. I called John again, and he called back to report, "They say that unless you're planning to change your orientation, it will be in the magazine." Another Sunday passed, I called John, and he called me back to say, "They said it's too late."

It was a great life lesson for me, one that has come in handy ever since. The Buddha said it best. "When you cling, you suffer." I had clung to the expectation that the article would appear and give me a platform from which I could reach a much larger audience with my loving kindness approach to the issues around homosexuality.

My open letter to Anita Bryant was eventually published by Sol Gordon at Syracuse University in his annual family life magazine, *Impact* (available in my book *On Being Gay*). Many Gay and Straight people responded well to the tone and the open hand outreach. A short while later, I was flown to Miami to be the grand marshall of the Gay Pride Parade, and to appear on the television talk show, *To the Point*. (You can watch this debate on my website and YouTube.) John Hansen, who represented Anita Bryant, was a decent guy with conservative religious beliefs, a wife, and children. I had gone to dinner with him the night before and had asked him to share his religious beliefs. John spoke of God making "man." I gently corrected him and said that God made man and woman. I saw John get flustered with the liberal insistence that the word "man" didn't include women.

The next day, Shirley Spellerberg, the conservative wife of a brigadier general, asked John to share his theology. Once again, John said that God made man. I whispered, "and woman." He stopped and got flummoxed, and Shirley Peters, the liberal, asked him not to use language that didn't include women. Back and forth they went, with Shirley Spellerberg urging John not to be distracted. I stayed quiet and smiled.

The conservative Shirley opened the program with, "Welcome *To the Point*. This is Gay Pride Month, although I can't imagine why anyone would be proud to be a homosexual." I waited for the right moment to explain why I was proud to be Gay. I genuinely believe that John was also a guy who would have loved to be able to say that he was Gay. But, to do so, he knew he'd have to give up his family and his religious community. Not only that, but he'd also have to jump back into the Gay community to look for love and fulfillment. He had explained on the program that he had Gay experiences but there was no love to be found, just selfish sex. It broke my heart that John hadn't experienced the happiness and fulfillment as a Gay man that I had experienced. I wanted to help him, but I knew you can't help people who aren't interested in being helped.

Those couple of days in Miami, I learned that I was a much better openly Gay television guest than I was as the grand marshall of the Gay Pride Parade. It's easier for me to ask the Holy Spirit for help in being effective in a televised debate than it is to seek inspiration to sit and wave to strangers from the back of a convertible.

Chapter Thirteen

How and Why My Message Changed

MY CAREER AS AN educator on Lesbian, Gay, Bisexual, and Transgender issues began when I came out, and flourished when I started speaking publicly. I spoke at prestigious universities and at small colleges, including Harvard, Oberlin, Indiana University, the University of Southern California, and nearly 200 others. In the beginning, I spoke for no fee, happy for the opportunity to tell my story. Soon thereafter, I began asking for an honorarium and travel expenses. There was rent to pay.

Colleges brought me in to increase the awareness of their students, faculty, and staff about this new "Gay" minority group. In the beginning of my college speaking, very few faculty, staff, or students were out of the closet. I would typically get invited by a Straight staff person, often someone in the counseling department. I recently heard from a retired counselor at Allegheny College who had invited me in to speak to the students and conduct workshops with administrators and staff after his daughter heard me speak at Kenyon. As more Lesbian, Gay, Bisexual, and Transgender students came out, it was their student groups who arranged for my talk.

The invitations to speak at colleges and at conferences were very steady for a decade. A couple of speakers bureaus asked if they could represent me, but I didn't get any requests through them. Initially, I was very nervous, intimidated more by the Straight men in the audience than by the women. The male students represented the threat of being bullied I had felt since childhood, despite having lots of Straight male friends all throughout my life. But I was on a mission to create a safer world for Lesbian, Gay, Bisexual, and Transgender students, faculty, and staff, and I had to get past my fears, which I did through prayer. I turned it over.

I felt that I carried a great burden on my shoulders. If I was the first openly Gay person the students and faculty met, I had to be conscious of every stereotype, and defy them. I didn't want anything to get in the way of my message, which was basically, "We're not unlike you, and we want the same things in life that you want. We didn't choose to be Gay, any more than you decided to be Straight. Being Gay describes who I am, not what I do. We want to grow to our full potential without worrying about discrimination. We want to feel safe and valued at home, in school, at work, and in church. We want to be able to love another person not in the shadows, but in the sun." Given the total lack of sophistication about homosexuality in the culture at the time, it was the necessary strategy. So, I dressed in a sport coat and tie. I watched how I crossed my legs, how I smoked a cigarette, and how I held a glass. It was exhausting worrying about such things, but I knew that the slightest thing could get picked up, whispered about, and cause me to lose control of the audience. They had no one to compare me against. For most of them, I was the only openly Gay man they had ever met.

A message arrived today on LinkedIn about a college presentation I made thirty-five years ago. ". . . You certainly changed my world, and—by extension—every LGBTQ+ student with whom I have interacted in twenty-nine years as a school counselor. I have been a loud and proud ally ever since you spoke at the University of Maine in 1988. Forever grateful that I went to your lecture with an open mind and open heart . . . I have mentored literally thousands of students with the empathy that I left your lecture with that night."

In the beginning, my typed fact sheet was my anchor. If it flew away, I feared I'd be lost. But before each presentation, I had to calm and focus myself. For hours before, while showering and getting dressed, all I would think about was what I was going to say. I usually needed to use the restroom before each talk or workshop. Once I sat down at the venue, it would totally break my concentration if a college student approached me to say, "Hi, I'm from our student newspaper. Can you answer a couple of questions for me?"

The opening joke that always broke the ice with a college audience was the one about the three women who were playing cards. When the host got up to get snacks, Mrs. McCarthy said to Mrs. Salvatore, "Did I tell you about my son the doctor? He has a new, bright red Porsche." Mrs. Salvatore said, "Isn't that nice. My son, the lawyer, has just bought a huge, yellow sailboat." Mrs. McCarthy said, "You must be very proud. But let's not talk about our sons in front of Miriam. Her son is a homosexual, poor dear." When Mrs. Leibovitz took her place at the table, she said, "Have I told you about my son? He's Gay and he has two lovers. One has a new, bright red Porsche and the other has a huge yellow sailboat."

When I look back at my presentations at colleges, which began with classrooms and grew to addressing thousands at UCLA, I can see how the content of my presentation changed as I matured, and as the culture changed. Initially, I had my typed notes with names and dates listed in the order in which I wanted to raise them. I'd begin with facts, then share a personal story, and end with something uplifting, such as the chapter "I Like It" from my book *On Being Gay*, or my children's rhyming story, *Grogg is a Frog Without Polliwogs*.

What I didn't realize until a few years later was that the content of my talk was far less important than my presence. The members of the audience may or may not remember what I told them about how the Bible had been misinterpreted, but what they would remember is me. "Could this guy be my brother/fraternity member/roommate/friend?" They were far less interested in what the anthropologist and zoologist Ford and Beach discovered about homosexuality in mammals than they were in whether I dated in college, had sex with a woman, how my parents responded, and did I wish I was Straight?

Although I'd prepare myself with prayer, my stomach still did flip-flops as I walked to the stage. Yet, as I spoke, I would start to feel more in control and immersed in my message. I think I've known how to read a room since I was in kindergarten. I tend to look at the faces in the audience, taking a moment to focus on individual people and make nonverbal connections. I could clearly see that most of those folks were listening intently, nodding along or showing empathy. By the end of my career, I described what was happening as a dance between me and those in the audience, whether the group was huge or small. So often people would approach me at the end of the talk to say something like, "I could have listened to you for two more hours."

I loved working with college students. Their minds weren't yet locked to opinions to which they'd cling. After giving several dozen college talks, I learned that what worked best was getting personal from the start and being totally vulnerable. If I could lay myself out there, confidently putting myself in their hands, they would do the same with me. I used humor to help students drop their defenses and feel safe. I never directed humor at the audience but at myself, and at the absurd notions people had about what it is like being Gay. For instance, I'd tell them that just prior to one of my earliest talks, the professor of human sexuality at one college asked me to meet with him in his office. We were chatting amiably, when out of the blue he said to me, "I'm not attracted to you." "Well, I'm not attracted to you either," I replied. He asked, "Why not?"

"Everyone has types," I said, "and you're not my type. In addition, I'm assuming you're Straight, and I'm not attracted to Straight men." A more honest answer would be that I don't allow myself to be attracted to Straight men. However, I don't think he was totally straight with me.

In the beginning of my speaking career, I'd have one hour to share information and answer questions. I was always asked to leave time for questions, and the first question would invariably be, "How did your family respond?" That one question allowed me to do an endearing and funny talk about my folks, my grandparents, and my cousins.

Not long ago, Carson Kressley, the television personality who was on the original series *Queer Eye for the Straight Guy*, came to Fort Lauderdale at my request to present me the Legacy Award from the Stonewall National Museum & Archives. He told the audience that when he was a student at Gettysburg College and heard me speak, I provided him a role model of a proud, happy Gay man. "If he could be like that," he said, "so could I."

Most people know that the scariest thing for many Straight men about Gay men is that we're going to find them attractive. So, I told them that one day in Chicago, I got into a cab and asked the driver to take me to the Sheridan Hotel. "Are you married?" asked the cab driver. "No, I'm Gay," I replied, as it wasn't yet possible to marry. "I'm okay with that," he said, "as long as you don't come after me or my kids." "No offense," I replied, "but why would you think I'd be attracted to you?" Everyone laughed because they knew that Straight men feared being the object of another man's lust, even those who wouldn't likely be noticed by a Gay man.

I'd say, "These guys with beer bellies hanging over their pants will say, 'If a homosexual ever comes near me, I'll kill him.' First, you don't have to go directly to killing them. Saying 'No thank you,' should work. Secondly, don't worry about it. Gay people have taste."

After each talk, especially when they were open to community members such as the mayor, police chief, and parents, I'd usually have a long line of people who wanted to speak with me. One by one they'd step forward into a safe space and ask a question or tell me something. If it was an adult, I assumed they were going to tell me that a son or daughter might be Gay. "What advice can you give me?" I never rushed through an answer. I'd recommend books and organizations, and I'd give them my address and home phone number. Years later, it would be my e-mail address, cellphone, and website. I still do the same. A few years ago, the US State Department during the month of June showed every Thursday a half hour of my two-hour video presentation *Understanding and Managing Gay and Transgender Issues in the Workplace*. I would call in on Zoom and answer questions for half an hour. At the end, I'd always give them my e-mail address and website if they wanted further information.

As I reflect on my early presentations, I realize that not only did I feel a great weight to be the "perfect" ambassador for the Gay community, but I was also desperate to be accepted. I was defensive because I expected pushback, and often got it from some of the male students. I had been through hell with *The Michigan Catholic* and no longer would tolerate being a victim. I took solace in the applause and standing ovations as they gave me the satisfaction that I had done a good job representing my community, and that they liked me. I was accepted.

During this time, it was not uncommon for a daytime television talk show host to have Gay people on their program. When the man or woman were stereotypically Gay it drove me crazy. "I spend all of my time trying to defy stereotypes, and you, in 15 minutes, are seen by millions of people who have the stereotypes reinforced." I felt this for some time, until I began to understand that my hunger for acceptance as a Gay man by all levels of society was not healthy for me or realistic.

It was through my speaking engagements over the years that I matured. I grew from someone who had a hair-trigger defense system into a man who became comfortable with himself, with other Lesbian, Gay, Bisexual, Transgender, and Queer people, and with those heterosexuals who just didn't get it. My maturing didn't happen just because I got older, but rather because I got better informed about all aspects of sexuality. I was exposed to audiences from different cultures around the world, and I learned to trust myself and my instincts. It also happened because my spirituality became more sophisticated. The Buddha taught that when we cling, we suffer. If I clung to acceptance by Gay and Straight people alike, I would pay the consequences.

At the end of my talk, I would tell them the story of being asked by God, "Brian, did you sing the song I taught you?" And then I'd ask, "What's your song, and are you singing it? If not, why not?"

Ray will tell you that he's heard me speak a hundred times and it's never the same presentation. It's true. Like my cooking, the recipe changes depending upon what ingredients I have on hand, and how confident I am that the result will be delicious. There are components to my presentations that are always there but are never exactly the same. When limited by time, I've learned to drop things I used to think were very important and add last minute tweaks to make the talk more relevant to a specific audience. My original talking points on the sheet of paper I carried from talk to talk is in my collected papers at Cornell. If I could easily retrieve it, I'd bet there's not a single item that I used to feel was essential for Straight people to know that is now part of my presentation.

In 1981, I gave my first speech to an audience of sexuality professionals. I was just thirty-three years old when I was invited to be the first Gay person to give the plenary address at the annual conference of the American Association of Sex Educators, Counselors, and Therapists, (AASECT). I had only been speaking publicly for seven years, and much of my talk was telling my story so that the audience would have a face to go with the issue. I made participants laugh by sharing my childhood aspiration to be a saint and made some cry when I told them about drinking the turpentine. This audience would be more sophisticated and knowledgeable regarding sexuality than any group to which I would ever speak. As I prepared for the keynote, I didn't fully grasp that the three different types of professionals in the room might see and hear me differently. The sexuality educators and counselors were probably on the same page with me, but some of the sex therapists made their living by treating Gay men and Lesbians who didn't want to be homosexual.

When I finished my story, I sensed a strong, warm, loving feeling of acceptance in the room. And, then I said, "I feel that if you're not good on the Gay issue you're in the wrong profession." The atmosphere in the room immediately changed. Those who agreed with me applauded, but there were rumblings of pushback among the others. In the midst of this awkwardness, Mary Calderone, the aged grande dame founder of the Sex Information and Education Council of the United States (SIECUS), and the daughter of Edward Steichen, the World War II photographer under whom my father served, stood up in the middle of the audience and said in a booming voice, with her right hand index finger pointing at the ceiling, "He's right!" igniting a strong fire of affirmation in the room.

David McWhirter, MD, the openly Gay psychiatrist who with his psychologist husband, Andrew Mattison, conducted the study and wrote the book *The Male Couple*, made his way through the crowd at the end of my talk and said, "That was amazing! Great job." Dave became a role model for me of an unapologetic, self-loving Gay man. He and Drew became close friends with Ray and me despite their living on the other side of the country.

I've trained police officers and prison personnel, but the toughest personal challenge for me was when I was asked to speak to all the coaches at Brown University. Gay men and Straight or closeted coaches weren't a good mix for me growing up. I knew that with the Brown athletic department, I couldn't use my reliable formula to get them to like and accept me, and thus homosexuality. That's not what they needed to hear.

We met in a large locker room, with my host, Toby Simon, the human sexuality professor at Brown, standing nearby, smiling with pride before I opened my mouth. The women coaches all stayed in the back of the room and said nothing during the entire time we were together. I know that it had to be very awkward for them because people generally assumed that women coaches were Lesbians. The male coaches sat or stood in front of me, many with their arms crossed. It was the one time in my life that I took a beta blocker before speaking, as I was so scared of the confrontation and rejection I anticipated. I wish that I hadn't because I count on the edge to keep me focused.

"We are each other's worst nightmare" I began, getting some smiles in return. This was long before many Gay people were coming out in sports, and there were no known Gay Olympians. So, I created my own scenario for them. I assured them that I wasn't there to have them change their personal values on sexuality, but I wondered what their reaction would be if the star player on their team came out to them as Gay. The person I described was an individual who enabled them to win games. It was worth their while to stop that star from transferring to a more welcoming school. All that I was asking them to do was assess the environment in the locker room. "Start listening to how often the word 'fag' is used, and how often you catch yourselves saying, 'Alright ladies, out on the court.' Now, I'm asking you to imagine that one or two of your star athletes are Gay but they're not telling you because they've watched you let the word 'fag' go unchallenged. To what degree do you think your Gay athletes are affected by the atmosphere in the locker room, gym, and playing field?" It was the perfect approach.

Chapter Fourteen

Five Queers and Me

My Aunt Alice and Uncle Lenny had finished a delicious meal with their daughter Kathleen and her husband Bob in their home outside of Boston. As they were about to depart, Kathleen said, "Oh, you can't go. You must watch *The Lou Gordon Show* with us. This guy's great."

My aunt and uncle stayed, and they all sat in front of the television waiting for the program to begin. There he was, Lou Gordon, the talk show host out of Detroit, and his special guest that night was me, the Gay man whose column had just been dropped because I had come out. None of them were expecting that, and it was how they found out that I was Gay. Kathleen wrote me a beautiful note saying how proud she and her parents were of me. She'll always have a special place in my heart for that greatly appreciated early affirmation.

Another person who saw me on the program that night was Michael Crinnin, who was so excited about me that he urged Sol Gordon, the human sexuality professor at Syracuse University to invite me to speak to his class. Once I met and began working with Sol, my sense of self and my career got a booster rocket ride beyond anything I might have imagined.

Sol liked me; he took an interest in my success, and gave me a national platform. I became good friends with Sol and his wife, Judith, who had narrowly escaped the Nazis. The fact that Judith liked me made a huge difference to Sol. She and Michael attended most of my presentations over the years. Sol made me a regular speaker at his Annual Workshop on Human Sexuality at Thornfield. I went on to serve as staff at the workshop for the next thirty years. Sol published and promoted my open letter to Anita Bryant in response to her Save Our Children campaign, and it became one of the most reprinted essays on what it means to be Gay.

Sol Gordon was well connected in the field of sexuality and collaborated with many of the most renown educators in the country and beyond. He was a master performer with an extraordinary understanding of all things sexual, and he knew how to court controversy to draw attention to his work. Sol and Judith wrote many books for children that explained sexuality in the easiest of terms, such as *Did the Sun Shine Before You Were Born?* Sol also had chapters in several sexual anthologies. Every time I'd come to speak at Syracuse, Sol would have me stay with him and Judith. He and I would stay up on the evening I spoke, have a little wine and cheese, and read through the first draft of a chapter he might be working on. I'd help him with copyediting or provide other assistance. I believe it was Sol who raised my speaking fee to $500, plus travel expenses, and that launched me successfully into the world of consulting.

On Valentine's Day, 2016, Ray and I were helping two women friends, Alix Ritchie and Marty Davis, celebrate their fortieth anniversary. At their party that included most of their friends, Alix and Marty were gracious enough to tell everyone that Ray and I would be celebrating our fortieth in a few months, too. While standing at the bar with my friend, Bryan Rafanelli, the super-talented event creator who designed Chelsea Clinton's wedding, a mutual friend walked up and asked us how we knew one another. I said that we were neighbors in Provincetown.

Bryan replied, to my complete surprise, "I was in Sol Gordon's class on human sexuality at Syracuse University. Brian, here, was brought in to speak about being Gay. When he finished, I said to myself, 'I think I'm Gay.'" By the way, it was Bryan and his husband, Mark Walsh, Deputy Chief of Protocol for the US (2011–2017), who paid out-of-pocket to have the White House bathed in the colors of the rainbow flag for Gay Pride in 2015.

In those early days, with Sol as my mentor, I was invited to speak at a sexuality conference in Hawaii over the Christmas holiday. Ray flew with me and had a grand time getting to know fellow Kansan Betty Dodson, the "women's guru of self-pleasure," as well as many others in the field of human sexuality. Betty danced with us in her black leather outfit with studded collar.

Sol's teaching assistant, Alison Deming, directed Sol's annual summer workshop. After one year of trying to hold it in Syracuse University classrooms, Alison insisted that it be moved to Thornfield, the Episcopal Church retreat facility on Lake Cazenovia outside of Syracuse. Initially, as remained true with his class, I would fly in; Sol would pick me up, I'd stay with him, and then I'd give a presentation at Thornfield the next day. The format of the weeklong workshop at that time was that the first weekend would be a SAR (Sexual Attitude Reassessment), an intense experience designed to help sexuality professionals get in touch with their attitudes and feelings about a range of sexual topics and behaviors. The SAR consists of watching explicit films on all aspects of sexuality and then processing your feelings in a small group to which you had been assigned. It's a training required for certification by AASECT.

Once the SAR ended, it was Sol's workshop during which he would speak to the group at least once a day; introduce them to his featured guests, who would arrive, make their presentation, and then leave.

During this time, I came up with a powerful guided imagery activity in which I'd ask participants to close their eyes and imagine growing up Straight in a Gay world (Gay family, Gay church, Gay high school, etc.) I'd lead participants through various life experiences, such as going on a date and kissing their same-sex partner "good night." I'd say to the group: "In this world people like you are called 'breeders.' You'd have to always be secretive—at home, at school, and at work—because you aren't attracted to members of the same sex. You're attracted to people of the opposite sex. Eventually, you meet a person of the opposite sex that you love and want to be with. They love and want to be with you. So, you rent a two-bedroom apartment, telling people that you are roommates. One day, you find out that your beloved has been in a horrible automobile accident and has been taken to the hospital. You rush to the hospital to discover visitation is restricted to family." After each set of imagined experiences, I'd ask participants, "How do you feel? And who do you tell how you feel?"

At the end of the guided imagery, I'd ask participants to open their eyes and tell me with a word or two what feelings came up for them. Typical responses were: "Lonely." "Scared." "Depressed." "Hopeless." "Angry." For some people, it was a very emotional experience and the first time that they really got what it was like to be Gay at the gut level. It worked every time. More than one corporate executive from outside the US told me that my guided imagery helped them to really understand how a Gay person might feel very isolated and alone. (You can watch the guided imagery on the video, *Growing Up Gay and Lesbian*, on my website, www.brian-mcnaught.com.)

At Thornfield, I'd lead the group in the guided imagery, process their feelings, and then tell the audience my story. I always trusted that if I could win over just one heart, I was creating an ally, and a safer world for LGBTQ people. At Thornfield I saw Toby Simon cry, and fully grasped the idea that many potential allies have never had the opportunity to understand the powerful personal impact of keeping such a secret. From the discussions, I also realized that individuals who are "in the closet" about a different issue such as a hidden disability, often related very easily to the guided imagery because they too had lived their lives keeping secrets.

One year, as I was packing up at the end of my presentation, a beautiful woman with a comforting and understanding face approached me and said, "Brian, I won't hold you up. My name is Mary Lee Tatum, and I've got to tell you something. You did a great job describing what others must face as Gay people, but you really didn't tell us how hard it was on you. You've got to have some pain in there." I was taken aback, and I cried, which is something I rarely do.

"No one has ever asked me that," I said.

"Oh, sweetie," she said as she took my cold hand into her warm ones, "can we promise to talk about this at another time, because I know you've got to go?"

That brief exchange with this remarkable human being began an intimate friendship that continued to grow over the years into a most joyful dance of our souls.

I came home and told Ray about Mary Lee, as I always reported everything of substance about my time away. I would see her again soon at a Workshop for Advanced Sexuality Educators at the Airlie Conference center convened by Mathtech which had just completed an evaluation of sex education programs in the US. This workshop was another pivotal moment for me because I met people who would play key roles in my life and career. Pam Wilson, another very well-known sexuality educator with whom I've created a soul-to-soul and career connection was then on staff at Mathtech. Pam helped design the workshop and invited me to participate. The idea was that advanced educators in the field would make presentations to one another and give each other feedback. Mary Lee, who was teaching one of the most nationally respected sex ed programs at George Mason Senior High School, was a key member of this group. I also met Debra Haffner, a participant who went on to head up SIECUS and to create the Institute on Religion and Sexuality.

Mary Lee Tatum and I became very close very quickly. She had a warm, funny, and magnetic style that drew me and others to her. Her students at George Mason High School (now Meridian) in Falls Church, Virginia, adored her and loved that someone who looked like their middle-aged aunt could be so warm and comfortable with the topic of sexuality. Mary Lee grew up on Whidbey Island, Washington, married her college sweetheart who became a Presbyterian minister, and the couple had two beautiful daughters, Cindy and Lisa. When the girls were teenagers, Mary Lee's husband came out of the closet and contracted HIV. Mary Lee stood by him and cared for him until he died from AIDS. "ML," as some people called her, was on a similar spiritual path as mine. She was a Presbyterian who was loved by many people on Capitol Hill, not because she had any money, but because she was a politically savvy liberal, a pioneer in the field of sexuality education, a great piano player who played everything by ear, and she stayed up on all the news of the day.

I'm looking at a picture of her now, taken, I think, at her daughter Lisa's wedding. I remember dancing with her there, both of us a bit tipsy on white wine, but nevertheless spinning round and round the dance floor.

Mary Lee and I talked on the phone daily at 5 PM, each of us with our glass of Chardonnay. Ray and I invited her to visit us in Gloucester, where we moved when we left Brookline. She came a couple of times, once coinciding with a visit from my parents who fell in love with her immediately, as did Jeremy, the Irish setter. As Mary Lee joined our family of friends, she was the older, wise sister, and I her impish younger brother.

After I had participated for a couple of years, Sol decided to let go of the Annual Workshop on Human Sexuality, and turned over the reins to Alison Deming, a marriage and family therapist in Syracuse. At the time, there were a few key people who had been regular presenters at the workshop—me, Mary Lee, and Bill Stayton, an American Baptist theologian and sexologist, who led the SAR. Alison asked us to redesign the workshop so that it would be a more intensive experience with staff who would remain with the group the entire week, rather than have presenters come in for their presentation, and then leave. Only Sol would come to give a presentation and leave.

We planned to show SAR films on different topic areas throughout the week interspersed with a variety of presentations, activities, and experiences designed to help participants confront their attitudes, feelings, and potential biases so they could become more open and nonjudgmental as sexuality educators or counselors. So, the new and improved Annual Workshop on Human Sexuality was established.

The first year of the new design, Mary Lee and I co-facilitated one of the SAR small groups and there met the participant, Carol Dopp. A couple of years later, we invited Carol to join us, and she became an essential component of the staff. Mary Lee and I became quick friends with her. Carol thinks of Ray's and my home as her home when she visits, which makes us very happy and relaxed. Carol has kept all the photos and paraphernalia from the Thornfield workshop. She's currently head of counseling and the sexuality educator at the Holderness School in New Hampshire.

Pam Wilson joined our team soon after we redesigned the workshop. She came to Thornfield the first year as a participant but ended up co-facilitating one of the SAR groups with Alison. Pam and Mary Lee had previously led SAR groups at the Paul Fleming Institute, so she was well trained. Coincidentally, that year Ray attended Thornfield and was in Pam and Alison's small group. A few years later, Pam permanently joined the staff at Thornfield, and we were lucky to have her. She was now a sexuality education consultant who had written the *Our Whole Lives* junior high curriculum for the Unitarian Universalist Association and the United Church of Christ. She also joined Ray's and my family of friends. Every time we'd go to Washington, DC for a march or to honor the AIDS Quilt, Pam, who lived nearby, would join us as a strong, committed ally, not just there but in my life henceforth.

There were other terrific staff members at the time, Dr. Dick Cross, a retired MD who introduced the first sexuality training for doctors at Rutgers University, Linda Roessler, RN, who lived in Elmira and worked with people with disabilities, and Gail Hompesch, our registrar and sign language interpreter.

Bill Stayton not only showed the sexually explicit films, many of them created by Glide Memorial Church in San Francisco, he also incorporated a sophisticated training on the topics of body image, masturbation, heterosexuality, homosexuality, Transgender issues, sex and disability, and sex and aging. Bill is one of the best sexuality teachers I have ever known. His complete acceptance of every form of loving sexual expression, combined with his theological degree and love of his faith, helped me embrace more completely the sacredness of my lovemaking with Ray.

I learned a great deal about myself, about sexuality, and about the stories of other people in the thirty years I spent a week at Thornfield. There was an intimacy that encased the grounds when we were there, like a snow globe with no snow, but lots of sparkles. The towering pine trees and the pristine lake had witnessed the gathering of other groups, but none, I would bet, who came together as a close family in such a short period of time. That happened because the staff modeled being vulnerable in our honest sharing of our stories. I had been telling my story to college audiences around the country, but being with Mary Lee, Pam, Alison, Bill, Dick, Linda, Carol, and Gail, I dug a lot deeper each year, and left my script of "things every heterosexual needs to know" at home.

Mary Lee and I were the only two staff members who had private rooms. We shared a bath and spent hours upon hours talking and laughing. Mary Lee used to swat my arm and say, "You fool," which made me feel very special. To help her feel the same, every morning I'd go down to the cafeteria and bring her up a cup of coffee, and every night I'd bring her a glass of white wine.

In one popular small group exercise, we'd ask participants to take a large sheet of paper and create representations of the five most significant moments in their sexual development. Some people talked about having their first period, and others talked about being sexually abused by their uncle. My five items would change from year to year as I probed deeper and deeper into my life, and increasingly let go of the need that week to be the perfect Gay ambassador.

At Thornfield, I came to understand that I had experienced unclear parent-child boundaries which led to a lot of sexual confusion, not about my sexual orientation but more about what was normal. I also learned that I had intuitive group facilitation and counseling skills that I was able to enhance as I carefully watched how the other staff members managed the needs of the participants. Within a short time, some people asked to be in Brian's group. One year, in fact, a woman came and insisted on being in my group. "My husband was here last year and was in your group. He came home and said he was Gay. I want to know how this happened."

Although I was initially on staff to be the authority on LGBTQ issues, I broadened my knowledge of all other aspects of sexuality and gender. Prior to going to Thornfield, I had only seen one woman's genitals, and I didn't know any Transgender people. At Thornfield, I saw films depicting women's vulvas many times over the years and became friends with many Transgender individuals.

Jackie and Michael were the first Transsexual people that I truly got to know. Initially, both Jackie and Michael attended the workshop as presenters during the session on gender identity, role, and expression. However, we decided that we wanted them to attend the whole week to provide a richer experience for everyone. Being able to spend seven days with Jackie and Michael, and several other Transgender people over the years, allowed me to get to know them as full human beings and to better understand the challenges they faced. In the opening session of one year's workshop, with all of us sitting in a circle to introduce ourselves, Jackie identified herself as a Transsexual woman and a man named Ray shared that he was a cross-dresser and that he played the guitar. Michael just gave his name, as we planned because we wanted participants to get to know him simply as Michael before learning that he was Transgender later in the week. The next day, Carol saw a woman playing the guitar. She introduced herself and the guitarist told Carol her name was Roberta. Carol said, "You should meet Ray. He plays the guitar, too." Roberta just smiled.

At Thornfield we got to interact with people representing different points along the Transgender continuum. Comfortable with her identity as a woman, Jackie dressed for comfort, feeling that she had nothing to prove with her clothing. Roberta, however, was very conscious of her presentation. She dressed impeccably every day and paid careful attention to her hair, make-up, and nails. Roberta told us she was in bliss all week because she didn't have to worry about how others would react to her especially since they first got to meet Ray, and because the environment at Thornfield felt so safe and welcoming. She dreaded the thought of going home after the workshop and living as Ray. It was these kinds of experiences, the movies, talks, and listening to people tell their stories that helped build my confidence as a sexuality educator outside of Thornfield. (My book *Sex Camp* guides you through the week at Thornfield as if you were there.)

For several years, I was the only openly Gay person among the staff and the participants at Thornfield, and I felt the weight of responsibility to get it right. I didn't have the option of pulling back or of being unavailable. The retreat center was perhaps fifty yards from the main two-lane road, and the driveway was circular. From the first year on, I walked that driveway in circles dozens of times as different participants asked if they could talk privately. The closeted Gay people were excited to have at least one person with whom they could speak honestly. Most knew that coming out was the only path to living a happy, authentic life, but opening the closet door was terribly frightening at that time. Many closeted folks eventually came out in their small group when they told their stories.

As the years passed, the Gay movement matured, and heterosexuals became more conscious of the issues. I would continue to walk the driveway with people, but they were generally less afraid, and more often wanted help thinking through how to come out at work, or how to end their heterosexual relationship. The time eventually came when no LGBTQ person needed special time with me. I did walk, however, with the parents of a Gay or Transgender person, or the Straight spouse of a Gay person. I could clearly see in the lives of the people who were LGBTQ the seven stages of homosexual identity formation that Australian psychologist Vivienne Cass observed from her work with Gay clients.

In the article "Homosexual Identity Formation" in the *Journal of Homosexuality* (4:3, 1979), Cass proposed that the homosexual person goes through seven stages from confusion to synthesis. In stage one, there is identity confusion. The individual questions the possibility that they might have some same-sex attraction. Stage two is denial. "Not me. I don't even want to think about it." Stage three is identity comparison. "Maybe I am, but if I am, what will happen to me?" Stage four is identity tolerance. "I know I am and it's time that I started exploring what my new life will be like." Stage five is identity acceptance. "I'll be okay. I can do this." Stage six is identity pride. "We're here. We're Queer. Get over it." Rainbow flags are hung, and decals applied to cars. Stage seven is identity synthesis. "Okay, so now how do I integrate my sexual orientation into the other areas of my life, such as family, faith, work, neighborhood, and parenthood?"

I could easily see the progression through those stages in myself, changes in myself, in many Thornfield participants, and in the LGBTQ movement itself. Anita Bryant and AIDS brought Gay people to identity pride very quickly. I see myself and the LGBTQ movement as having one foot in pride and the other in synthesis. We move back and forth depending on the obstacles we face.

Many people who came to Thornfield were often from Planned Parenthood, school guidance counselors, AIDS educators, coaches who had been assigned to teach human sexuality, clergy, and others who had heard from friends that it was a life-changing experience. I loved it when there were openly Gay people in the group even if they didn't get assigned to my small group. It was fun to sit together at meals, and to have their company at late-night gatherings around a bonfire on the beach. It was around that fire, and on the raft offshore, that some of the most intimate stories were told.

However, the summer we decided we were ready to stop offering the workshop, there were five openly Gay male participants in the group who had both feet planted securely in identity pride. These guys didn't know one another prior to their arrival, but they each eventually identified themselves as Queer and sat as a group at the back of the room separate from everyone else. They made no effort to connect with me, and I didn't feel any encouragement to join their group.

Almost every year, on "Brian's Gay Day," a group of Gay men would drive in from Syracuse, be present for my talk, and then stay for lunch. In my presentation I gave an overview of Vivienne Cass's stages of homosexual identity formation, told my story, showed a few very moving video clips, and ended with a special activity. I'd ask people to yell out all the pejorative names that LGBTQ folks are called, and I would write those words on the board. Then I would erase one hateful word, saying "I'm not an 'abomination.' My name is 'Brian,'" which I wrote on the board. Then I'd extend the colored marker and eraser and invite participants to come up to write their name on the board if they identified as a Lesbian, Gay, Bisexual, Transgender, or Queer person. Always, at least a handful of individuals, including Jackie and Michael, walked up to erase a derogatory word and write their names on the board; sometimes the group included someone who had been struggling with their identity during the week. When I finished, everyone was deeply moved and often the room got very quiet, with many people crying.

One of the Queer men who sat in the back said in frustration to Carol, "How come he gets people crying and we get nothing when we do workshops?"

"Because he's Brian," Carol said.

One of those Queer men was in my small group. During group, I explained how much my presentation takes out of me, "So I may not be my best as a facilitator for this hour." I got wonderful feedback from the Straight people in the group, and a respectful smile from the one Gay man. I told the group about my history of being the only Gay man every year, and how nice it was to no longer be alone. Somehow, I found the courage to add, "Sometimes, though, I feel more isolated and lonelier than when I was here by myself."

That night, the Queer guy from my group approached me and said, "We get that you are like an ambassador to Straight people, which is very different from the roles any of the rest of us have."

And there you had it. I had heard it before. I'm thought of by some people as an "apologist," someone who speaks or writes to defend or explain something controversial. Some people find my letter to Anita Bryant to be "apologist," failing to remember that it was written thirty years ago. When I wore a sport coat and tie, for some Gay men I was an "assimilationist," who was working too hard to blend in. Some people called me the "Gay Mr. Rogers." Now, that was an honor.

My focus as an educator on homosexuality had primarily been to help Straight folks get past their fear of Gay and Transgender people. But I also dedicated much of my time to helping Gay and Transgender people come out to their families, their employers, their friends, and their church. An apt metaphor would be me in a swimming pool encouraging people to jump in, telling them how wonderful and liberating it feels, and promising that I'll catch them and teach them to swim.

From the mid-1970s to the beginning of the AIDS epidemic in 1981, I strove to provide a positive image for both Gay people and Straight people. There just weren't many nationally known Gay role models at the time, nor were there books by Gay authors that Gay people felt comfortable giving to their parents. My nonconfrontational tone and temperament were unique and badly needed. The authentic John Boy Walton approach with Straight people enabled them to lower their guard and listen. Had I come on stage angry and accusatory, I'd never reach one person, Straight or Gay. Nor would I ever have been invited to speak at any college or be asked to provide training to corporate managers.

It has taken many different voices and strategies to achieve the progress we've made in the US on LGBTQ issues. I feel that the will of the Universe put me on my right path to make my unique contribution.

With the AIDS epidemic, a lot of Straight people were better educated about homosexuality than they had been before. No one thought they'd throw up when the Gay person walked into the room, but many thought "Gay" equals "AIDS," which equals "death." Pat Buchanan, White House communications director for President Reagan, wrote in a June 23, 1983 editorial in the *New York Post*, "The poor homosexuals—they have declared war upon nature, and now nature is exacting an awful retribution."

When working with corporate managers, I'd usually ask that every person who would be attending my presentation be given my book, *Gay Issues in the Workplace*, in advance of the training, and asked them to read the book on public transportation. The CEO of S. C. Johnson and Sons, when introducing me and talking about the importance of the day, told his upper-level managers that when he pulled out my book on the plane, the man sitting next to him got up and moved. An AT&T senior manager told the group that on his flight he helped a woman get her heavy suitcase into the storage bin. She sat next to him while he read my book. When they landed, the woman instructed the executive not to touch her suitcase.

AIDS had to be addressed in my workshop or presentation on LGBTQ issues in the workplace. I hated having to do so because it took up a lot of time I didn't have to spare in the program. Plus, I hated the assumption that if you were Gay, you had AIDS.

The epidemic changed public awareness, and though the two issues of Gay equality and AIDS got linked, public compassion for Gay people also increased. Night after night, and week after week, Straight people would see pictures on the news, or in the newspaper or magazine, of Gay men with AIDS being cared for by their partners and by Lesbians.

Gay people changed, too. AIDS brought Gay people together as nothing else could, including the assassination of openly Gay San Francisco City Supervisor Harvey Milk. Many Gay men, Lesbians, Bisexual, Transgender, and Queer people across the country got very angry. We stood defiantly in Vivienne Cass's stage six, "identity pride," for our own preservation. The story of AIDS had its villains, including the president of the United States, Ronald Reagan, who didn't say the word "AIDS" until 40,000 Americans had been diagnosed as HIV-positive, as well as pharmaceutical companies whose slow trials and high prices caused many unnecessary deaths. Conservative William F. Buckley advocated in a 1986 column that everyone detected with AIDS be tattooed on the upper forearm and buttocks.

Lesbians came out of the woodwork to care for their Gay male friends. Act Up formed to engage in nonviolent, attention-getting protests. Movies and plays were written and shown, such as *Philadelphia* and *Angels in America*. Movie stars such as Elizabeth Taylor made clear their support. But Gay people would never, ever be the same as they were before the epidemic. "We're Queer. We're here. Get used to it."

The five Queers who sat together in the back of the room at Thornfield all worked for AIDS organizations where no explanations were made for being Gay. No ground would be given. Too many young friends had been buried for other Gay people to worry about being accepted. Many parents, clergy, and undertakers had been heartless during the plague. "He's not our son." "I will not preside at the funeral, nor can they be buried in a Catholic cemetery." "I won't take the body." Senator Jesse Helms proposed that the CDC not fund any programs that "promote, encourage, or condone homosexual acts." He argued, "We have got to call . . . a perverted human being a perverted human being."

Gay men being simply tolerated or accommodated was no longer acceptable.

At Thornfield, the Queers were outnumbered by unknown Straight people who might not yet get it. Each of the guys joined the pack, and I was not of their pack. I wasn't visibly angry enough. I was a Gay man who had too many Straight friends. The staff understood what was happening with the guys with a chip on their shoulders. They had seen and worked with angry Gay men before, but nothing more could be done than to show loving kindness with the hope that each guy would know he was considered part of the family. Whether they chose to join in was up to them.

Chapter Fifteen

The Mayor's Gay Liaison

IN 1982 I WAS selected from a group of applicants to be the mayor of Boston's liaison to the Gay and Lesbian community, with the understanding that I could continue to speak on college campuses, and write my column. Elaine Noble had helped create the role, and the previous liaison, Robin McCormack, worked part time. Robin was drawn to the police department and spent most of his time as liaison there. I stepped into the role as the only full-time Lesbian and Gay liaison position in the country. Shortly after starting work, I recommended to Mayor Kevin White that we create a Gay and Lesbian liaison position in the police department. A Straight, White, physically imposing Lieutenant Don Devine took on the responsibility. He was a jewel of a Straight man. When my older brother, Michael, died at forty-one from a gun accident on Father's Day 1983, Lt. Devine arranged to have a Mass said for my family.

To succeed in my job of helping to make Boston a safe place for LGBTQ people, I needed the full support of Gay and Lesbian community leaders, many of whom were bar owners or managers. Ann Maguire was a tough as nails (with a marshmallow center) manager of Somewhere, a Lesbian bar. She was also a local, blue collar Irish Catholic, but when I asked for her support, she said she'd give it only if the previous liaison, Robin, gave me his blessing. Robin managed the popular bar Buddies. I called, made an appointment, and walked across town to talk with him. I was told he was upstairs and would be right down. I waited for over an hour, decided he was playing games, which he was, and I left. I knew the owner of the bar, Michael Campbell, another Irish Catholic, and he liked me very much, so I had one vote of confidence there. Robin never gave me his support.

Why was it important to build a coalition with Lesbian and Gay community leaders? Boston was the political soul of the country. If you look at who ended up heading national LGBTQ groups, most of them were from Boston. John Ward, Gary Buseck, Amy Hoffman, Cindy Rizzo, Eric Rofes, Kevin Cathcart, Urvashi Vaid, Richard Burns, Stephen Tierney, Tim McFeeley, Kevin Jennings, Larry Kessler, Elaine Noble, Barney Frank, Gerry Studds, Bob Farmer, Arline Isaacson, Annie Silvia, Peter Lombardi, Sue Hyde, and others. I'm not including here the names of the bar owners who had enormous clout and made it financially possible for many political efforts to succeed.

One reason LGBTQ people made such progress in Boston was because of the progressive leadership of four-term Mayor Kevin White. I had to play my best game when I worked in his administration. He was astute, had a photographic memory, and knew when to accept the counsel of his advisors. When I escorted Mayor White to the first Human Rights Campaign black tie dinner in Boston, I spent my time in the car with him going over the names of people he would see, and why he should know them. Throughout his stay at the dinner, as we walked through the crowds, he didn't miss a beat. When we ran into Michael Campbell, I said, "Mayor White, you remember Michael Campbell." "How is Buddies doing?" the mayor responded to Michael's delight and astonishment.

Here are three examples of why I needed community support. The owner of an after-hours bar called the Loft, Joe D'Onofrio, served alcohol after the cut-off time in Boston. The police began raiding his bar. He called me in the middle of the night and threatened to have "another Stonewall" if the police raided him again. I asked all the bar owners to meet with me to discuss the issue. They all agreed that D'Onofrio was deliberately provoking the police into creating a huge political mess. I asked the bar owners and managers to speak to him, because his behavior was going to impact them. I urged the mayor not to let the police raid the bar again, and I gave him my rationale. At the end of his administration, Mayor White thanked me for helping him avoid a huge mistake. He didn't elaborate, but I assumed it was this incident.

After that I got a call from a good friend in Minnesota who told me he had "the Gay plague." He said he had Kaposi's sarcoma and pneumocystis pneumonia. Although I couldn't spell either, the call was all it took for me to start researching, including a call to the Fenway Community Health Center that catered to Boston's Gay community. The director, Sally Dean, urged me to help coordinate the city's response. As was the practice, I typed up a proposal to create the Mayor's Task Force on AIDS and had it reviewed by two people who oversaw my work. At the time, there were only three cases of HIV recorded in Massachusetts, and I was asked if I wasn't overreacting. The research I provided on what was happening in New York and San Francisco was enough to get the "okay."

With the help of Lisa Savereid, my boss in the mayor's office, I reserved the conference room for the first, and subsequent meetings of everyone in the city and state that I thought could be of help. Because of the work I had done building support among community leaders, I got no pushback from those few who thought of me as "a company man." This city task force was the first of its kind in the country. At the time, AIDS was casually referred to as "The Four H Club," homosexuals, hemophiliacs, Haitians, and heroin addicts. So, the task force reflected those targeted groups. It included the state epidemiologist, the city epidemiologist, a representative from the Fenway Community Health Center, Stephen Tierney, from the Board of Health and Hospitals, Dr. Don Butterfield, one of the few openly Gay doctors in the city, Larry Kessler, head of the new AIDS Action Committee, a doctor who worked directly with the Haitian community, the head of the Red Cross in Boston, Annie Silvia, head of the newly formed community AIDS Task Force, and a renowned doctor from Los Angeles, Jerry Groupman.

The job of the Mayor's Committee on AIDS was to share information, eliminate misinformation, and guide one another from our own areas of expertise. The head of the Red Cross, Peter Paige, credited the Mayor's Task Force with creating a workable set of guidelines. The nurses at Boston City Hospital said that what they needed at the hospital wasn't information on HIV, but training for the staff who had never seen two men hold hands. I took that one on. We wrote the state's first "safe sex" brochure in Ray's and my Brookline living room. I ran the meetings in city hall, provided each person an agenda, and wrote a regular report to the mayor. I also wrote a periodic column for *Gay Community News* to help keep the city's Gay community informed. One of my favorite Gay men, Bob Andrews, who respected my insights on other issues, asked "Brian, why is this happening?" Bob was one of the early deaths from HIV in Boston.

There were some Gay men who thought AIDS and "safe sex" were a government plot, supported by untrustworthy Gay people, to curtail the sexual exploration and activity of Gay men. At the funeral of Dave Stryker, the typesetter used by *Gay Community News* and Detroit's *Metro Gay News*, one member of the Fort Hill Faggots for Freedom stood up and yelled out, "Don't trust them. Fuck like bunnies." Fortunately, reason prevailed, saving thousands of lives.

A third reason I needed community leaders' support was to help me with the Boston Project, an unprecedented exploration of how well the city was meeting the needs of the Gay community in several designated areas. With the mayor's blessing, we put together panels consisting of two or three representatives of the Gay community along with two or three city representatives in the areas in question, for example the police department. At public hearings LGBTQ people could tell the panel about their experiences with the police department. All the testimonies were recorded, and then transcribed by my assistant Katherine Graves. Each panel was also required to make recommendations to the city, based upon what they heard. My brother, Tom, who worked in the mayor's press office, was a great help in pulling together data on how many people testified in each issue of concern, and in getting printed *The Boston Project*, one book of testimony, and another of recommendations. Lisa Christie also helped me reach out to community members.

As the mayor's liaison to the Gay and Lesbian community, I needed to build a bridge to the staff at *Gay Community News*. *GCN* was created each week by a politically left-leaning collective that offered input on what was going on in the city and country, and what needed attention. The editors and staff were nice enough people, but I always felt they kept me at an arm's length. I never felt any trust, affection, or gratitude. Nevertheless, I shared with *GCN* up-to-the-minute reports on what was happening with AIDS from not only the perspective of the Mayor's Task Force, but from what I was hearing from across the country.

We finished *The Boston Project* just before Mayor White retired, but made sure the new mayor, Ray Flynn, and the new mayor's liaison to the Gay and Lesbian community, Ann Maguire, received a copy. I was proud of what we did, but I don't think it was ever given the attention it deserved.

My time serving as the mayor's liaison happened in our final years living in our great apartment at 1035 Beacon Street. As mentioned earlier, our home was a safe and welcoming space for family and friends including Congressman Gerry (pronounced "Gary") Studds. When he called me at city hall to ask if he might stay with us to avoid the press during his censure for having sex ten years earlier with a page, I said "Yes." I then called Ray at his Lehman office to see how his visiting mother felt about it. She said "No."

I didn't blame her. Ray's mom and dad were with us from Wichita, Kansas, for the first time. Their youngest son, David, who was living with us, was Gay but not out to his folks. Ray's father and mother both grew up on farms. They were Roman Catholics who had disowned Ray for two years after he came out to them. By the time of their visit in 1983, they had reconciled themselves to Ray's homosexuality, had suspicions about David, and kept a wary eye on me for being so public about being Gay and Catholic.

Soon upon their arrival, Ray's dad spotted people saying the rosary outside the women's health clinic next door where abortions were an option. He went down three flights to give them money in support of their efforts. When Ray called his mom to see if they'd be comfortable with Gerry as our guest, she felt overwhelmed. Ray called me back to relay his mother's feelings and we decided that he and David would take their parents to our small cabin on Franklin Pierce Lake in Hillsborough, New Hampshire on Friday. Gerry and I would stay in the apartment in Brookline.

In the middle of the night, Gerry woke me up, standing there in his underwear, and told me that the women's health clinic next door was on fire, and that our apartment was filling with smoke. Gerry threw on a trench coat, and I put on some clothes, and we hid in the alley hoping not to be seen by the press that had arrived to report on the fire. A few hours later, I called Ray at the cabin, explained what happened, and told him we needed to come to the cabin. He agreed and prepared his folks. David spent the weekend avoiding his parents so that he didn't get confronted with the question, "Are you Gay?"

On the way up, we stopped to pick up the newspapers that had Gerry's face on the front cover. The controversy was not just the censure, but also Gerry's refusal to apologize, saying that the experience was consensual, and the page was of age. Once we arrived, Ray's mom made herself scarce, and Ray's dad kept asking, "Senator Jerry, why won't you apologize?" In retrospect, it was a very funny scene with David in the canoe avoiding his parents; Ray's parents thrown into an internationally covered event; and Gerry maneuvering to find what quiet space he could find. He was very grateful and gracious.

We all snuggled in on Saturday night, and after a hearty breakfast, I headed back to Boston with Gerry and David. Ray stayed with his folks but was angry with their lack of support. And yet they did the best they could given their limited knowledge and experience of homosexuality. We felt their disappointment for many years, which compared to my folk's full acceptance, was especially painful to Ray.

In 1986, when Ray and I had been together for ten years, his mom and dad visited again, and we took them to the lake, which they loved. At an afternoon cookout, as we held hands to acknowledge our gratitude before we ate, Ray's dad added, "And God, it's not too late to send two good women into these boys' lives."

"Dad, now stop it," Ray said angrily. "Okay, okay," his father responded.

Before Ray's dad died, he made sure that I knew he considered me a son. On one of his final days, while Ray and I were with him, he asked for "The Jesus, Mary, and Joseph prayer." Ray had no idea what he was talking about, but I had been taught by the Sisters of St. Joseph at Holy Family in Grand Blanc, and I knew what he was asking.

"Jesus, Mary, and Joseph, I give you my heart and my soul. Jesus, Mary, and Joseph, assist me at my last agony. Jesus, Mary, and Joseph, may I bring forth my soul in peace with you."

Ray's dad, Art, smiled with appreciation. Ray said to me bewildered, "How do you remember that?" "Oh," I said, "I can do the Acts of Faith, Hope, and Charity. Isn't it nice though that I knew what your dad was wanting to hear?"

Before she died, Ray's mom, Mary, told him, "Having two Gay sons was God's gift to me." If you give people time to listen and think it through in their own way, they can change.

We left Brookline in 1983 and moved into a "summer house" built by a wealthy person in 1860. It needed a huge amount of work that we initially did ourselves. I steamed off the layers of wallpaper and pulled up the carpeting on all three floors. We named the house "Bachelors' Hall" after a series of hunting prints that hung on the dining room wall. The grand three-story home, with stone on the first floor, and shingles on the next two was the site of cousin reunions, a McNaught family Christmas, Fourth of July parties, Thanksgiving gatherings, and elegant Christmas parties. We used it as well for retreats, workshops, and parties of the AIDS Action Committee, and for the first social gathering of people with AIDS in Massachusetts.

It was after we moved to Gloucester, which was a year before my work with the mayor ended, that I became a "buddy" to people with AIDS. I was trained for the task by Peter Lombardi at the AIDS Action Committee.

My first assignment was with a hospitalized man from New York. He had wasted away to skeletal form and didn't have long to live. I brought him a cute stuffed rabbit, and he sighed saying it was the first stuffed animal he'd ever had. He told me about his life before contracting HIV, noting that he'd had a beautiful, muscled body and great abs. He was really into the arts, loving ballet, opera, and theater. As I sat and listened to him I reflected on my longtime desire for a well-muscled body with great abs. One day you have them and the next day they're gone.

This man, my first AIDS buddy, died not long after my first visit. Ray and I drove to Maine to be present for his burial. Once we were seated in a pew, a woman next to Ray asked, "How did he die?" Ray responded, "I don't know." He looked at me and I nodded. It was not our place to give out information without the parents' consent. For many years in the beginning of the epidemic, there was great fear and shame associated with AIDS. After the burial I watched five guys, all in black trench coats to protect them from the rain, standing around the grave in silence. They were his closest friends from New York.

Jimmy was my second AIDS buddy. He was a florist and seemingly healthy. I met his family. Often, I'd pick him up and we'd sit with our feet dangling in our pool in Gloucester. Jimmy and I talked a lot about death and whether there's a hereafter. When he died, his mother called me to say that Jimmy wanted me to give his eulogy, but the family didn't want me to say that he was Gay or that he died of AIDS. I accepted the request because it was what Jimmy wanted, but I knew I needed a way to honestly affirm his life.

On the day of the funeral Jimmy's relatives were all in the front pews, and his friends were all in the back. It's never made sense to me that when you die, customarily your aunts and uncles who you haven't seen in years are given privilege over the people who knew you best and loved you the most. When I spoke, I naturally made eye contact with both groups, sending different messages with facial expressions to each. I spoke about Jimmy the florist who treasured the flowers that were most unique, even those that others might disdain. His life was about celebrating his own unique beauty and creating joy with both friends and family by arranging flowers that spoke specifically to each. He never allowed his own flower to lose its place or its luster. "All of you," I said, "were flowers carefully selected by Jimmy for his life's bouquet." The family in the front rows thought it was quite a beautiful tribute, and the guys in the back of the room smiled and nodded affirmation.

Chapter Sixteen

Four Great Responses, and a Death Wish

WHEN MY COLUMN IN the Boston Gay newspaper, *Bay Windows*, focused on being Gay and Catholic, and the *Boston Globe* did a front-page feature on me as a Gay Catholic, I got many responses but five stand out in my memory. The first is that of Ron Robin, a Boston disc jockey who called and asked if we might meet. Ron's real last name is Polcari, and he came from a very traditional Italian Catholic family. We became fast friends, and we remain very close today. Ron now owns the MEWS restaurant in Provincetown. He and I, and my Irish setter, Jeremy, used to walk around and around the beautiful Riverside park and river a couple blocks from Ray's and my home in Brookline. Ron's wonderful, free-spirited partner, Dennis, had contracted HIV, and it was destroying Ron. He also struggled greatly with being both Gay and Catholic.

Ron remembers our conversations better than I do and reminded me how helpful our strolls were to him. Dennis eventually died of AIDS and Ron's very tender heart was broken. But he knew he wasn't alone in his grief, and, as a Gay man came to trust his relationship with God.

It was Ron who suggested that we record one of my college presentations, especially since there were so few people talking publicly about being Gay. Ron got his friend Tom, who was a cameraman at a local television station, to come to our home in Gloucester and tape me giving my entire presentation while sitting on the sofa in our living room. We then arranged to record me giving my presentation to a student audience at Cornell University. Tom and Ron spliced together the two recordings and created one of the first educational films on Gay issues, called *A Conversation with Brian McNaught On Being Gay*. We named our production company TRB for Tom, Ron, and Brian.

The video *On Being Gay* did very well, and was used in schools, churches, and businesses across the country for many years. I'll often hear from high school sexuality educators how they used the video every year, and of how helpful it was. My older sister Kathy, a beloved first-grade teacher, was in a large audience of primary educators engaged for the day in diversity training. The first film up was mine. She was so surprised and excited that she stood up and announced with pride for everyone to hear, "That's my brother!" The DVD is available for free viewing on my website and on YouTube. Subsequently, Ron and I did a radio program together when Ray and I had a summer home in Provincetown. Later, after I started providing training in corporations, Ron and I created the video *Gay Issues in the Workplace*. And then, when I was recorded speaking at Merck, Ron's husband Ed Teo, from Singapore, managed the sale and distribution of all my DVDs.

Another person who responded to the publicity of me being Gay and Catholic was Gregory Maguire, who was still a college student when we met, and unbeknownst to me, had a crush on me. Gregory and I spent time talking about how I reconciled being both Gay and Catholic. I didn't hear much from or about him for a while until I read *Wicked* and delighted in his great success as the author. Gregory is married with children. He and his husband live in Concord, Massachusetts. We stay in touch.

Tomie dePaola, the revered larger-than-life prolific children's author and brilliant illustrator, ordered a copy of my book, *On Being Gay*, and sent to me a stack of signed copies of some of his most famous books, including *Strega Nona, Old Befana, Oliver Button is a Sissy*, and *The Hunter and the Animals*. We arranged to meet in Brookline in my apartment, and quickly became friends. Tomie invited Ray and me to visit him in Wilmot Flat, New Hampshire, and he and Bob Hechtel joined us in Gloucester for Thanksgiving dinner a couple of times and for a Fourth of July celebration. It was through Tomie that I learned that one of the inspirations of my life, Leo Buscaglia, was a Gay friend. Once when my folks were visiting we all went to Tomie's big Christmas party in New Hampshire. Mom and Dad loved it. Tomie had one of the most wonderful laughs you can imagine. He, too, was on a deeply spiritual path.

Tomie used to tell the very funny story of two children's librarians who went on a search for his home. Tomie was working in the garden, probably wearing a big straw hat. The women stopped and asked him, "Is this Tomie dePaola's house? We've driven so far, and we just love him." Tomie told them, yes, it was Tomie's house. The women then asked, "Do you think it would be okay for us to take a picture?" Tomie said, "Certainly." The school librarians politely then asked him, "Would you mind getting out of the way?" I love that there are so many Gay men and Lesbians who have been authors and illustrators of children's books, from Hans Christian Anderson to Maurice Sendak.

Matthew Flynn, the fourth surprise from my piece on being Gay and Catholic, was one of the most remarkable priests Ray and I had ever met. A Trappist monk in St. Joseph's Abbey in Spencer, Massachusetts, Fr. Matthew showed us how much fun and how happy God is. I don't recall how Matthew made contact, but once he did, he became a treasured member of our family. Matthew had a profound impact on Ray's and my spiritual journey. He gave us the book *Awareness* by Anthony de Mello, a Spanish Jesuit, who helped us bridge Eastern and Western spirituality. That coaxed us to look deeper into ourselves as spiritual beings. The fact that Matthew was an openly Gay, celibate Trappist monk whose spirituality enabled him to dismiss church teaching on several key issues made him a trusted messenger of the divine.

In our home and in our presence, it was safe for Fr. Matthew to be Gay. We were two Catholic-raised boys who shared his values of loving kindness. Matthew left his "disco clothes" at our house and had credit card bills sent to our address. He'd come to town, go dancing in a Gay club, come back and change, and head back to Spencer. On Saturdays, Matthew and our dog, Jeremy, would lie in front of the fire and listen to a performance of the Metropolitan Opera. He'd use up most of the firewood we painfully hauled up three flights in heavy bundles, but it was Matthew, so we just laughed.

Our first and second Christmas together, Fr. Matthew (whose baptized name was Paul) invited us to cut down our tree on the grounds of the abbey. And for at least eight years, Fr. Matthew would come for a special pre-Christmas dinner at our apartment in Brookline. Matthew was very extravagant with his gifts. His favorite shop was called Marian Ruth in Brookline where he bought us Bill Sax pottery, and a whole set of Arabia Valencia china. During the summer, Fr. Matthew would stay at our cabin on Franklin Pierce Lake in Hillsboro, New Hampshire. Once when we returned, we found a huge television antenna stretched across the beams inside our cabin. We laughed again.

Of these four visitors, Ron Robin and Matthew Flynn had the most profound effects on our lives. The first employee group in the country to want to address Gay issues in the workplace needed a trainer, and the National Gay and Lesbian Task Force referred them to me, and to my video. As a result, I was asked to design the first workshop on "LGBT Issues in the Workplace." When I point out to Ron, as I've done many times, the huge number of people who have been impacted by his idea to film my presentation, he, like me, sidesteps the compliment.

Fr. Matthew met us at a time when Ray and I were very angry at the Catholic Church. In Boston, in January of 1984, the conservative Bishop Bernard Law was made the cardinal, and he promptly ended Paul Shanley's ministry to street youth, most of whom were runaway Gay kids. Cardinal Law, in my eyes, had a very pious image that he projected while being the law-and-order cop for conservative Pope John Paul II and Pope Benedict XVI.

What most surprised me about Cardinal Law was that in previous assignments, he was known as a fighter for civil rights who once opened a clinic for battered women. But when it came to Gay civil rights, he was tone deaf. He personally opposed Dignity and any legislation that advanced the cause for homosexuals, including those with AIDS. Gay people in Boston hated Bernard Law, as did Gay Catholics across the country.

Once when I was shopping in a mall, I walked through the area where televisions were sold. There must have been fifty different TVs all showing Bernard Law's face, wearing a look that I saw as practiced humility. He was speaking against something, and it drove me so crazy I lost my serenity. I walked around angrily, stopping at every TV in the showroom to change the channel. When I told that story at a Dignity convention people laughed and cheered, but I said, "You know what? I should have just kept walking. My reaction stopped me from enjoying my shopping. It took time away from my joy. Changing the channel wasn't going to change Bernard Law."

Fr. Matthew helped Ray and me to still love and embrace the teachings of our brother, Jesus, despite clerics like Cardinal Law. The Sermon on the Mount could still provide us guidelines for spiritual living without us liking the boss of the Boston archdiocese. Like Hermann Hesse's *Siddhartha* both Ray and I were looking for experiences that could teach us our truths. Just as Siddhartha left the comfort of his home, Ray and I walked backwards out of the Church of Rome. It was a terrible time to be a Gay Christian. Ronald Reagan was president, Jerry Falwell filled the airwaves with his "Moral Majority" salvos, Fred Phelps and his Southern Baptist family stood outside the funerals of Gay men holding signs that read "AIDS is God's Punishment," and "Gays go to Hell." It was hard to find any well-known spiritual teacher who had the clout to publicly fire back saying, "You can't have Jesus. He's not on your side."

So, like many Gay Catholics and others in repressive denominations, Ray and I explored on our own where the truth was to be found. What balm was there that would heal our wounds? We read and read, mostly Buddhist teachings by Thich Nhat Hanh and Pema Chodron, but also the *Tao te Ching*; and we listened repeatedly to Joseph Campbell talk on making "the hero's journey." Every homosexual, Bisexual, and Transgender person of faith is called to make the hero's journey, to leave the closet, to confront self-hate and doubt, and to claim their sacred space in the front row of God's heart.

When my first book, *A Disturbed Peace—Selected Writings of an Irish Catholic Homosexual* was published, a copy was sent, as previously said, to every bishop in the country. Serendipitously, Cardinal Law and I both had aisle seats on a plane heading to Boston. After takeoff I introduced myself and asked him if he remembered me from our work together at the Call to Action. "No," he said. "That was some time ago." Then I asked, "Did you read the copy of my book that was sent to you?" He asked, "What book was that?" I said proudly, "*A Disturbed Peace—Selected Writings of an Irish Catholic Homosexual.*" Now quite uncomfortable, Law said, "No, I never received that book." I looked quizzically, and said, "It was published by Dignity and a copy was sent to every bishop in the country." Focused now on the papers he had in front of him, he said "I never got it." I let go of it. I had made my point and didn't need his affirmation to love myself or to trust that the Holy Spirit was using this time to try to speak to the soul of Bernard Law.

The fifth significant response I got to my column on being Gay and Catholic, and *The Boston Globe's* feature on me was a handwritten sign above our mailbox on the first floor of our apartment building. It read: "Get Out of Town, McNaught. I Hope You Die of AIDS." Someone knew where I lived, but I responded to that as I had to every threatening letter I received, at *The Michigan Catholic* and beyond. I tucked it away in my archives and moved on.

Chapter Seventeen

Are You Cuddling with Me, Malcolm?

MALCOLM BOYD'S BOOK *ARE You Running with Me, Jesus?* was one of the earliest and most significant planks in the bridge I crossed to freedom. By "freedom" I mean truly loving myself as a Gay Christian and being grateful for my life. There's no question in my mind that my homosexuality is in harmony with the basic message of every celebrated religious leader. And I don't accommodate myself with unwelcoming religious teachings. I embrace as perfect my manifestation of God's empathy and loving kindness. I no longer waste my time trying to convince religious conservatives that they've misinterpreted passages of the Bible that they think condemn homosexuality. I stay focused on the behaviors Jesus called us to do in our lives, and to help others embrace with confidence the same self-love.

If I was asked to name the most significant choices or best actions, I've taken in my life to grow into the man I am now, I would list: coming out of the closet, quitting smoking, quitting drinking, defending myself as a conscientious objector, going on my hunger fast, entering a relationship with Ray, backing away from the Church of Rome, and reclaiming and reaffirming my relationships with Jesus and the Holy Spirit.

Like Siddhartha who eventually returned to the place where he started, I no longer have animosity for the Catholic Church, and I'm very grateful for the religious education I got from sixteen years of parochial schools. I don't believe the words of the Apostles' Creed, and, as said before, while I love the tradition of sharing bread and wine in memory of the great spiritual teacher and my best friend, Jesus, I don't really believe that the host and wine are the body and blood of Christ. I'm not drinking blood when I sip from the chalice. I feel that I still deserve the Christian Leadership Award, and maybe too the Buddhist Leadership Award, and the New Thought Leadership Award. Everyone who makes the hero's journey deserves all the Leadership Awards.

Backing away from the authority of the Church of Rome and its influence on me didn't happen quickly or easily. It has been a very long, slow process in which I'm now able to accept the difference between a Catholic community of believers and the Vatican Curia. Malcolm Boyd was one of the first to help me see that my being Gay was a very good thing. In *Are You Running with Me, Jesus,* Malcolm writes about being in a Gay bar, and he asks Jesus if he's in there with him. That's the critical question, isn't it? Is Jesus with me as I am, and is he a source of loving support and affirmation? It was critically important for me to create a one-on-one relationship with Jesus.

I don't recall who wrote to whom first, and when I say "wrote" I don't mean e-mail. That wasn't easily available to the public until the late 1980s. One of us secured the address of the other to compliment a book or column, either Malcolm's *Are You Running with Me, Jesus?"* or my *On Being Gay.* Malcolm also read my column and he asked me to write a column to convince Doubleday to continue printing his autobiography, *Take Off the Mask.* I never imagined that Fr. Malcolm Boyd and I would become pen pals, and spend social time together. I have his twelve letters to me but not copies of my responses. He visited Ray and me when he came to the eastern part of the country.

Then, both Malcolm and I were invited to speak at a conference of the Metropolitan Community Church leaders and members. Malcolm, my friend, Heather (now Sky), and I were asked to do a trialogue sermon. (Really bad idea.)

Malcolm and I were put up in the same home of a member or supporter of MCC. I'm now so completely spoiled by how the Wall Street firms took care of me with fancy hotels that I don't know if it's still common practice to have a speaker stay in the home of a local person. It was, and possibly still is, a means of saving money. There had to have been others who were asked to stay in this house too because Malcolm and I had been assigned different couches. At some point after everybody went to bed, I got up and asked Malcolm if he wanted to cuddle. "Yes," he said enthusiastically. So, he scooted over, and I laid down spoonlike next to him. It felt warm and wonderful to be held by a spiritual Gay man that I admired, by a soul with whom I felt connected. The intimacy was sacred. After a while, I got up, gave him a kiss, and went back to my couch.

The next day at the conference, in the middle of the service, Malcolm, Heather, and I stood at the microphone and Malcolm started us off. We should have practiced the trialogue because all of us were used to speaking on our own, particularly Malcolm and me. I nudged my way into Malcolm's reflections, and he stepped back in to clarify a point. When it was over, Heather disappeared and I found her crying with her partner, Nancy Wilson, the future moderator of MCC. She was very upset with Malcolm for dominating the sermon and giving very little time to her to make a point. I tried to comfort her by listening and saying that I understood, and was sorry that I didn't step in and say, "Heather, what do you think?"

When I first started speaking at colleges, I had the full hour or ninety minutes to myself. I was able to spend most of the time on the personal, while also explaining that *arsenokoitai* and *malakoi* have been misinterpreted in the Bible as referring to homosexuals, when in fact they refer to pedophiles. I had time for questions that deserved complete attention. When women began asserting themselves in Gay organizations, which was the right thing to do, it changed everything, from the order of the letters in the acronym to the name of organizations. GLBT became LGBT. The National Gay Task Force became the National Gay and Lesbian Task Force. If I was a Lesbian, I'd be pounding on the door until I felt fully represented in what was known as the Gay civil rights movement. Thus, it generally became practice on college campuses, and at "Sex Camp," to have a Gay man and a Lesbian share the allotted time or they would invite a Gay man and Lesbian to speak at different times.

Rather than have the college find a Lesbian speaker, I proposed that my friend and most respected colleague, Bianca Cody Murphy, join me on stage. Bianca was no meek woman who would defer to me. She was a doctor of psychology, a professor, and eventually head of the psychology department at Wheaton. Even though we were good friends we spent time talking through our presentation and clarifying how we would divide the time. Not every college invited a woman to join me, despite my encouragement, but learning how to share the time was a very good lesson for me.

Chapter Eighteen

Was Jesus Fully Man?

JESUS AND I HAVE always been friends, sometimes very close and at other times not best friends. When I first focused on him, I was very impressed, and I identified with his values. Feed the poor, clothe the naked, visit the imprisoned. Blessed are the peacemakers, the merciful, the pure of heart. How could you not want to hang out with this guy?

Initially, Jesus was an entity I thought I'd never meet because he was a God, and I wasn't. He was a king who lived in a castle, a rich man who owned a super huge yacht, and I just had a shack and a leaky rowboat. I was a Catholic boy who tried to be as good as St. Francis, and a Gay boy who tried to be as good as gold. For many years, I learned about Jesus from the nuns, the brothers, and the priests. I was told that the priests were the representatives of Jesus. That part was confusing and caused spiritual conflict because I had met a lot of priests who weren't great manifestations of the Jesus I knew.

Then, my friend Jesus got kidnapped by televangelists, and conservative politicians. He got commercialized. Honk if you love Jesus. His personality seemed to change with his celebrity status. He was described by some preachers as the source of wealth and power. His church, the one in Rome, seemed to have lost its way. People who thought they were the sole representatives of Jesus in the Vatican wore outrageously extravagant clothes. They had jeweled rings on their fingers that they expected other people to bend down and kiss. The Jesus I knew would never do that. He washed the feet of others.

I was told that I could never be like Jesus, but I could try. Enough! Sorry, Jesus. This isn't working. I walked away and started looking for other friends who shared my values and who promised I could reach their same level of spiritual enlightenment. Otherwise, why try? My new mentor was Siddhartha who through trial and error, and a lot of focused work, became enlightened. I started reading books by Buddhists about the path to awareness. Jesus was a friend from the past who I missed, but how could I walk with him if he's God and I am but a lowly human? How could I possibly do as you have done?

One Sunday, many years ago, an American Baptist congregation invited me to give a presentation during the service on growing up Gay. That day an Army chaplain, the son of two parishioners, happened to be visiting and was asked to share some reflections before I spoke. He seemed to be a very nice man who spoke about walking with Jesus down a path to understanding. When it was my turn to speak, I thanked the chaplain, and said that I shared a similar vision, but before I accepted his invitation to walk with him to Jesus, I'd want to know whose "Jesus" this was, and where was he leading me? I explained that I had accepted too many invitations in the past to walk with Jesus to a place where I was called "seriously disordered," and an "abomination."

"I don't walk those paths with a Jesus I don't know," I explained. And the chaplain smiled and nodded knowingly.

Emotionally and spiritually wounded Gay people of faith aren't quick to return to the site of their abuse. There are Gay and Lesbian Catholics who go to Sunday Mass, but the majority of Gay Catholics will say they are in recovery, and no longer enter a church.

What's often misunderstood is that being unchurched doesn't mean unspiritual. In fact, people who must examine their faith as outsiders usually go a lot deeper than those who don't have to think about it. With the help of teachers such as Joseph Campbell, I came to realize that my religious beliefs were suspect because they were reactionary rather than authentic reflections of an unbiased mind. I hated the Catholic Church for many years not because of what it did to me. I'm a big boy who suffered great disappointment but not devastation. But there are plenty of people who have been knocked to the mat by religious abuse, and that's what still ticks me off. I expect so much more from Christians. "See how they love one another." Is that still true?

On my own, then, after I decided to see God manifested in all sentient beings, dogs, cats, butterflies, and orchids included, I decided that there were things I had been taught that no longer felt useful or true. Several years ago, at a conference on young adult ministry, I had the privilege of meeting Fr. Gustavo Gutierrez, the Peruvian prophet of the theology of liberation. He taught that if the passages of the Bible and the tenets of your faith don't reflect your daily experiences, you should choose to trust your daily experiences. That is where you'll find communion with God. I asked him, "Father, what guidance would you give to Gay people who struggle to find a place in the church's theology of sexuality?" He replied that Gay people must trust their own experiences as the truths of their lives.

I ended up putting my faith in the love, blessing, inspiration, and the grace of my life rather than in the doctrines of my church. I embraced my own divinity and that of all living things. Jesus, then, was divine, but also a very enlightened, compassionate rabbi who walked the talk. Then, it became much easier for me to restart my formerly close relationship with him as a friend. I believe that Jesus, like other enlightened spiritual standouts in human history, invited us to follow the example he gave us, saying "Do as I have done." "The kingdom of God is within you." He said these things because he knew we could do it. We could experience the enlightenment that he experienced.

Jesus was fully human, and divine like me, and it was exciting to feel an intimacy with him again. We were soulmates, and I once again trusted him. As taught to me by both Siddhartha and Fr. Gutierrez. I dismissed the interpretations of his life and teachings that didn't ring true for me.

To help me imagine Jesus as really, truly fully human, and therefore someone I was able to fully emulate, I allowed myself to imagine Jesus doing human things, like farting, burping, sneezing, throwing up, and maybe even having a wet dream. I hope not to offend, but if he was fully human, he didn't look like a Ken doll beneath his robes. He had a penis.

"Brian McNaught, you don't create quite the impression you think you do."

Jesus also had to have had a sexual orientation unless we want to think of him as asexual, which means that he had no sexual feelings. Apparently, it was uncommon for a thirty-year-old Jewish man at that time not to have a wife, and Jesus chose twelve men to hang with him wherever he went. It's not impossible to imagine Jesus as homosexual. Different authors have done so. I think though that he was Bisexual, not that he ever acted on it. Are you still with me?

In my search for awareness, it felt important to me to experience Jesus as a peer, and not as a celebrity you weren't allowed to get close to, as it stipulates in the contracts of many well-known people today. To fully appreciate him, and to take his words to heart, he had to be open to the idea of sharing intimacy with me, not just prayer but through touch, too. Do you think Jesus hugged? I imagined he hugged his most beloved disciple, John the Evangelist. So, why not hug me?

Many years ago, while lying in bed at night, I fantasized about inviting Jesus into my bed to cuddle with me. I imagined his face and his body, Middle Eastern features, maybe 5'5" tall, long hair and a beard. If he was going to be fully human in my mind, I wanted to imagine being able to touch him, as he was lovingly touched after the crucifixion when he was being prepared for burial.

As was true with Malcolm, I wanted to feel the warmth of the body of Jesus as I held him. I felt the intimacy and then he gave me a kiss as I had Malcolm, and he went off to be on his own.

Although I never created this fantasy again, for me this experience was one of the most important steps of my spiritual journey. From that moment forward, we fully shared our humanness.

I know that I'm not the only person who has experienced these feelings with thoughts of Jesus. Some nuns have reported having such experiences in prayer. I imagine other spiritual Gay men can also tell us of their similar fantasies. I shared my experience here because it helps explain how I've been able to build this bridge, one plank at a time, to span the chasm between being Gay, Catholic, and a friend of Jesus, as I am a friend of the Buddha—although I never imagined cuddling with him.

It merits explanation that when I say that I'm Catholic, I'm not unlike the millions of people who consider themselves "cafeteria Catholics." Not everyone eats everything that's been served to them. They pick and choose what satisfies their hunger and thirst.

I don't go to Mass except at Catholic weddings, funerals, and workshops. I don't go to confession, but I do go to communion if the opportunity arises. I don't believe Jesus was the sole son of God, but I believe in the Holy Spirit which is like the Tao that permeates and gives life and meaning to all things. I don't think it's important to believe Mary was a virgin, nor that she was born without original sin. I don't believe Jesus or Mary ascended into heaven. I don't believe in a fiery hell, purgatory, or limbo. I do believe in angels, in miracles, and in souls. The Bible, in my mind, is no more or less the word of God than are my columns, and it's not a history book.

A Christian is a follower of the teachings of Jesus. A Buddhist is a follower of the teachings of Buddha. A Taoist is a follower of Lao-tzu and his *Tao te Ching* (the Book of the Way and How It Manifests Itself in the World.) I'm all of the above, but it took a long while before I was able to identify again as Catholic.

Why would I call myself a Catholic? For the same reason I call myself a McNaught. It's the name I grew up with, it's where I find my happiest childhood memories, and I see no reason to change my name just because I rarely agreed with my father, as good a man as he was. I'm also a Michigander, though I haven't lived there since I was twenty-eight. "Oh, how I wish again, that I was in Michigan, back home on the farm."

A quick story about what we call ourselves, my sister-in-law is Judith McNaught, the second wife of my older brother, Michael, and a very successful historical romance novelist. She told me that she once got a letter from one of her fans that gave her a heads up that there was a homosexual writer with the name "McNaught" and that she should tell him to change his last name to something else. She wrote back, "He had it before I did."

Chapter Nineteen

"Stop This Shit"

SPEAKING ON COLLEGE CAMPUSES over an eleven-year period helped me feel confident about the content of my speech and about my stage presence. I've talked about feeling physically sick from fear. Additionally, I was addicted to nicotine since freshman year in high school, and I needed to have a cigarette just before I went onstage and immediately after. I'd also pee, even if I didn't feel the need, before every speech. I never wanted to feel as if I had to go during my talk. So, I would pray, pee, and smoke, but what I mostly did was self-hypnosis. I focused, focused, focused on what it was I was going to say and to whom I was going to say it. I did research in advance so that I could personalize my talk, but I worked to build within me a "song" the audience wouldn't forget.

People tell me I'm a natural public speaker, and they're correct. Since early childhood, I was a light that wouldn't be hid beneath a basket. I entertained friends, classmates, and visitors to our home with confidently told stories and humor. As said earlier, a lot of big names visited our house as we were growing up, and I wasn't afraid to speak up. In fact, at one party I cornered the CEO of General Motors, Jim Roche, and asked when GM was going to get out of South Africa to help end Apartheid. I remember hearing my father call out, "Will someone rescue Jim from Brian?"

I imagine it would be very hard to be an introvert and speak confidently to thousands of college students. I had to get their attention, get them on my side, and get them to see themselves as beautiful Gay people or beautiful allies. So, each time after praying that God would shine the light through me, I'd pee, and have a cigarette before I walked into the auditorium. I sat and waited for my bio to be read, hoping for applause as I walked to the microphone. It's hard to mount the stairs to the stage, or to enter from the side into a completely silent space. Dead man walking.

If I were to pick out the most memorable college presentations among the 200 I did in the decade after I was fired, the list would include Northern Michigan University where I had received a death threat, speaking for the first time to Sol Gordon's class of 500 students, and speaking to 2,000 fraternity and sorority members at UCLA and to a similar, but smaller group at UC Berkeley.

I had to fly to Northern Michigan in a small plane that seemed to be an endless journey. I began my talk with the question, "Did you know that there's been a credible death threat made against me while I'm speaking here tonight?" The women particularly were aghast. It had been rumored that the threat came from someone in ROTC. The head of ROTC made clear to every member that he was going to be there that night. Apparently, the fraternities had a contest to see who could get the most members to come listen to the Queer.

"Making such death threats is called homophobia," I said, "and there are three known causes of homophobia. The first is that the individual was abused as a child by a same-sex adult, and the individual assumes that every person who is attracted to same-sex people is a pedophile. So, someone might be angry at me for something that happened to them as a child. By the way, the overwhelming number of victims of sexual abuse are young girls molested by a man in their family. The second cause of homophobia is that someone belongs to a group whose approval they seek, and who senses that everyone else in their group hates homosexuals. That can happen in a fundamentalist church, the police, or even ROTC. The third cause of homophobia is self-hatred by someone who thinks they might be Gay. So, the first guy who boos me tonight, I want you to look at him and understand what he's going through." The women cheered.

Speaking to Sol Gordon's class for the first time was a little overwhelming because I had never spoken to so many people at once, and I was told a large number of them were jocks looking for an easy "A" grade. Getting academic credits for listening to someone talk about sex was a no-brainer. The auditorium stage was huge, and I had only recently come out. Could I flap my wings and fly, and if I couldn't, how would my failure affect Gay people in the room? One of Sol's teaching assistants at the time was Dr. Sandy Caron, who went on to teach human sexuality at the University of Maine. Her kindness and encouragement that night relieved a lot of my anxiety about failing, and fortunately, I soared.

The talk at UCLA was outdoors in a stadium, and all the students sat 100 rows away from me. A friend suggested that I should have said, "Will all of the Gay people please stay seated, and the Straight students move down here in front of me?" At UC Berkeley, the auditorium was packed. Just before I walked onstage, a staff person whispered, "We didn't tell them what this was about."

That's happened twice to me. One time in Orlando a company was having trouble in a particular department because a Lesbian employee was picking up on the bad vibes. The company scheduled two days of training. On the first day, the small group of participants had their feet up on the chair in front of them, were reading newspapers, and talking. It was clear defiance. The manager who brought me in introduced me and then left the room. Halfway through my guided imagery, in which I have members of the audience close their eyes and imagine being Straight in an all-Gay environment, one of the guys yelled, "Stop this shit!"

I looked at him and said, "I'm going to finish this exercise." That was a big mistake, because after his rude outburst no matter how commanding my voice might be, I lost everyone's concentration including my own. I should have stopped the exercise, asked everyone to open their eyes, and asked what was going on.

The major issue was that they hadn't been told what the workshop was about, nor how I could help them from getting disciplined for anti-Gay or anti-Trans behavior at work. Once I stopped, listened, and talked with them, everyone calmed down and I could proceed. Once again, when I started talking about my own life, I got their undivided attention.

At the end of the workshop, I gave the manager who introduced me a description of what happened. I told him that there were no managers in the room. "Tomorrow, I want to have all of the managers here, and I need you to tell all of the participants in advance what the topic will be and why." The second day went beautifully.

With both the college and corporate presentations, I started taking more time to prepare the client and asking them, "What would be a home run for you?" Generally, the answer was the same, "Raise their awareness so that we can have a more welcoming work environment." I told them that there were three important components of a successful presentation: 1) The most senior person in the company needs to introduce me, explain why we're doing the presentation, and stay in the room; 2) students, employees, and managers needed to know that their presence was required. Otherwise, the only people who would show up would be those who agreed with me. If they wouldn't mandate it, the president or CEO could send out a message to all managers that read, "I'll be there and will be very disappointed if I don't see you;" 3) people need be told in advance that the presentation doesn't seek to change anyone's moral values. "If you insist that your religion forbids you from attending, be aware that the speaker is going to outline unacceptable behavior toward Gay and Transgender people. If you engage in such behavior, you won't be able to say, 'I didn't know.' And there will be consequences for any inappropriate behaviors."

In 1988 I started declining invitations to speak on college campuses. When I began speaking in 1974, I was twenty-six, and there were very few of us traveling the country at the request of universities to help them create a safer, more welcoming environment. Twelve years later, I was thirty-eight, and there were dozens of LGBT people represented by speaker's bureaus. I felt the students needed someone closer to their age to serve as a role model.

Chapter Twenty

First Workshop on Gay Workplace Issues

WHEN I RECEIVED THE letter in 1986 from the Sexual Orientation Equity Committee of Bellcore (Bell Communications Research), among the first of such employee resource groups (ERG) of its kind, asking if I would be interested in creating an eight-hour workshop for them on Gay issues in the workplace, I was beyond ecstatic. I first thanked God, called Ray, and then Mary Lee.

God was behind it. Ray was delighted for me. And Mary Lee jumped at the chance to be a part of this groundbreaking sex education opportunity. I typed out a response to Bellcore saying I'd be very happy to create such a workshop, and I recommended that I teach it with a straight woman who was a highly respected sexuality educator. We'd then have a male and female, and Gay and Straight team, optimizing our chances of reaching the maximum number of participants. Next, we set a time for a telephone call to talk through the details prior to them meeting with their department head.

Mary Lee was over the moon with excitement and agreed to help me with the design. This was going to be the first such workshop ever offered in the corporate world. There may have been other diversity trainers who mentioned "sexual orientation" and "gender identity" in their list of marginalized groups, but there was not a focused training on growing up Gay, the challenges Gay people faced at work, and how to be a Straight ally.

The head of the department at Bellcore who was open to such an idea was Bob Martin, a man with a PhD from MIT. The SOE (sexual orientation equity committee) met with Bob to make the case for a diversity class on Gay issues in the workplace. Bellcore had mandated that every employee take one eight-hour diversity training annually. Although there was a plethora of options, sexual orientation was not one of them.

Bob told the SOE to proceed and to bring him the proposed workshop design for review. That's when the SOE contacted the National Gay and Lesbian Task Force and learned about my work. They ordered my video, *A Conversation with Brian McNaught On Being Gay*, and then they reached out to me.

Based on my own experience, I thought the workshop should include: 1) an introduction on why this was a business concern; 2) clarification that the workshop was not attempting to change personal religious beliefs; 3) building empathy for what it's like to be Gay in a Straight world by leading the participants through my guided imagery activity and by telling my personal story; 4) education to help participants understand the differences between sexual orientation, sexual behavior, and sexual identity, as well as the differences between gender identity, gender role, and gender expression; and 5) outlining strategies for creating a safe and comfortable workplace for LGBTQ employees, for example using inclusive language and challenging offensive language and/or behaviors.

Mary Lee was on board with all of that, and suggested two additional activities: one in which the employees evaluated the safety and "Gay-friendliness" of the atmosphere where they worked. Would they feel safe enough to come out if they were Gay; and a second activity that gave employees opportunities to practice being an ally. We would provide scripted scenarios in which small groups identified the problem and corrected it.

I pulled it all together and composed the rational for the workshop: "In the war for talent, in order to attract and retain the best and brightest people, the company has to create an environment in which every employee feels safe and valued." I used those same words at the beginning of every corporate training for the next thirty-nine years.

When I sent the workshop outline to the SOE committee, they liked it a lot but wanted to see the exact scenarios we would use for the ally activity. I got input from the SOE on real problems that have or might come up at work and did some brainstorming with Mary Lee. We developed three plausible scenarios. The SOE then set up a date for Mary Lee and me to fly to Newark from Boston and Washington, DC, and be taken by car to Piscataway, New Jersey, to meet Bob Martin and the SOE members. Our job was to talk Bob through the workshop and address any questions or concerns he might have.

We began by discussing how our professional backgrounds enabled us to conduct the workshop. Mary Lee and I did so and added accolades to each other's credentials. After the introductions, the members of the SOE committee, some of whom were Straight, some Gay, and some Bi, but no one openly Gay or Bi, listened carefully to Mary Lee and me talk Bob through our workshop design. He was very impressed and suggested that we begin with a pilot workshop and see through the evaluations how the employees responded. What exercise did they like most and what did they like least.

After the evaluations were tabulated, (remember, these are IT people) we would meet with a senior manager in human resources to go through them. We made some tweaks here and there, were given the go-ahead to set dates for future workshops. We charged $5,000 plus travel expenses.

The pilot workshop included some familiar faces of folks from the SOE committee, but also many people we didn't know. In my mind, everything had to be perfect. I not only listened carefully to everything both Mary Lee and I said, but I watched the time and the faces of the participants. At the end of every workshop, the participants were asked to fill out evaluations. In the beginning, Mary Lee and I, and some members of the SOE read them very carefully. After a while, though it became very clear that the training was a huge success.

I say that so casually. I'm one of those people who can look at forty evaluations on which thirty-nine people gave us perfect scores, but I focus on the one person who didn't. One "nay" vote could gnaw at me. Mary Lee was far more laid back. "They liked it."

After the pilot workshop, when we got dropped off at the Embassy Suites, Mary Lee and I fell into chairs in the bar, had a glass of Chardonnay, reviewed what happened and talked about how we felt. "Don't over-react to one bad evaluation," she told me. "It's not about you. It's about them." That was great advice, which I eventually learned to follow. I did though like reading the personal messages some participants added to their evaluations. They were anonymous, so people could comment freely. "My brother is Gay. I wish he could have been with me today." "I didn't know it wasn't a choice." "You two work well together."

Mary Lee and I were a really great team, but neither one of us was used to co-facilitating. So, we had to work out some ground rules and be very open about how each of us played our assigned roles and managed our time. I had a larger and more prominent role in the workshop because I was telling my personal story which typically evoked emotional responses. Mary Lee did more of the education and skill building and she tended to run over the time on some of her segments which caused me to have to speed up or shorten the next activity. We had to work out these kinds of kinks that are common with co-facilitation, but there was great love and respect between us. "Breathe, Brian."

One night, we came back to the Embassy Suites, and Grace Evans, a Straight ally and very active SOE leader, came in with us. Mary Lee sat at the piano and played songs that I knew, so I started singing, and Grace joined in too. We were usually in Piscataway for two workshops in a row, so at the next visit most of the SOE committee members joined us standing around the piano too. We were developing a great feeling of collegiality.

Our workshop, "Gay and Lesbian Issues in the Workplace" became very popular, primarily because it was so intimately personal, which computer geeks weren't all that used to at work. We were told, "This is the first diversity workshop in which I didn't feel judged or made to feel guilty." Mary Lee and I both had welcoming personalities. No one was ever going to feel singled out for the question they asked nor for the opinion they shared.

These IT employees understood the cost of discrimination. All of them knew the story of Alan Turing, the father of the modern computer, who broke the German encrypted code in World War II, and saved hundreds of thousands of lives. Afterwards, though, when the police responded to a break-in at his home and discovered he was homosexual, he was charged, found guilty, and forced to take castrating hormones. He committed suicide by eating a cyanide-laced apple. Where might we be today if he had been celebrated, rather than judged as a Gay man?

The training was limited to forty people at a time; Bob Martin had made it mandatory for his 2,000 employees, so we got scheduled a year in advance. Mary Lee and I were careful to give ourselves a break between scheduled engagements, but we nevertheless spent six days together every month, plus the week in July at the Annual Workshop on Human Sexuality at Thornfield ("Sex Camp").

Each week that we'd return to Piscataway, the Embassy Suites was our home. After such frequent visits from us, and the joyful after-work singing at the piano in the lounge, the staff of the hotel became fond of Mary Lee and me, and enjoyed checking us in, and serving us a drink and dinner.

After conducting the training for several months, one Bellcore employee told us, "It's harder to get into your workshop than it is to get tickets to *The Lion King*." When Bob Martin retired, he wrote to me "You ran a superb course at Bellcore in the late 1980s. My wife asked me to write memories for the kids and grandkids, including life-changing events. I just finished describing your magnificent course. I don't know if Grace ever told you, it became the most well-received course in my eight years at Bellcore."

Not long after we started doing workshops for Bellcore, I heard from a human resource person at Bell Labs who was married to a Human Resource person at Bellcore. "I've heard great things about your workshop on Gay and Lesbian issues in the workplace. Can we set up a date for a pilot?"

Mary Lee and I flew to the site of the Bell Labs pilot and began conducting the workshop with forty participants. Compared to the Bellcore pilot, it was so much easier to get and hold everyone's attention. In the beginning of the workshops at Bellcore, I would ask, "By show of hands, how many of you know someone who is Gay, Lesbian, Bisexual, or Transgender?" In the late 1980s, not a lot of hands went up. However, the same question at the Bell Labs pilot resulted in most of the participants raising their hand. We then learned that more than half the class were Lesbian and Gay employees who had flown in for the event. Within a couple of weeks, we got invitations to do the training in all the places from which they traveled.

Then, of course, we heard from AT&T, Hewlett-Packard, Motorola, Eli Lilly, and dozens of other companies across the country. Some corporations, such as Bell Labs, Hewlett-Packard, and Motorola wanted the exact same eight-hour workshop, while others said they could only set aside four hours, some two hours, and some just one hour. When the time was limited to four or less hours, I did the training on my own.

In 1996, AT&T spun off Lucent Technologies. Lucent still wanted to maintain the eight-hour format. At one point, I had five part-time consultants, two teams of two, and someone with me, to provide the exact same workshop, the only difference being that the Gay or Lesbian presenter would tell his or her story. We also added at the end of the program fifteen minutes for a Gay, Lesbian, Bisexual, or Transgender employee to step forward to tell their colleagues their experiences of working at the company.

Many of the personal accounts from the employees were about why they felt it was unsafe to come out. Some of the speakers feared they'd lose out on a promotion, and there were those who said they were out in their department, and everything was fine. I'd ask, "Will you tell us what department you work in?" Those who had no trouble being out usually worked in the office of human resources.

Mary Lee was so much more than a colleague; she was a soulmate and best friend. She visited us once in Gloucester when my parents were there, and I was so pleased that Mom and Dad got to meet this most significant person in my life. When Ray and I held a party for our tenth anniversary, Mary Lee couldn't make it, and I was, of course, disappointed. Not long thereafter, when Ray and I traveled to Washington for the 1987 March on Washington, Mary Lee hosted a beautiful tenth anniversary party for us at her home in Falls Church, Virginia. She also invited us to her second daughter Lisa's wedding. That's when I feared I'd throw her into the crowd with our wine-induced, spinning dance number.

On June 1, 1991, Ray and I were at the neighbors' for dinner. When we went to the office on the third floor of our home, our phone answering machine was blinking red with sixteen messages. The first one I played was from Matt and Martha Reese asking me to call them, and the next several were from Carol Dopp, Mary Lee's and my good friend from Thornfield. I called Carol, holding my breath. The news was the worst I'd ever received. Mary Lee was dead. In a horrendous rainstorm, she'd lost control of her car and hit a tree. There was no question that she died instantly.

When I got off the phone, Ray and I fell into each other's arms. "No. No. No." I kept saying.

"I'm so sorry, Brian. I'm so sorry," Ray said.

As I started calling mutual friends who needed to know immediately, such as Sol Gordon, Pam Wilson, and Alison Deming, I heard Ray crying very loudly in a nearby bedroom. He was crying for me.

It was only by chance that Ray was in Gloucester that weekend. It enabled us to comfort one another. He had been promoted to head up the Lehman Brothers office in Atlanta as an openly Gay man. He was living in a hotel and had to fly back to Atlanta on Sunday. When he got there, there was a message from Mary Lee on his answering machine. She was checking in on him, thinking he'd be alone again that weekend. We still have that tape. That Sunday is a blur to me.

Mary Lee's daughters, Cindy and Lisa, called and asked me to give Mary Lee's eulogy, along with Karl, the beloved minister at her Presbyterian church. I didn't imagine I'd be able to speak without bawling, but I gratefully agreed. On that Monday, I called Grace Evans at Bellcore, and all the diversity and inclusion people in the corporations where Mary Lee and I teamed up. Many of them drove from out of state to be at her funeral.

My mother had died of lymphoma in April of that year, so there was no comfort to be found from her. When I went to the airport on Tuesday, I was so upset and tearful that I couldn't talk to the airline person at the ticket counter. I wrote down "Washington, DC" on a piece of paper. "My best friend died," I whispered. "She drove into a tree." While kindly expressing her sympathy, the woman handed me a ticket for the next available flight. Carol picked me up at the airport.

She drove me to see the tree, where there were a lot of flowers from the students at George Mason High School. We both concluded that Mary Lee must have dropped something and reached down for it. Mary Lee was an open-armed Mother Earth who was also a total klutz. Her mind was often elsewhere, and she'd constantly ask, "Where are my glasses?" "Brian, do you have my plane ticket?" "Now, I have something to give you, but I can't remember what it is."

Once, when Mary Lee and I were scheduled to conduct two days of trainings in Columbus, Ohio, I flew from Boston to Washington National, where she was supposed to join me for the flight to Columbus and sit next to me. I waited and waited for her and was certain she was going to miss the flight. Finally, with the help of airline personnel, she limped to the gate.

"What happened?" I asked. She replied, "Oh, I tripped on a plastic cleaners' bag and fell down the stairs. Why do they make those things so long?" When we landed in Columbus we went directly to the hospital where they determined she had broken a bone in her foot, and she needed a cast. "Let's cancel," I said. "No, I'll be fine." Yes, she'd be fine because I'd be pushing her wheelchair for the next two days, even when she was facilitating a workshop activity.

The caregiving went both ways. Once when we had just checked into our rooms at the Embassy Suites in Piscataway I doubled over in horrible pain. I could hardly breathe. I called Mary Lee, and we got a ride to the hospital. She stayed with me nearly all night as they determined I had kidney stones. I forget what they gave me or did for me, but Mary Lee and I were both bushed when we entered the workshop room a few hours later. Nevertheless, everything went very smoothly.

I had no notes when I climbed the steps to the lectern in the church to give Mary Lee's eulogy. I looked out and saw Lisa and Cindy's red eyes, but expectant smiles directed at me. The church was packed, with people listening to speakers outside. I told them that when I went downstairs to use the restroom a young woman tearfully told me that Mary Lee was her best friend. "No," I thought, "Mary Lee was my best friend." Everyone laughed in recognition. I pointed out that the church was filled with people for whom Mary Lee was their best friend.

After explaining Mary Lee's and my relationship, I recalled for everyone the storyline of the movie *Defending Your Life* with Meryl Streep and Albert Brooks.

The two strangers who had just died met in the waiting room for heaven. But, in my version, before she gets there, Mary Lee must take a bus and she was digging frantically through her pocketbook and pockets in search for her admission ticket. Her pockets were filled with uncapped Magic Markers, so her hands got covered with different colors. She pulled all kinds of things out of her purse until she finally found her ticket in her coat pocket. Lisa and Cindy were laughing, as was the rest of the church as I reflected on why Mary Lee was so attractive to us, and why she made us feel so happy.

When she got to heaven, she called everyone "sweetie" even the angels. In the movie, everyone sits with a panel of judges who watch the film of their life. It was here that I was able to recall all the wonderful things Mary Lee had done for others. "In fact," I said, "Mary Lee's life movie was so endearing, kind, and loving that word spread and people were crammed into the room, as we are now."

I continued to capture Mary Lee with humor and descriptions of our interactions, such as when she stopped me after my presentation at the human sexuality workshop at Thornfield and made me cry by asking about my unspoken personal pain, and at the airport in Columbus, going home, where Mary Lee yelled at me to try to get us into first class because of her cast. I yelled back that I was doing that very thing, and she should relax. In response, she shot me the bird, not just a little bird but a very big, high, shaking one, to which I replied with my own high flying, shaking raised two middle index fingers. The church was filled with laughter.

When I finished, I walked past Cindy and Lisa who were both smiling and mouthing "thank you."

When I sat down next to Ray, who had flown in from Atlanta for the funeral, he said "Great job. Perfect." And I said to him in all earnestness, "It wasn't me. I was up there, but I didn't do it. I didn't give that perfect celebration of Mary Lee's life." Many of us have had the experience of writing, saying, or doing things that we feel are beyond our intelligence, spiritual level of awareness, and skill. That's the Holy Spirit. Call it intuition or an out-of-body experience, but what I felt was the flow of light through the cleanest window I could manage. God gave Mary Lee the send-off she deserved.

Chapter Twenty-One

Use What the Universe Gives You

As hard as it was to imagine the workshop without Mary Lee, I had engagements lined up for the rest of the year, and into the next. With extraordinary courage and grace, Mary Lee's daughter, Lisa, when asked said "Yes," she'd like to represent her mom in the first workshops the following week. When we arrived at the Embassy Suites in Piscataway, I was asked by the desk clerk, "Where is Ms. Tatum?" I explained with great difficulty that Mary Lee was in an accident and had died. "This is her daughter, Lisa," I said.

Lisa and I went to our rooms, and then came down and had dinner together. The server was very kind but solemn. The next morning, we had our breakfast and were picked up as always by Jean Van Ness, an elegant older employee with beautiful white hair, who took great pride and pleasure being our ride back and forth each day. Jean expressed her sadness and condolences. During the workshop, Lisa was a trooper. I explained at the beginning that my co-facilitator, Mary Lee, had died and that her daughter stepped in to help guide us through the training. The people in the workshop responded with love and respect.

When Lisa and I got back to the Embassy Suites, we learned from our dinner waiter that management had called all the hotel staff together to let them know that Ms. Tatum, whom they all loved and looked forward to seeing, had died. Do any of us know the extent of our impact on others? Lisa was very moved to learn this. I wasn't at all surprised. Mary Lee was warm and welcoming to everyone.

The following week, my good friend, Carol Dopp, stepped in to co-facilitate the workshop. Carol would say, as I do, that "Sex Camp" totally changed her life. As said before, Carol was in Mary Lee's and my small discussion group her first year. A couple of years later, she was on the staff. At this time, she was a highly-regarded high school sexuality educator and counselor, with a great working knowledge of a range of sexuality issues.

Once again, I explained to the workshop participants that Mary Lee had died, and that her dear friend and mine, Carol, whose credentials I shared, was with us for the day. Carol, like Lisa, did a great job, but wouldn't be able to work with me on a regular basis because of her school obligations.

As our workshops at Bellcore were winding down, Lucent Technologies, contacted me and requested enough workshops across the country to fill a year although I had promised myself to take a week off after two weeks of training. I needed a new co-facilitator for these eight-hour workshops, so I approached Pam Wilson, who was also on staff at Thornfield and a good friend who'd marched with me at Gay marches in Washington, DC.

Pam is a Straight Black woman, a superb sexuality educator, and another person with warm, welcoming energy. I was excited about Pam joining me and she was a perfect match. We worked well together, and although our friendship and mutual respect were already established, we grew much closer as we began this joint venture. From that point on, Pam worked with me for every eight-hour workshop.

Pam was not only a co-facilitator in the workshop, but she was also my gentle, loving tutor on the elements of racism. With her permission and encouragement, I asked about her early life and what racism she experienced as a child. We talked about her mom and dad, two brothers, and two beloved nieces. Pam helped me start to see the world through her eyes. When we'd go to dinner, for instance, I'd notice that she was the only Black person in the room. I shared that being with her gave me heterosexual privilege for as long as the meal lasted. We looked like a Straight couple.

There wasn't anything I couldn't ask Pam, nor she me. One time, after she had just returned from a Caribbean vacation, she said to me, "So, what do you think?" I replied, "About what?" Her eyes got big, "About my tan. Look," she said as she pulled her blouse away from her shoulder, exposing a much lighter brown strap from a bathing suit. "Oh, wow. You did get a great tan," I said with some astonishment and embarrassment. It didn't occur to me that Black people got a change in color from sunbathing. But, of course, it made perfect sense.

Pam and I talked about how Black people's pigmentation impacts their opportunities in life, as well as their safety. Pam looks to me like Halle Berry. Richard, her IT wiz and senior manager husband, has darker skin. As a result, he is pulled over by the police so often that he just sighs and automatically puts his hands on the top of the steering wheel. Once when Pam and Richard were visiting us, they went golfing. On the walk up to the clubhouse, a White man sitting on the grass said, "Go back to Africa where you belong." Richard, who is all muscle, turned back and asked, "What did you say?" "Free speech, man." Fortunately, when Richard told a manager of the golf course what had transpired, the White man was banned for life from the golf club.

I like to think of myself as enlightened on issues of diversity. I have the right attitude, but just a peripheral understanding of how people different from me live. I'm not afraid to ask questions nor to apologize for a mistake. That attitude has enabled me to learn. Thanks to my tutors such as Pam Wilson and Deb Dagit, I feel more confident as a person who seeks to help change the world. But I must respectfully ask questions and be willing to acknowledge my unconscious racism, sexism, and ignorance about living with disabilities seen and unseen.

Our invitations to speak at the Lucent manufacturing facility in Massachusetts, and at other Lucent facilities across the country, was due to the lobbying efforts of the LGBTQ Employee Resource Group, LEAGUE. The Bell Labs training, which led to the AT&T training, introduced me to LEAGUE members across the country. Each time Pam and I did a full day workshop, or I did a four-hour training, we'd arrange to have a LEAGUE member speak for ten or fifteen minutes at the end of the session. That's how I got to know the Lesbian and Gay United Employee (LEAGUE) members so personally, especially Steve Mershon, Kathleen Dermody, Ryk Koscielski, Jim Deacon, Margaret Burd, Art Nava, Sandy North, and John Klenert, among others.

In 1991, I most reluctantly moved to Atlanta from Gloucester when we sold our beloved house in Massachusetts. I was leaving Jeremy behind, as he was buried on the property around our pool, as was Bing Crosby, our yellow canary who loved singing with Joan Baez. It was an amazing home, with lots of great stories to tell. At one black tie Christmas party, we had every major player in the Gay movement in Massachusetts drive an hour to attend. The house was decorated extraordinarily, with a carved ice reindeer standing at the side of the walk in. Before the party began, I met with the catering staff and told them that most of the people they would see that night were Gay, and if that made them uncomfortable, they needed to leave, or work just in the kitchen. They were terrific.

Brit, our yellow lab, and I were eager to join Ray in Atlanta. He had found a house which we totally renovated. It was in Ansley Park, on 15th Ave. and Peachtree, across from the Christian Science Church and the High Museum of Art. Not long after we finished renovating the house, we had a few guests come for a cookout, and one of them greeted me by saying, "There's the godfather of Gay diversity training, according to *The New York Times*." Apparently, their business writer, in doing her column on corporations and their diversity initiatives on Gay issues, talked with a variety of heads of diversity and inclusion, as well as Lesbian and Gay trainers who I had invited to sit in on my workshops when they indicated interest in doing the work. I didn't reject the moniker, and used it, but I always chose to interpret it to mean that I was the man who helped launch the work of others in the field.

In 1991, my mother, my best friend, and my 101-year-old grandmother died, and I moved to Atlanta. It was a huge year of transition for me. We quickly made very good friends with whom we've remained close after all these years. Atlanta was a great place for young Gay men to live and was the destination of Gay men and women throughout the south who were looking for a place where they'd feel safe and welcomed.

It was in 1991 that I spoke to a group of AT&T executives in San Francisco. I thought, "What can I teach the people in San Francisco about being Gay?" As it turned out they knew very little accurate information despite living among Gay people. I've learned not to make assumptions about my audience and I got reminded on that trip to use what the Universe presents you.

As I was being introduced to an all-White audience, a large Black homeless man walked to the front of the room and said, "I have something in my pocket," which immediately made me and others think it might be a gun, "and I need $20 to get a prescription." I stood up, embarrassed by my assumption, gladly gave the man twenty dollars, put my arm on his shoulder, and helped guide him to the door. Once he was gone, I began by saying to the senior managers, "That was scary, wasn't it? How were we supposed to know how to handle the situation? No one taught us. It's the same for managing Gay and Lesbian issues in the workplace. Many of us don't know how to handle a situation, and that raises anxiety. Today, we're going to answer all the questions you might have so that the topic is less scary."

A similar thing happened to me when I was speaking to a large group at Los Alamos, the historic and well-known government research facility. As I began my presentation, all the lights went off. There were no windows in the auditorium, and the only light that came in was when the door to the room was opened. I said, "This is how a lot of Straight people feel about homosexuality. They're in the dark and it can feel unsettling." People laughed and sat down. I kept speaking, trusting that the lights would eventually come back on, which they did.

Chapter Twenty-Two

"I Don't Know What to Do With You."

WHEN LEAGUE HAD THEIR first gathering of its members from throughout the country, they did so in Florida in 1993. Because I had traveled to all their locations, I was the only one who knew them all by sight. They knew each other only by name and voice from conference calls. When AT&T spun off Lucent Technologies, the LEAGUE members who were reassigned created new LEAGUE chapters in their new sites. They became one of the most effective corporate Employee Resource Groups in any category, and their conference became an annual event at which senior managers would not only speak but stay for the entire weekend.

The format of the conference usually included me providing a pre-conference four-hour training for Straight managers, and then LEAGUE would have two days of plenary speakers, workshops, and a gala dinner.

For this first gathering, Ron Robin, who, as you recall, created my first video, approached me about creating a video featuring LEAGUE members who'd talk about what it was like for them at work, and what they hoped their company would do to improve the workplace atmosphere. Ron also filmed my workshop and had me speak to the camera as a segue between interview topics. The resulting video, *Gay Issues in the Workplace*, became a pioneering corporate resource.

Also in 1993, I wrote, and St. Martin's Press published, my book, *Gay Issues in the Workplace*. That book is now in the Library of Congress, and a copy was given by the Human Rights Campaign to every US congressperson who signed on as a sponsor of the bill to end workplace discrimination based on sexual orientation and gender identity. From then on, I asked every company that invited me to speak to provide each workshop participant a copy of the book. Not only was the book filled with helpful information but having it on one's desk communicated to others that your office was a safe space, or at least that you had some awareness of the issues.

Gay Issues in the Workplace provides the rationale for addressing the issue in the workplace by outlining the ways that homophobia and heterosexism impact productivity and lessen a company's ability to attract and retain the best and brightest talent. The book also provides: 1) examples of Lesbian and Gay employees who were either out or afraid to be out, and what they considered to be helpful in creating safe space, 2) all the words and definitions one needs to know to comfortably address the issue, for example using the words "sexual orientation" rather than "sexual preference," and 3) an outline of the eight-hour workshop. In the book, I encourage others to use my ideas and workshop design.

It was also in 1993, when I was scheduled to speak in Denver, Colorado, to AT&T one day and to Hewlett-Packard, the next day that the local public access television station, KBDI, asked me to tape two one-hour presentations. I happily agreed. They said to bring a different tie and shirt that I would change into after the first presentation. The studio audience, many of whom were members of the Denver chapter of P-FLAG, Parents and Friends of Lesbians and Gays, would be moved around for the second presentation.

I spoke first on *Growing Up Gay and Lesbian* and then changed clothes before speaking on *Homophobia in the Workplace*. As I prepared to create these videos, I repeated my plea that the Holy Spirit flow through me. I was excited to be part of something that could reach so many people. It was still very scary for people to come out, especially in small towns. KBDI put both videos up in the satellite of public access stations where any of the stations around the country could show the programs in their areas for free. And they did, including in San Francisco and New York. We saw a promotion for it in a New York TV program guide. A lot of people told me they watched the program in their parents' home, some with their parents and some quietly alone.

TRB Productions (Ron and me) also had the right to reproduce and sell the videos, with the KBDI television station getting a share of the profits. We now had four videos for sale, and Ron's husband Ed Teo, from

Singapore, took charge of receiving orders, mailing them out, and keeping the books. Four years later, KBDI asked me to do another presentation that we called *Gay/Straight: Can We Talk?* All of these are available on YouTube and on my website for free.

It was probably in 1993, after Pam and I had done several full-day workshops for Sheila Landers (the much-loved head of diversity and inclusion for Lucent Technologies in Merrimack Valley, Massachusetts) that *The Wall Street Journal* did a feature column, including caricatured artwork of Sheila and me, about Sheila's commitment to train everyone in the facility, including second- and third-shift employees, on this issue. Sheila introduced us at every workshop and told her colleagues that she wanted to make sure her young son Christopher would never have to worry about telling her anything about himself. The *Wall Street Journal* piece generated a lot of congratulatory phone calls and inquiries. I'm delighted that Sheila and I can continue to be the president of each other's fan club on Facebook.

My mantra from the beginning of my unintended career of being an educator on Gay, Lesbian, Bisexual, and Transgender issues, initially in the Catholic Church, then on college campuses, then in the City of Boston's mayor's office, and finally in the workplace is that ignorance, by which I mean lack of familiarity, is the parent of fear, and fear is the parent of hatred. If people are given the opportunity to safely listen to new information, shared not with anger but with loving kindness, you can turn a person's life around, and that of their family members and friends. I have a lifetime of examples, but three stand out.

The Lucent employees on the third shift complained to Sheila that they didn't have access to diversity training, so Pam and I agreed to do a couple of workshops between 11 PM and 8 AM. Our bodies protested but we both understood the need. The first participants to come in, we were told, all came from the same work group. In that group was a man that everyone suspected was Gay, but he wouldn't come out, and he was missing work because he found the environment to be very hostile. One of the first things we do in the workshop is ask the participants to tell us whether the environment for LGBT employees is welcoming or unwelcoming. White collar office workers around the country, and throughout the world, would tell us or me that the environment was somewhat to very welcoming. Blue collar factory workers feel freer to put it out there. They'd say the workplace is somewhat to very unwelcoming for Lesbian, Gay, Bisexual, and Transgender employees.

Next question. "If I confided in you that I was Gay, what might you think is best for me? Stay in the closet. Tell a few close friends. Tell the manager. Or, come out to everyone." That day, both the closeted Gay employee and their manager were in our group. One of his colleagues replied, "If someone came out to me, I couldn't guarantee they wouldn't lose their hands in a machine." Okay, now we'd never heard anything that extreme before. Throughout the workshop, I kept my eye on the man who made that declaration.

In the beginning, when I made the case for why this is a workplace issue, he didn't pay much attention. He mostly stared at the floor, but when I started to tell my story, he looked up. His face became more animated; he held eye contact with me; he laughed when the others laughed; got choked up when the others got choked up; and became thoughtful at the end.

The next day, I heard from Sheila that after we left that morning, the guy who said a Gay person might lose their hands in a machine if they came out to him, walked up to the guy everyone thought was Gay, and asked, "Are you Gay?" The Gay man, like most Gay people at the end of the workshop, was feeling more empowered and said a definitive "Yes." And then the guy who made such a threatening comment in the beginning of the training said to him, "I'm really sorry about all of the things I've said or done."

We only lived in Atlanta from 1991 to January of 1994. Ray was promoted to be the head of global equity sales at Lehman, but it meant we needed to move to New York City. Prior to our move, I was on my way back to Atlanta after doing two days of training in New Jersey. My seat assignment was on the aisle. When I sat down, drained from that day's presentation, the man next to the window looked over and smiled. Before long, we were chatting away as I'm prone to do. Big secret, right?

"Are you heading home?" is usually the opening question. "Yes," we were both returning home, me to very liberal midtown Atlanta, and he to the very conservative Cobb County. Cobb County became infamous when the International Olympic Committee removed all venues from the county because the county government wouldn't back down from its public statement that homosexuals were not welcome in Cobb County.

"What do you do for work?" I asked. It turns out that he was well-known as a leader in Christian values in the workplace. He had received one of President George H. W. Bush's "Thousand Points of Light" awards and had been featured in both *Inc.* and *Fortune* magazines, among others.

"What about you?" he asked. "What work do you do?"

I explained that I helped create safe and welcoming environments for Lesbian, Gay, Bisexual, and Transgender people in the workplace.

If you could read the bubble over each of our heads it would say, "Of all the seats on the plane I could have sat in . . ."

My seatmate could have then pulled out a book to read, but he asked instead, "Why would a company bring you in to address that issue?"

"Imagine you're Gay," I said, "and you come into work and find on your computer a handwritten note that quotes Leviticus 18:22, 'A man shall not lie with a man, as with a woman. Such is an abomination.' How much work would you get done that day?"

"I wouldn't get any work done," he thoughtfully replied. "I'd be thinking all day, 'Who put this on my desk?'"

"That's why they have me come in to help make sure that regardless of one's religious beliefs, everyone understands that you have to treat colleagues with professional respect."

"What exactly do you do in these workshops?" he asked.

I gave him my explanation of how homophobia and heterosexism impact the work environment. I then gave him a mini sexuality education, explaining that the company is taking a stand on one's sexual orientation and identity, not on one's sexual behavior. I shared the words that are "welcoming" and those that are considered unwelcoming, and then told him that I tell my story. "I put a face on the issue."

"I don't know any Gay people that I'm aware of," he said. "If you're willing, why don't you tell me your story?"

Never missing an opportunity to help someone become an ally, even a socially conservative Christian businessman, I told him my story of how I've always known that I was attracted to men, and of how I wanted to be God's best friend, and of healing service to others.

"Did you date girls?" he asked.

"Yes, I had girlfriends from kindergarten through college."

"This is very personal," he said, "but have you ever had sex with a woman?"

"Nothing is too personal for me," I smiled. "Yes, in college I had my first heterosexual experience. I felt nothing."

I then told him about my work for the Catholic Church as a weekly columnist and reporter, about drinking the paint thinner, about coming out, about my folks' reaction, about being fired, about Dignity, about Ray and the many years we'd been together, and about my take on what makes a person a saint.

When we landed, my seatmate said to me, "Brian, as sure as I'm sitting in this seat, I know that God had you sit next to me, and I'll never think about this issue in the same way again." He then pulled out of his briefcase the copy of the *Fortune* magazine that had featured him, and he signed it for me, and I pulled out a copy of *Gay Issues in the Workplace* and signed the book to him. For a couple of years, we exchanged Christmas cards, and then drifted apart.

Over the years, I have had the same experience multiple times. Coming out and telling our story is the Holy Spirit giving the necessary wisdom to the person who fears or hates us. No one should be found guilty for being uninformed. However, if they continue with their oppressive behavior after their heart has been touched by the Spirit, then they're responsible for their behavior. Some people, though, don't understand how to incorporate the new information into their daily living.

Early in my career, I joined other sexuality educators at a gathering of private school teachers. I was asked to do morning and afternoon presentations on "Growing Up Gay and Lesbian." My morning session had a relatively small audience, but word got out and the afternoon presentation was packed, standing room only. As my friends and I were in the parking lot saying our "good-byes" and preparing to leave, a car came up towards us, stopped, and out jumped a woman who came straight to me and asked, "May I have a moment, please?"

"Sure," I said. Always say "yes" to the Universe.

"Quite frankly, I strongly opposed you being invited to speak here today. It's totally against everything I believe in. I refused to go into either of your talks, but I stood outside this afternoon and listened. I need to tell you, Brian, I don't know what to do with you. I'm a conservative Christian who believes homosexuality is wrong. But I heard you speaking your truth from your heart today. How can I go home and tell my children that I've changed my position on this? If I do that, then everything else I've taught them falls apart. I don't know what to do with you."

"Thank you for taking the time to tell me this," I said. "I can't solve that problem for you. What I can tell you is that I'm now a card in the hand you've been dealt. God wanted you to meet me. It's now part of your faith challenge to decide how you're going to respond."

Chapter Twenty-Three

Me, Maya, and Intimacy

IN 1999, I WAS invited to speak to the business council of the Human Rights Campaign at their meeting in San Francisco. They were a new group and wanted me to tell them about my work as an LGBTQ diversity trainer in corporations over the past twelve years. As a result, my friend, Kim Cromwell, unbeknownst to me, recommended that I be invited to do a presentation at the prestigious Linkage Conference in Atlanta in the year 2000. The Linkage Conference was a big deal. The major keynote address was to be given by Maya Angelou. The event attracted a huge audience of corporate human resource personnel, many of whom were Black women. This was a change and a bit of a challenge for me because my audiences tended to be White, with a sprinkling of racial diversity. Although my work with Pam had increased my awareness of racism and other issues affecting Black people, I recognized that I still walked my path as a White, privileged Gay person. I worried that these Black women and men might not relate to me as easily as my typical audience. Could I trust that all kinds of different people in my audience might identify with to my story? We're basically singing soul to soul regardless of our external differences, are we not?

Maya Angelou spoke immediately before me. She was a Black woman, international superstar, magnificent author, and poet, beloved not just in the Black community, but in most any community. It was scary to have to speak right after her. Her presentation was great, delivered beautifully with sophisticated artistry, but it wasn't particularly personal. After she left the stage to a standing ovation, I was introduced. On my way up the stairs, I said to God, "Do with me what you will." I began by laughing with the audience about the challenge of speaking in Maya Angelo's echo.

My talk was very personal, as it always is. I first asked the audience members to raise their hand if they had a Gay, Lesbian, or Transgender person in their lives. As I expected, more than half of the people did so. I thanked them and said to the others, "I think you know someone who is Gay, but you just don't know you know them." After explaining why this issue was a corporate concern, I began telling them my story. As I've said more than once and intend on reminding people until my ashes are scattered, it's through our stories that people truly get to know us, and once you truly get to know another person, it's very difficult to consciously do harmful things to them. Every great spiritual guide has told us stories to teach us their truths.

When you and your audience are in sync, you and they can feel it. No one is left out. Everyone senses that something very special is happening, that they're part of the dancing of souls. That's always what I work for when I speak. I hope to bring us all to the next level, the highest vibration, of being soul to soul, innocent, vulnerable, empathetic, grateful, and loving. When I finished my talk, I too got a standing ovation. Later, I was told by Kim that to my surprise I got a higher rating in the participants' evaluation forms than did Maya Angelou. I suspect that's because it's easier for me to be totally accessible. It's easier to experience intimacy not so much with "Brian" but with that part of me that manifests the Divine, angel to angel.

Following this talk in Atlanta, I received more requests for presentations and workshops. Some were one-shot deals, such as with the Federal Reserve, Sandia, Brookhaven, and Sony, but most were requests for multiple workshops at multiple sites. Motorola and Hewlett-Packard especially wanted extensive training, which is when I brought in my two teams of trainers.

Before Ray, I, and our dog, Brit, moved to New York, I received a very emotionally compelling letter from a seventeen-year-old girl who had just seen my video, *Growing Up Gay and Lesbian*, on television in her home outside of Detroit. She told me that her father died of AIDS and that she was living with her grandparents who were fundamentalist Christians. They refused to let her talk about her father, and they took all the pictures of their son off the wall. Her name was Vicky.

I, of course, wrote back immediately, promising to be there for her. I kept Vicky's letters, as I did everyone's, but regrettably I didn't have copies of my responses. The writers of the letters had either read one of my books, heard a presentation, or had seen one of my videos, and they reached out because they needed to know they'd be all right. I was a Gay lifeguard or lifeboat. Some letter writers were young and felt stuck in a homophobic setting. Others were in heterosexual marriages, or were leaders in religious organizations, such as the Salvation Army, in which they felt they had no other option but to stay in the closet.

There used to be a resource called the *Gayellow Pages*. It listed the contact information for every LGBTQ organization in every city in the country. When I'd write back to people in need, I'd suggest that they reach out to this or to that organization, or Gay religious group, and to go to a Gay bookstore or a Gay bar (if they were adults) to get the support they needed. I also recommended they contact P-FLAG and I gave them the names of books that might help. Most important to all of them was my promise that I'd be there for them. And I was. Whenever I got a letter or an e-mail, I'd stop what I was doing to make sure the person seeking comfort got it, day or night.

Vicky needed a lot of help. She called me a couple of days after she got my response to her letter, and we ended up talking regularly in the late afternoon. We did so because each time we'd seem to solve a problem, another would come up. Once she graduated from high school, she'd be eighteen and then be able to move out of her grandparents' home. Vicky never asked for money. Once she sent me an afghan she said she made, and a cassette of her singing. All she wanted was my time and attention. She'd send a letter and I'd answer, or she'd call, and I'd talk. When my dad died, she said she wanted to come to his funeral, but would be out of town. Her cousin, Judy, came in her place. Ray warned me that I was getting too involved, but I got defensive of this teenager in need.

I wrote about Vicky's journey as a Straight ally for my next book, *Now That I'm Out, What Do I Do?*, also published by St. Martin's Press. But because she was underage, I needed her to sign a release giving permission for her story to be told. After several failed attempts, I called my friend Henry Grix in Detroit whose law firm had an investigator. He replied quickly that there was a Vicky with the same last name living at the address to which I sent flowers for her graduation, but she was twenty-eight, not eighteen. It broke my heart to learn that I had been so deceived, and that it was Vicky who came to my father's funeral. I let my editor, Keith Kahla, know immediately that the chapter on Vicky had to be pulled from the book.

My friend, Armistead Maupin, author of the *Tales of the City* series, had also been scammed, and he wrote a book about it. He and I talked on the phone, and it felt as if we both had been taken advantage of by the same person. Armistead contacted *20/20*, the television news and feature program. They stepped in, had me listen in on their conversation with Vicky, and they determined that it wasn't the same person who was deceiving Armistead. After I hung up, I pulled way back to take a serious look at my need to be needed.

It was at this time that I began seriously exploring the issue of codependency, of needing to make everything "right." Why did I continue to talk to this young woman every day? Because, when I help someone, I get warm fuzzy feelings. Vicky gave me the opportunity to feel as if I was helping her. Her real gift to me was enabling me to figure out how to start setting better personal boundaries. I'm a middle child who excelled at helping people. I still am, but I've gotten much better about taking care of myself in the process.

Sometimes you succeed and sometimes you don't. A Lesbian employee of one of my clients asked me to go to dinner with her during one of my overnight stays. During our dinner, I gave her 100 percent of my attention, listening and offering stories from my own life that affirmed her. She undoubtedly wrote an e-mail "thank you." I returned to that site several more times that year. On the third or fourth visit, I saw the woman in the cafeteria at lunchtime. I gave her a big smile and a "hello" wave. She came over to me with an angry face and said, "Every time you come here and don't seek me out, you stab me in the heart." What? "I'm sorry," I said. "I had no idea."

I didn't give this woman any more attention than I gave anyone who wanted to go to dinner while I was in town, or to any person in need, but she misunderstood my sharing with her as the beginning of a more intimate friendship. I had made her feel special, and then I didn't. Those of us who are able to give our complete attention to others need to be aware that such focused listening might be rare for them and might seem far more intimate than they typically experience with people, and they might misread it.

Maybe it's my age, religious training, spiritual seeking, family background, the security I feel with Ray, or a combination of them all, but I love people and always have. I want to do good by them, and I forgive every person who has consciously or unconsciously harmed me. To the best of my ability, I don't think about the past in anything but positive ways. There are names you could throw at me that would get a negative reaction, but I know that's about me, not them. Judgment is a slippery slide to the basement when a minute ago you were vibrating at the highest level of awareness. Ray has the same skill of letting go.

I forgave Margaret Cronyn immediately after she told me my column was dropped. She was in a horrible position, having just been made editor, and then having to punish someone she loved. The former employee who yelled "Faggot, faggot, faggot" at me after I came out was a wounded soul and hurting. The person who said he was going to bring a gun to kill me at Northern Michigan University and the one who said he hoped I died of AIDS might both have been closeted Gay men whose fear of themselves made them lash out at me. Everyone in my life has done the best they could, including Vicky, and more recently the good friends who borrowed all our savings, spent it foolishly, and now can't pay us back. People ask, "Why aren't you angry?" "Why don't you want revenge?" Sometimes, I can get angry, and I do want revenge, but that is not the person I aspire to be. So, I say the Prayer of St. Francis and the Serenity Prayer; I forgive. I stop the dramas that creep their way into my consciousness, and I fully accept that no ill will was intended. I believe deeply that anger solves nothing and stops me from living in awareness, and that revenge is a never-ending cycle of violence.

I've received many slurs, threatening letters, obscene phone calls, and disapproving glares since I came out publicly at age twenty-six. Although each of those things hurt, I never would have made it to seventy-six in one physical, emotional, and spiritual piece/peace if I didn't learn to forgive. I'd be constantly looking in the rearview mirror and missing the great splits in the road ahead of me. This largely intuitive ability to forgive and to look forward with optimism has helped me successfully change hearts, minds, and behaviors on one of the most threatening topics in our society—homosexuality. We've made great strides politically and socially, but the work is not done. It will never be done. To keep moving forward we need to remind ourselves that the messenger is the message. If we are happy, spiritually whole, grateful, loving, and kind people, our message is that it's possible to be Lesbian, Gay, Bisexual, and Transgender and be happy, spiritually whole, grateful, loving and kind.

Chapter Twenty-Four

Same Heart Beats in Tokyo and Mumbai

I NEVER PLANNED OUT MY life and couldn't achieve what I've described in this memoir without the involvement and support of many people. I don't know how exactly God works through me or any of us. I see myself as one tiny piece of colorful glass in a kaleidoscope, amidst all of you, the patterns of which are constantly changing. I never said "No" to an invitation, whether it was to speak, be interviewed, sit one-on-one with a person in need, write a book, contribute a chapter, make a video, write a magazine article, host a radio program, interview Gay and Lesbian leaders on TV, or create a dinner party for people with AIDS.

Many people have told me that my writing is helpful to them because they see their own feelings articulated. I love to write and to speak. I believe the Holy Spirit, or the Tao, or the Universe, uses my talents to communicate messages that it wants others to pay attention in order to grow toward their full actualization.

Franciscan Father Murray Bodo wrote *Francis, the Journey and the Dream*, a story about St. Francis of Assisi that grabbed my soul. It was about simplicity. People who have visited the homes Ray and I have lovingly renovated and decorated might raise an eyebrow when I say that I resonate with "simplicity." We do love beautiful antiques and have collected treasures throughout our life. However, those who truly know us understand that possessions mean little to us. We're simply caretakers until the next person has the treasure in their lives. Our hearts are simple.

We have lost our retirement funds, but we're still happy because of our love of simplicity and each other.

My work as a speaker on LGBTQ issues in the workplace took me across the country working with extraordinary people, Gay and Straight, who worked in human resources or diversity and inclusion, or were part of an Employee Resource Group. Some of the names that come to mind are Todd Sears at Credit-Suisse, Ana Duarte McCarthy at Citi, Karen Whiteside at Eli Lilly, and Tom Millner at DuPont. And through those people and that work, I encountered strangers with whom my angel danced, and I grew into the human being I am today. Hopefully, I helped them to do the same.

Two clients stand out, Merck and Chubb, although picking just two makes me anxious because there are dozens of others with whom I soared. At Merck, I got to work with Deb Dagit, and at Chubb with Kathy Marvel. Deb was head of Merck's office of diversity and inclusion, and Kathy was a leader of Chubb's LGBT Employee Resource Group. Both became dear friends.

Deb asked me if Merck could videotape my two-hour presentation for in-house use. "Of course," I said. "May I have a copy so that I might make it available to the public?" That's how the four-part series of *Understanding and Managing Gay and Transgender Issues in the Workplace* came to be. Deb is a little person, a brilliant, gracious, clear-thinking, and compassionate dynamo, and now a highly regarded and sought out consultant on issues of disability in the workplace.

Besides securing several presentations for Chubb employees, smart, beautiful, articulate, and very committed Kathy invited me to train members of the Employee Resource Group at Chubb. Greg Sampedro, another beautiful soul at Merck, asked me to do the same. I designed a "train the trainer" session to prepare each LGBT participant to tell their own story as a teaching strategy in the workshop just as I've told mine. "You don't have to be sexuality experts," I told them. "You can show clips of my workshop to provide information on sexual orientation and gender identity, and to review proper vocabulary. The most important gift you'll give people in your training is your story."

We practiced and practiced. Me telling my story is what changed hearts around the world. When I was at *The Michigan Catholic* my mom would run every Thursday to the mailbox to find out what family secret I was telling the world. She once said to me, "Do you know what your initials stand for?" I replied, "Blessed Mother?" "No," Mom said. "Big Mouth."

Remembering that conversation always makes me smile, but it doesn't stop me from telling the intimate details of my life. When we make ourselves totally vulnerable, like a dog that lies on its back with his legs splayed we invite others to look closely. Something extraordinary happens when you and your audience are in sync. It brings out the very best in people. The pattern we all make together as little colorful pieces in that kaleidoscope is always brilliant, if we say "Yes" to telling our story.

You might wonder, "Why do these people have to practice telling their own story?" It's important for them to think through the most specific stories from their lives that will help the audience see them as full human beings, and to understand what it's like for them to work in their specific workplace. There's not enough time for them to start with their grandparents and end with the birth of their new niece, as interesting as those stories might be. Once they outline their stories, they must practice delivering them comfortably and within the allotted time.

When I conducted workshops at Chubb, Kathy Marvel always came to speak during the last fifteen minutes. Kathy would tell her Chubb colleagues a compelling story about her mother's funeral. She had asked her life partner, Candy, to stand in the back of the funeral home while Kathy stood next to her own mother's coffin. "It was hurtful for both of us," Kathy would say. "I wanted her with me, but I was afraid of the ramifications at work if Chubb employees came to the funeral." Kathy hit on two things the participants needed to know, "How is your life different from mine?" and "How does being a Lesbian impact your work?"

In this work I've met and always tried to encourage individuals, Gay and Straight, who had what I call "fire in the belly." Such individuals in both colleges and corporations focused their time and attention on getting everyone educated on this issue. They have taken actions ranging from advocating for training, inviting me or another speaker on the issue, educating coworkers one on one (each one teach one), speaking at the end of a workshop, or becoming a trainer within their corporation.

I began working internationally when an employee from London who happened to be in New York attended my presentation at J.P. Morgan. He was so impacted by what he witnessed happen in the room that he invited me to come to speak at J.P. Morgan in London. Of course, I'd say "Yes." This work was poignant for me because I heard stories from Ray about what it was like to be openly Gay on the trading floor. In my London presentations, I'd say, "I know nothing about investment banking, but I do know how to help you make your workspace and home more welcoming to Lesbian, Gay, Bisexual, and Transgender people. And, if you're working in asset management, I can increase your chances of attracting the attention of wealthy Gay Men and Lesbians." American Express had me do exactly that.

When I worked with investment banking firms, I'd share Ray's experience at Lehman Brothers. After he came out at work people began to censor their conversations with him. They quit asking him on Monday morning about his weekend as they had in the past. They seemed nervous about saying the wrong thing or perhaps they worried that Ray would give them too much information. Ray didn't know how to interpret their silence which felt like disapproval.

"It's like knowing a few words in Spanish and trying to use them with a Spanish-speaking person," I'd say. "The fear is that the person will come back at you very quickly with words you don't understand. 'Why did I try?' Ray's colleagues weren't sure what they'd hear in response from asking, 'How was your weekend?' Ray would probably say 'Oh, thanks for asking. Brian and I went to see a movie I think you'd enjoy.' However, some people might fear that Ray would say, 'Oh, it was great. We had sex in the kitchen, watched porn, and then I tied Brian up in the basement.'" The audiences always laughs with recognition not that they thought that's what we'd do, but because their lack of information created a lack of confidence.

Once my invitation to speak in London was confirmed, Frank Howell, an openly Gay leader at J.P. Morgan, notified Gay people who worked at the other banks in London that they were welcome to come to my presentation, which they did. Nearly every bank in London then booked a series of workshops. I credit Frank Howell for opening that door.

When I spoke at these banks, I always hoped to have senior managers in the group. There's a huge gap between corporate policy and corporate culture. For a bank, or any institution, to become a place where LGBTQ people feel safe, and trust that their work will be valued, training needs to begin with the most senior people in the organization. The message must come from the top that the company takes this issue very seriously. Otherwise, middle managers in the smaller offices don't pay much attention to the reminders they get from Human Resources.

J.P. Morgan and Chase merged and brought me to Bournemouth, a beautiful summer escape, but it was midwinter when I spoke. There I trained the support team employees, often referred to as back-office workers. I was in Bournemouth a couple of times, and after doing four workshops I had reached the bulk of the employee group. The next time I was in London, a Gay employee from Bournemouth took the long train ride to the city to tell me in person what a huge difference the presentations had on changing the environment there. "There are no more jokes about Gay people. Employees feel comfortable coming out now. We can't thank you enough."

One exercise in my training really helped banking managers understand why it's so difficult to come out even in their very welcoming environment. I did this with every group. Imagine, if you will, 200 well-dressed executives sitting with their senior managers. I have already asked them to assess how welcoming the environment is for Gay people in the workplace. I described this activity in an earlier chapter. Most often, participants gave me politically correct answers: their work areas were very welcoming to LGBTQ people, and that they would encourage Gay employees to come out to everyone. To challenge their assumptions, I would ask, "You're sure nothing bad would happen to a Gay employee who comes out here?" "No, nothing bad will happen," they assured me.

I'd push further, "How many of you think you can pick out a Gay person?" No hands go up. "How many of you know Straight people who satisfy Gay stereotypes?" Several hands go up. "Okay, I agree with you, most people can't pick out Gay people, but I have the gift of excellent Gaydar. I've been watching all of you since you walked into the auditorium, and I'm going to now pick out the Gay men in this room." There is sudden silence. You can feel the tension. I let the silence sit and then say, "What's going on?" A woman employee will say, "They're all afraid that you'll say they're Gay."

"Why would you be afraid?" I ask. "You just told me that your office is very welcoming, and that Gay people should come out. Why would you feel anxious then about me saying that you're Gay? Are you afraid that people will treat you differently? Maybe when you walk into the men's room it will get quiet? Maybe you won't get picked to represent the bank to a new customer? What you've told me is that you would treat a Gay person with professional respect, but you don't trust that your colleagues would be as accommodating as you. If you can get in touch with the fears you had that I might label you as Gay, you'll understand why it's so hard for a Gay person to come out at work."

I took me a long time to recognize that all my speaking and writing on LGBTQ issues was a career, perhaps because of Mother's early question, "What do we tell people you do?" And Dad's question, "When are you going to get a real job?"

I used to have anxiety dreams about getting a real job. But, when awake, I always trusted that there would be an angel in the places God wanted me to work, and it was those angels, such as Subha Berry and Roman Matla, both Straight allies, who wouldn't give up until they got me to speak to their senior managers in Mumbai and in Singapore. Jason Kendy got me to Japan, and David Golden got me to Hong Kong. In Australia, it was the leadership in the LGBTQ Employee Resource Group that ensured I'd speak in both Melbourne and Sydney.

I'd say to audiences in other countries, just as I say to those in the US: "The horror of growing up Gay is having a secret you don't understand and that you're afraid to tell your parents for fear they won't love you anymore." Once, when we were in Cambodia, I asked our personal guide, "How are Gay people treated in Cambodia?" He was a very intelligent and well-spoken man, so I was stunned by his response. "We don't have any Gay people in Cambodia. They all live in Thailand. It's because of the fertilizer they put on their mango trees." People used to say the same uninformed things in the US in the early days of the recognition. "We don't have any homosexuals in Montana. They're all in San Francisco," although they never mentioned fertilizing mango trees. Maybe, perhaps, "It's in the water."

I said to our Cambodian guide, "Can this be a teachable moment? Percentage wise, Cambodia has the same number of Gay people as there are in Thailand. It's just easier to be out in Thailand, especially if you're Transgender." He didn't respond, so I continued. Ray knows that I'm never going to let go of an opportunity to educate others on LGBTQ issues. "Tell me, if you were Gay, how would your parents react?" He said very quickly, "I'd have to move away." This man was the breadwinner in his extended family. Everyone lived on his raised platform with a thatched roof, and car batteries providing electricity for what every family considered necessary, a refrigerator and a television. And yet, were he to come out as Gay, he imagined he'd be forced to move away.

When I was in a foreign country to speak, I'd always educate myself about the laws, history, and culture of the country and the city. I'd go to their museums before I met with them. I'd also find out in advance what their office practices were, such as whether it was common to put a picture of the person they loved on their desk. That's a good example of being in the closet in the US but not in Singapore. In that country, as well as in India and Japan, it was less likely that employees would talk about their personal lives at work. They were used to LGBTQ Westerners doing so, and the Gay nationals with whom I spoke wanted to be able to do so too.

Many of the nationals in my audiences came in assuming that I was there to make life easier for American, British, Canadian, and Australian Gay people who had been transferred to work there. They understood that LGBTQ nondiscrimination was the corporate policy of their firm's headquarters in New York, London, or Zurich, but they didn't easily see the connection to them in their locale. But, as I said in Tokyo, as an example, "I'm also here for the Gay Japanese who sit among you, and who are growing up in your homes. This training is not just about how to create a welcoming and inclusive work environment for Lesbian, Gay, Bisexual, and Transgender employees. It's also about how to create a home in which your child can tell you who they are." That personal connection always got the attention of the women, especially. Moms and dads everywhere want to protect their children from harsh treatment. That's why after my presentations in Singapore and Japan, groups of local women would stay afterwards to ask the questions they didn't feel comfortable doing so during my talk.

One thing I had affirmed for me in my most wonderful global travel is that no matter where you are in the world, we're all the same soul, all manifestations of the divine, and despite what seems to be differences there is no difference in a parent's love for their child. In Tokyo, for instance, there is uniformity in dress and in behavior, with people living with the mantra, "The protruding nail gets hammered." In other words, don't do anything that calls attention to yourself, such as coming out.

In Japan, then, it wouldn't be religious views that made it difficult to come out, it would be the fear of defying the cultural norm. So, I said to them, "What if the protruding nail gets promoted? The thinking behind diversity initiatives is that everyone brings something unique to the table. What do you think Gay Japanese people bring to the table?" That night, Jason Kendy took Ray, me, and a group of Japanese colleagues out to his favorite restaurant. Before we left for our hotel, a young Japanese man pulled me aside to whisper, "Thank you. I'm Gay too. I think what you said today will help."

Ray and I flew from Tokyo to Mumbai the next day. Unlike the order, formality, and courtesy of Japan, India is like an explosion of confetti in which you're surrounded by multicolored saris, the smells of incense, food being cooked on the sidewalks, and fresh fish on ice in the open market. We saw monkeys, camels, cows, chickens, and multiple phone lines strung together hanging down each side street, and behaviors, such as the constant honking of cars and the seeming lack of traffic laws. Here, the ability to come out might be influenced by your religion, as well as by your caste. But the same thing holds true in India as it does in Japan. Despite the clothes we wear, ignorance is the parent of fear, and fear is the parent of hatred. Despite different styles of living, such as how one boards a train, the horror of growing up LGBTQ is the fear of losing the love of your parents. And despite the different Gods who are worshiped, a parent's heart beats the same song for their children everywhere.

Chapter Twenty-Five

What's Your Music?

A TRANSGENDER WOMAN FROM THE company's LGBTQ employee resource group had volunteered to check me in at the security desk. As we walked down the corridors to the auditorium, I noticed that every person we passed looked me in the eye and said, "Good morning." But no one made eye contact, nor wished "Good morning" to their colleague. I didn't raise the issue with my guide, but I imagine that you must put on several layers of emotional armor so as not to have your feelings hurt daily. This is a good example of the chasm between corporate policy and corporate culture.

Pam taught us at Thornfield that how you talk about sexuality is more memorable than what you say. "They are paying attention to your tone of voice and your facial expressions. Listeners remember your music. As an educator or parent, does your music say that sexuality is a natural and normal part of being human, or maybe it's something bad and dangerous." Pam expands on this theme in her book, *When Sex Is the Subject: Attitudes and Answers for Young Children*.

I loved this metaphor so much that I tailored it to relate to the workplace, and I use it with every audience. I begin by saying, "I often hear from the parent of a Gay child, 'Why did my daughter tell her Aunt Martha that she was Gay before she told me?'" I'd respond, "Most of us have in our lives someone we know who will love us no matter what. It might be a parent, but it also might be an uncle or grandmother. And why is that? Because of the person's music."

I explain that in every song there are words and there is music. "Your company has great words about protecting Lesbian, Gay, Bisexual, and Transgender people from discrimination." I'd often stop here and read to them their company's policy. I did the same when speaking at a college. "But, what's the music? What's the feel of the place? Do you think the environment feels different in corporate headquarters from what it does in the same company's offices around the country? They have the exact same words to guide behavior, but is the music, the feel of the place the same?"

I ask, what creates music? "I know the comfort level of every person in this audience. Tell me how I know?" They'd think about it for a moment and then someone would say, "Eye contact." Excitedly I'd reply, "Yes, exactly. Is the person looking at me, are they smiling, or are their arms crossed? Are they looking at their watch, or their phone? Are they laughing when everyone else is laughing? That's their music. And each of you, whether you're aware of it or not, have music around this and every other issue. And you know who's watching? Your fellow employees and your children if you have any."

"If ignorance is the parent of fear, how do we stop being ignorant about something?" I'll ask.

"By learning new information," someone will answer, or, if the audience is politely reserved, as could be true in Tokyo, I answer my own questions. "Today, we're going to share new information that can improve or enhance your music. If your music is welcoming your colleagues might then trust you enough to tell you that they're Gay, Lesbian, Bisexual, or Transgender; and your child might tell you his secret before he tells his Aunt Martha."

In my next presentation for a different client, I would tell the employees about my experience with a Transgender woman as my guide. Personal stories help make the point in a meaningful and powerful way. "What was the music she experienced where she worked," I'll ask, "welcoming or unwelcoming?"

When my corporate training on LGBTQ issues was in its infancy, I'd often get the question, "Why does someone have to tell me about what they do in bed? I don't come to work and talk about what I do in bed."

"When I tell you that I'm Gay," I'd respond, "I'm telling you who I am, not what I do sexually. If you tell me that you're Straight, are you telling me your sexual practices?"

I'd feel good that my music communicated to the assembled employees that they could ask me anything, and that my response would be said in a warm manner. No one in audiences in the US, Canada, or Great Britain would ask that question today because most of their employees are well educated on the subject and know the answer, but in cultures where the open discussion of homosexuality is very new, and for some people possibly threatening, I'd more likely be asked, "Why do we need to talk about what happens outside of the office?"

That would be my first question to the LGBTQ employees at Merck and Chubb who I trained to do their own workshops. "What do your colleagues need to know about you and why? Also, never forget that the messenger is the message. Your colleagues are going to remember the way your words made them feel and the attitudes you convey."

One of the blessings of the "train the trainer" exercise I developed not only provided me the opportunity to help them hone their stories, but it also gave the leadership of the group important information on their LGBTQ colleagues' music. Who do they send out to conduct the workshop?

There were basic questions to address before they were asked: 1) Is it a choice? 2) Are you trying to change my moral beliefs? 3) Why do you need to talk about it at work? 4) How did your family react?

Regarding question number one, a television talk show host once asked me, "Brian, when did you decide to be Gay?" To which I responded, "That day I thought it would be fun for me to get kicked out of my family, lose my job, and be condemned by the church." Using humor is an important component of my music, but you don't have to be funny to be a great trainer or ally.

That question disappeared as the culture changed. The western world became more knowledgeable about the topic. As Lesbian, Gay, Bisexual, Transgender, and Queer people started coming out at home, in school, and at work, there was an increased awareness that no one chooses their sexual orientation or their gender identity. However, as more Gay and Transgender people came out, the more we were on people's radar screens. That was good in a progressive company such as Ben and Jerry's, where their Gay employees were the first to get domestic partner benefits. Coming out also started momentum in liberal church discussions and actions, such as becoming a welcoming congregation. But it also raised hackles in Fundamentalist churches. For that reason, it became more important than ever to address question 2, "Are you trying to change my moral beliefs?"

Can a room have music? Can its song be welcoming or unwelcoming? You bet. As soon as I walked into the room in which I'd be speaking I'd know what had to be done to have it become more welcoming. That could include asking that the rows of seats in the back be roped off. If you have 100 people attending a training in a room that accommodates 500, and people spread out, it makes it very difficult to create the magic. We couldn't become a family if we didn't sit together.

When I spoke in Dallas at a corporate site, I arrived early in the conference room, as I'd always try to do. The space had to have the right feel. I didn't want the chairs askew, or empty Coke cans, or half cups of cold coffee sitting randomly around the room from the last group's meeting. On several occasions, I have vacuumed the floor. If it was a huge crowd, I'd need to meet with the technician to get the clip-on microphone I requested. It's hard for me to be creative if I have a handheld mic. I would also talk to the person filming the presentation. Often there were employees in other offices around the country watching the session through closed circuit. I wanted to make sure there were no technical glitches created by me.

There weren't random chairs in the room in the Dallas training room, nor empty Coke cans, but on every seat there sat a conservative religious anti-Gay brochure. I picked them all up, threw them in the trash can, and replaced them with my book, *Gay Issues in the Workplace*. I'm very grateful to those companies that ordered the books for each workshop participant. Usually, they'd be in a box in the front of the room, so I needed time to place them on the seats before we started rather than hope everyone would come to the front of the room at the end of the workshop to pick up their copy.

Once Gay issues became the topic of sermons in Southern Baptist churches among others, there usually would be one person in my audience or workshop who arrived with a Bible. I watch the participants as they file in, me smiling and saying, "Good morning." At the beginning of every workshop, I explain that I wasn't there to change anyone's religious beliefs. "You can believe that I'm going to hell but still treat me with professional respect at work. If we don't, we impact the effectiveness of the group, which then impacts the success of the company."

"Why do Gay people need to push it in your face?" I'd get asked occasionally in the late 1980s. My music would remain upbeat as I asked, "Give me an example of pushing it in your face."

"Talking about it. Talking about what they did over the weekend. Putting pictures of their girlfriends or boyfriends in their cubicle."

"Do you consider that flaunting?" I'd ask.

"Yes."

"If Straight people did the same things, would you consider them flaunting?"

"That's different."

"Why?"

"Because being Gay is not normal."

"Your company is not taking a position on what's normal, any more than they would take a position on divorce, birth control, or the sexual behavior of unmarried heterosexual people. The company is saying that if it wants to be competitive, it needs to create an environment in which everyone can feel safe and valued. That's why they insist upon professional respect. You with me? Good, let's move on."

If an employee raised their hand and started reading to me from the Bible, I'd put up my hand and say, "I know all those verses. But you need to remember that reading from the Bible to make a colleague or a consultant feel as if they were unwelcome is considered harassment and a violation worthy of suspension. But, that's why you're here, right? To learn what is welcoming behavior and what is not. Thank you for giving me the opportunity to address that."

It's essential when I'm dealing with disruptive participants that their colleagues approve of the way I'm handling the situation. They're there to learn and they don't want the music of the room to feel combative. If you respond with loving kindness to the person who felt the need to plant their flag, who knows? By the end of the workshop the person who brought in the Bible might end up an ally.

When I'd be given ten minutes with the executive committee, the one thing I knew they'd find most helpful was knowing what words are considered welcoming and show respect, and what words don't. There's a helpful glossary in this book that explains the meaning of all the words used today on these issues.

Knowledge of the proper use of words can make a huge difference in whether an LGBTQ person finds your music welcoming. Vocabulary is very important because often people don't speak up out of fear that they're going to use the wrong words. In the workshop or presentation, I'd try to help ease their fear. "We say 'sexual orientation' rather than 'sexual preference' because 'sexual preference' suggests 'choice.' The acronym LGBTQ stands for Lesbian, Gay, Bisexual, Transgender, and Queer. We all sometimes use the acronym but try to say the words 'Lesbian,' 'Gay,' 'Bisexual,' 'Transgender,' and 'Queer.'" I'd make sure I took the time to suggest that the word "Queer" ought not be used in business communication because though the word has been reclaimed by many people in the Gay community, it still feels like a pejorative to plenty of others, both Gay and Straight.

As the example that opened this chapter illustrates, lack of awareness on an issue such as being Transgender can make Cisgender (not Transgender) people afraid to even say "Good morning." Without such awareness the workplace culture can feel intolerably unwelcoming. Education is the only way to change the music in the corridors.

Transgenderism can be a confusing issue for some of us, but a simple explanation about the difference between biological sex and gender identity helps. There are a lot of words related to being Transgender, and it's important to be aware of them if the goal is to create a welcoming environment. What is meant by "Non-Binary," and how is that different from being Transsexual?

What are the components of our changing songs? The lyrics change as we become more informed. Our words also reflect our faith, our values, our family of origin. You've heard people say, "Oh my God, I sound like my mother!"

How and why does our music change? Our words usually reflect our music and vice versa. My music reflects growing up in Michigan in the McNaught household as the middle child; growing up Roman Catholic and loving parochial school; my neighborhood friends and foes; my exposure to difference in race, culture, religion; my sex education; my uniqueness; my life experiences; and the amount of love I've given and received. I would be a different man had I stayed with Dan, the Episcopal priest.

My music changed with my awareness. I grew more and more confident speaking and writing because I knew the words and the issues. My music changed also because of the appearance of angels in my life, and for me, the whispers from my soul. I've also long believed that I'm doing the will of God.

Chapter Twenty-Six

Sex In and Out of Camp

When we lived in Atlanta, Ray and I had two friends, Keith and Philip, who lived in a condominium across from our home. When we learned that Philip had AIDS, we were hopeful that new medicines might prolong his life. Keith was an extraordinary caregiver to Philip, and he'd share with us how his soulmate was declining. Sadly, Philip died soon after entering hospice care.

Ray and I have always been a dependably stable couple. Keith knew he'd find comfort with us. He sought refuge in our home, in our arms, and eventually in our bed. What started out as compassion on our part and need on his, evolved into a sexual relationship. We thought we might become a threesome relationship. Ray and I knew both Straight and Gay people in threesomes, so the idea didn't seem outrageous. We weren't looking for it; it happened gradually, and it was exciting.

Mary Lee, in talking with her high school students about sex, used to tell them about the cartoon in which Woody Woodpecker was busy doing important things when a female woodpecker walks by, batting her eyelashes at him. Woody's eyes pop out, his head opens, and his brains fall out. That was me. I was Woody and Keith was the male woodpecker who batted his well-developed young body at me. My brains fell out. Truly, I lost my ability to think clearly, to maintain my emotions, and to listen to the wisdom being whispered by my soul.

As hard as I tried to create equity in the relationship, asking myself questions such as "Who's going to sit in the back seat of the car?," the threesome didn't and couldn't work. Ray and I had been a couple for sixteen years and Keith needed to mourn the death of Philip. I didn't think that through at the time because my brain had fallen out. What I knew was—I was more taken with Keith than Ray was, Keith was more taken with Ray, and Ray was more taken with me.

As a result, I experienced an emotion at age thirty-eight that I had never felt as intensely before, and that was jealousy. My experience of that raw, highly charged feeling changed me. I lost my bearings and my prayer life. I was possessive, competitive, obsessed, and totally confused.

We invited Keith to move in with us, which he eagerly did because of his loneliness. He sold or stored some furniture, but also moved in some of his favorite pieces. He had his own bedroom and bath. The three of us did everything together—run four miles in the early morning, go to movies and out for dinner, entertain others, and travel.

At the time, I traveled a lot doing corporate trainings, and was always eager to get home. But I was also jealous of the time Ray had alone with Keith. I experienced jealousy as a five-alarm fire. On one hand, I felt very sophisticated sexually because the good Midwestern Catholic altar boys, Brian and Ray, were coloring outside the lines. Nevertheless, I was also not prepared for the daily reality of it.

It was during this time that I decided that I was an alcoholic. Ray was already in the program. I was never a drinker who had blackouts, horror stories to tell, or days of work missed. I relied on two glasses of Chardonnay each night to relax. I realized that I was dependent on the wine to relax. I started drinking a glass of orange juice at 5 PM when I would normally pour my first glass of wine. I was amazed to learn that the craving I felt was for sugar. Today, the wine and orange juice have been replaced by dark chocolate.

The great thing about acknowledging you're an alcoholic, I found, is that all pretense is gone. I especially loved hearing someone in an AA meeting say about themselves, "I'm just another Bozo on the bus." To me that meant, "Don't get carried away with yourself." Ray and I were seeing a very good therapist, who I also saw alone, and once with Keith. When I heard Keith say that he wouldn't mind being coupled with Ray, the sandcastle I had built got swept away. The imagined threesome was never going to happen, no matter how much thought and work I put into it. I called Ray after my therapy session with Keith and said, "It's over." Ray was relieved because he had been forced to deal with my roller-coaster emotions from the very beginning of the experiment. Keith found an apartment and we helped him move out.

After three years in Atlanta, Ray and I moved to New York with Brit, the yellow lab, when Ray got the promotion to be global head of equity sales with Lehman. It was an easy out after our breakup with Keith.

We didn't stay in touch with Keith. Ray was too busy, and I was embarrassed and hoped to erase the memory of my jealous behavior. However, Keith and I did connect not long ago on Facebook Messenger. I told him how embarrassed I was about the intensity of my feelings. He was gracious enough to acknowledge he was seeking refuge in Ray's and my relationship after Philip died, rather than spending time mourning and getting his head around being without Philip.

When we arrived in New York, I initially continued my regular contact with Vicky, and then I discovered that Vicky was not real. I wasn't the designer of a successful threesome relationship, and I wasn't the savior of a young girl trapped in the home of her homophobic grandparents.

You may wonder why I chose to tell you the story of Keith and of Vicky. When I read the stories, I cringe. However, if I had left out these stories, my memoir would be dishonest. Good things came out of both experiences. I grew up in many ways. I became more aware of my emotions, and I learned to keep away from situations in which my brain would fall out. Putting out for review the things I'd most like to forget keeps my window clean. I'm actually very grateful for the experience of both the threesome and of the charade. Not only did I quit drinking and start facing my co-dependency, I also got even closer to Ray, had much improved sex with him, and realized that the "prince of a boy" was slowly becoming "a prince of a man," with scars to prove it.

Embarrassment can be a great source of growth. When we publicly acknowledge our mistakes, we take off the mask. When we have scars, they can help remind us of where we've been and where we never want to go again. I don't regret my relationships with Keith or Vicky. Being engaged with them has helped me mature into the man who feels more confident in my own wisdom. Each experience, if we learn the lesson intended by the Universe, is a gold deposit in our soul.

We were only in New York for three years, but it was an extraordinary three years. We lived in a 3,700 square foot apartment on the fortieth floor of the Millennium Towers. We were on Sixty-Seventh and Broadway, just a block from Central Park, through which we ran every morning at 5:30. I'd walk through the park to the Metropolitan Museum of Art, the Fricke, and to Fifth Ave. where I'd often take refuge in St. Thomas Episcopal Church. It always felt like home to me, as opposed to St. Patrick's Catholic Cathedral—that felt chaotic. As I said before, I find great peace in an empty church with candles flickering and incense making magic in the air. Sometimes, I'd be lucky enough to hear the St. Thomas Boys Choir practice. Each Christmas, we'd go to *The Messiah* at St. Thomas.

When Ray took an early retirement from Lehman at age forty-five, we bought a house Ron Robin found for us on the water in Provincetown, a Gay mecca at the tip of Cape Cod. And, on a whim, we also bought a house on Baker Street, across for the Palace of Fine Arts, in the Marina district of San Francisco. Brit made the trip there from New York with our mover, Larry Reynolds, in the cab of his truck.

I continued to accept speaking engagements, doing workshops with Pam, and still had my two teams of trainers working more often than any of us imagined. I also continued to be away for a week each summer at the Annual Workshop on Human Sexuality at Thornfield.

On September 11, 2001, my plane from Provincetown to Boston landed at 8:30, because I was conducting a workshop for Chubb in the World Trade Center of Boston at 9. I was confused when a couple of participants in the back left the room, came back, and started talking to the people around them. I wasn't used not to having everyone's attention so I stopped and asked, "Can you tell me what's going on?"

"A plane flew into the World Trade Center in New York." I assumed it was a small plane. "Thank you," I said, and continued with the workshop. The senior manager opened the door and said, "Two planes have hit the World Trade Center. We need everyone to go home."

Traffic in Boston was at a standstill, the airport was closed, and no ferries would be transporting people to Provincetown. I made my way to a telephone in a hotel and called Ray. He was beside himself with grief, crying hard because he worked with several people in the World Trade Center. He was devastated as he watched the planes crash and the buildings collapse repeatedly on the news.

"Ray," I said, "I'm so sorry. I wish I could be there to hold you. But you've got to quit watching the television. You've seen what happened, and it's going to upset you further to watch it happen repeatedly." I had done the same on my birthday, January 28, 1986, watching the Challenger rocket explode again and again, always unconsciously hoping for a different outcome. Sometimes, the greatest gift you can give in these situations is to proactively create acts of loving kindness to those around you, and to send strong loving thoughts to everyone directly impacted.

When Mary Lee died, the staff at Thornfield pulled together with tender care for one another. Alison was the director of a program that had become a finely tuned, often life-changing experience. As a marriage and family therapist, Alison set the mood at Thornfield with her healing words, her joy and laughter. She did the same when we lost Mary Lee.

The staff was a tight-knit family who worked hard and played well together. When staff member Susan Vasbinder, who became my Lesbian counterpart, died, we asked permission from the Episcopal Diocese if we could plant a pine tree in her honor. They were very amenable. So, when Mary Lee died, we also planted a pine tree, next to Susan's. I would visit Mary Lee's tree every morning with a cup of coffee for her, and the whole staff would stand around the tree at least one night during the week and pour some white wine on it. Mary Lee was the heart of our training, and we missed her presence terribly.

I quit smoking in 1983 and quit drinking in 1993. As I said before, those were two of the most important choices I made in my life, shadowed only by my coming out as Gay, stepping out of the influence of the Vatican, and my relationship with Ray. I've described in this memoir the many things that have influenced my life. Among those, the Annual Workshop on Human Sexuality at Thornfield is near the top of the list. In those thirty years of seven-day SARs, I found my footing and grew into my skin. I started as a young man who sought acceptance and left a middle-aged Gay man who didn't need any affirmation of his sexuality but his own.

Alison and Dick Cross have both died, but we didn't plant trees because we were no longer conducting the workshop. The Episcopal Diocese sold the property, and all our scared spaces were demolished. Nevertheless, all the laughter, tears, love, and self-acceptance continue to inhabit the pine trees. I still have close relationships with Carol and Pam, who I see regularly, communicate with Bill Stayton, and stay connected to Gail and Michael on Facebook, so that part of the Thornfield experience continues.

Alison's daughter, Darcy, told me that she and her brothers went to Cape Cod for bags of sand and big jugs of sea water. Alison spent many years loving her summer life on Cape Cod. They brought them to Alison's simple home in Arizona, blew up a plastic swimming pool, put it in her living room, poured in the sand, and then the salt water. They brought

Alison out of her bedroom and into a chair at the edge of the pool. She stuck her feet in the water, thanked them, and laughed. She then said, "If I knew dying was this much fun, I would have done it sooner."

I look at Alison, Fr. Matthew, and Mary Lee every day, smiling at me from the picture frames in my mini mancave. My Grampa McNaught smiles at me too. They all have front row seats in the circle around my heart.

Chapter Twenty-Seven

Facing the Fear of Straight Men

Growing up, every Gay boy must develop an awareness of who in his world is safe and who isn't. His possible bully could be a "mean girl," but more likely it's a Straight boy or a self-hating Gay one. Most Gay men in the Western world have close Straight male friends. I certainly did and still do. However, it takes longer for me to become friends with a Straight man than it does a Gay one. I always ask myself: How comfortable am I with this man? Can I speak as freely as I would with Gay friends? My guess is that every group has people outside their group on probation, too. Does this White person get it? Does this Cisgender person get it? Does this able-bodied person get it?

Lieutenant Colonel Oliver North said that if Gay men were allowed to serve in the military "no real man will every enlist again." North, a US Marine, known best for the 1985 Iran-Contra scandal, believed that to be a *real* man you had to be a Straight man. What makes a man a man? One year, Ray and I gave a birthday present to our Straight friend, Jack, a framed photo of me fully clothed holding Ray fully clothed from behind, us each smiling happily on our twentieth anniversary. The two other Straight men at the dinner party called Jack the next day to tell him how uncomfortable they were seeing the photo of affection. These guys were both White, wealthy, successful, and well-educated. Jacked laughed at their responses. He and his wife, Jean, had already put the framed photo in a place of prominence in their home.

We Gay men know that we make a lot of Straight men uncomfortable, and it should come as no surprise to them that a lot of us are equally uncomfortable with them. I've never liked those feelings of suspicion and distrust I've felt on my journey to being fully human, fully male, fully Gay, and fully divine. I needed to do something about these negative feelings.

Ray and I had lots of good Straight male friends in Tupper Lake, New York where we moved from Provincetown. But the anxiety about the Straight stranger was always there.

When I learned about the Mankind Project Warrior Weekend that had trainings for both Straight men and others for Gay men, I knew I was being called to go. As the Buddhist teacher Pema Chodron tells us go to *The Places That Scare You*. That's where we'll learn some of life's most important lessons. I signed up for the training for Straight men.

Since I was at home in Tupper Lake, a Mankind Project leader asked if I might give someone a ride to the event. Always say "Yes." So, on my way, I stopped at Fort Drum to pick up Mark, another participant. He was a tall Army officer with whom I had a terrific conversation in the hours we still had to travel.

Mark wasn't very familiar with Gay men. In fact, I may have been the first Gay man with whom he'd ever had a real conversation. I told him that I felt anxious when first meeting a Straight man especially if they were southern and Republican. Mark was both, and we laughed about our odd pairing, with me being a Gay northern Democrat. Nevertheless, we talked the whole drive to the event.

When we arrived, it turned out that I was quite a unique participant. I was the oldest person there, the only openly Gay man there, and, because my sciatica was really acting up, I was the most infirm, using a walking stick all weekend. We had to haul our sleeping bags, clothes, and pillow up a long gravel driveway to the main lodge where we'd meet. I was very aware from the beginning that Mark was keeping an eye out for me.

The Mankind Project holds Warrior Weekend trainings all over the world. These trainings focus on helping men claim their male gender as good, powerful, and needed by the world. The training is based on the work of Carl Jung and the book *Iron John* by Robert Bly. You begin by having your identity and key possessions taken from you and are forced to face hardships such as very little food, Spartan sleeping conditions, and cold showers. On the first night in the dark with sleeping bags spread haphazardly across the floor, I tried to find my way to the restroom. I tripped over a guy who was stretched out across the path to the restroom, and I fell flat on my face. It hurt like hell, but I had to put up with the pain because the Weekend Warrior staff had taken my pain meds away from me when I arrived.

The next day we participated in team-building contests, and psychodrama experiences to confront the greatest emotional pain in our lives. We spoke to the child within and danced naked around a huge fire. We were told to pick a spirit animal guide. I chose the snowy white owl. We sat together in a smoke lodge. We were also asked to pick our archetype—King, Warrior, Magician, or Lover. I chose all four.

The weekend was a powerful learning experience for me, and exactly what I needed to own my masculinity. Oliver North should know that a *real* man is one who is Gay and spends the weekend with Straight men opening themselves up to complete vulnerability. We each did so. I watched the Straight men work on their own personal issues, their "shadows," most of them with far more difficulty than I had because of my many years at "Sex Camp," my years of telling my story to others, and the strong friendship I had with my teacher, Jesus. But the biggest prize from the weekend was carpooling, and making friends with a big, White, Straight, southern Republican. He was my guardian angel all weekend, and when we stopped for gas on the way back to Fort Drum, he found a small ceramic snowy white owl in the gift shop and bought it for me.

I'm aware that today's young Straight, Bisexual, and Gay guys are much more mature, laid back, and healthier in their relationships with one another than was my generation. They're more evolved because my generation built on the efforts of the previous generation to understand sex and gender. Mark and I don't stay in touch because we're both busy with our different lives, but he's part of my soul, and part of my sense of being a man.

Since that Mankind Project experience, with all the discussion today on being gender fluid, I've celebrated something that used to scare me, and which I denied for many years. In 1862, Karl Ulrichs, a German pioneer in the field of sexology, proposed that Gay men were a "Third Sex." I poo-pooed that for many years, as I was totally preoccupied with proving to the world, and to myself, that Gay men were *real* men. I felt no connection to gender-bending Gay pioneer Harry Hay and his Radical Faeries. And then a funny thing happened on the way to spiritual awareness. I now celebrate that I am both male and female. I have a male body, male hormones, male privilege, etc., but I'm also able to tap the female in my brain and in my soul. I am so grateful for that gift.

The ability of Gay men to tap both the male and female because of very clear and identifiable pathways between both lobes of the brain, enables us to give to the world the gifts we've been offering throughout history. In my last book, *On Being Gay and Gray*, I created an imaginary "Parliament of Snowy Owl Elders." A gathering of owls is called a parliament. Snowy owls represent wisdom. Elders are individuals in the community who are worthy of respect and looked to for guidance in most cultures, such as high priests, witch doctors, and shamans. Elder doesn't mean elderly. It's a description of accumulated wisdom that comes from the hero's journey through life experiences.

Am I a third sex? I hesitate to complicate things because I feel that the Lesbian, Gay, Bisexual, Transgender, and Queer communities have already given this culture far more challenging information than can be easily processed. But I could be a third gender. Sex is male and female. Gender is boy and girl, man and woman. I'm not sure what word to use to describe what I think happens in my brain, even as I choose words to share thoughts in this book. Perhaps that's why younger LGBT people prefer the term "Queer," because it says quite clearly, "don't ask."

Chapter Twenty-Eight

Manifesting the Result of the Work

MY INNOCENT COMPASSION AND my grateful love are my God nature.

In my ongoing pursuit of spiritual knowledge and growth, I began joining over 100 other gray-haired Gay men every Tuesday at noon at the Pride Center in Wilton Manors, Florida to listen to the most amazing storyteller and teacher, August Gold, a Jewish Lesbian from New York who was trained as an interfaith minister. She is a very funny, superb storytelling teacher who reminded me of myself working with an audience. August is a wise, aware, high vibrating soul, who became a friend. We were fellow spiritual beings who were sitting side by side next to a fire at the top of Mount Fuji. She insisted that I sit there with her, seeing in me a level of spiritual sophistication that escaped my awareness. "The only thing holding you back," she once said to me in a small discussion group, "is your brilliance." I seriously had no idea to what she was referring.

I paid for time with August for a one-on-one consultation. During that session, she gave me an exercise to help guide my thinking about my life's purpose. August asked me to write down twelve things that give my life meaning, that I couldn't live without. After I did so, she had me cut the list to just six essential things. I listed: 1) my relationship with God, 2) the innocence of my heart, 3) the gratitude with which I live, 4) my compassion for others, 5) being in nature, and 6) my love for Ray. August then had me reduce every sentence to one word. I came up with: God,

Innocence, Gratitude, Compassion, Nature, and Love. She then had me write those six words on individual index cards and make a sentence. I could add words for clarity.

As directed, I moved the cards around and around, as I now do with the letters in the online game, Words with Friends. Finally, I looked down at the order in which I had placed them and got a chill. I said to August, "My innocent compassion and my grateful love are my God nature." She smiled and said, "There you have it." For me, like sitting in the tent with the psychic from New Jersey and listening to the dream my therapist had of me, it was a peak moment of affirmation.

I've had many peak experiences in my fifty years of full-time advocacy. Sometimes, while sitting in my room in a high-end hotel paid for by the banks, I'd think back to when I was fired. I was hated by so many people. One woman thought she'd throw up when I walked into the room. One person wanted me to die of AIDS. I'd wonder, "How did I get here?"

I had a lot of help along the way from people whose names rarely get mentioned, but we've all contributed to and witnessed a seismic change in our culture. I was initially an embarrassment to many members of my family and friends, some because I came out of the closet, but also because I kept attention on the subject. "Gay, Gay, Gay, Gay, Gay! Enough already." No one ever said that to my face, except me.

There would be times when I'd wonder, "What would my life be like if I wasn't so totally focused on LGBTQ issues?" "I'm sick of telling my story. I've told it hundreds of times." But then I'd remind myself that I was channeling the healing grace of God into the lives of not just the people in my workshops, or those who read my books or watched my videos, but also to everyone they knew. The rippling of awareness is thrilling to imagine. That is a good feeling.

My ego has been a necessary component of my work, not because I felt I was competing with anyone for the cover of *Time* magazine, but rather because it helped give me the hutzpah to stand in front of a large group of strangers and tell them so many personal details about my life. Surprisingly, I've only choked up a couple of times when I talked about trying to kill myself by drinking the turpentine. I was looking into the eyes of the audience and spotted a woman who was crying. She instantly represented my mom.

I choked up too when I stood before Ray's former peers, presenting to them my two-hour training. Ray had retired in 1997. Seven years later, after hearing me report on my presentations to all the banks in London, including Lehman Brothers, Ray wrote to his friend, Joe Gregory, the president of Lehman, and suggested that I be invited to speak to all the senior managers in New York. Joe did that very thing.

Ray sat quietly in the audience and beamed with pride as he watched his peers laugh with me. When I spoke of my suicide attempt, I looked at Ray's loving concern and got choked up momentarily. It was a peak moment in Ray's life to have his peers be educated by me on how to create a welcoming environment. I shared his example of how it changed his social interactions at work. Suddenly, he wasn't asked, "How was your weekend?" I used that example throughout the world to help participants understand how openly Gay colleagues feel invisible.

Ray's colleagues had heard him talk about "Brian," and I talked across the globe about "Ray," but no one in that room of Lehman in New York, other than Joe Gregory had put two and two together. Finally, I said, "And the Ray to which I'm referring is Ray Struble, who is here with us today." Ray grinned with gratitude as necks craned to find his face. People waved and smiled. When the workshop ended to enthusiastic applause, Ray was surrounded by all the people with whom he once worked, happy that they could connect again with him, the new "Ray" who loved himself and didn't now need the affirmations. For Ray, it brought things full circle.

You never know what's going to happen when you're free-falling with the Universe. But you must be willing to share and be willing to listen. Ray and I were in a little café off St. Mark's Square in Venice when four women sat right next to us. They were all American and from the South. Like many ignorant northerners, I assumed because of their accents that they were conservative Republicans. Our meal was served before they ordered, so they were looking at our plates to see if it looked good. The question of, "What's that? It looks good," led to a ninety-minute lively discussion about us being Gay, and one of them having a Gay son, and how they were four active Democrats from Winston-Salem, North Carolina.

I don't remember in what city LEAGUE, the LGBTQ Employee Resource Group, was having its annual national conference, but I gratefully was a favorite of theirs, and usually gave a keynote address. On the morning of the first day of the conference, I was in the hotel's gym with some friends from the conference, clipping a good pace on a treadmill. There was a stranger to all of us on the treadmill next to me. When you're in a celebratory mood because you're surrounded by LGBTQ colleagues and friends, you don't want to have the experience ruined by an ignorant comment from a Straight stranger. Sadly, we expect it.

When I gave my keynote address a little bit later in the day, I said to the packed auditorium, "Some of you were with me this morning in the hotel's gym. There was a stranger in our group running next to me on the treadmills. After you left, he asked me what group was meeting in the hotel. Never one to miss such an opportunity, I told him that it was a gathering of the Lesbian, Gay, Bisexual, Transgender, and Queer employees from AT&T. 'Wow!' he said. 'That's terrific. I've got a Gay son and I'm going to call him and let him know that this is happening.' You never know who is already an ally or who, given the opportunity to learn, might become one."

It's important to remember that it wasn't all that long ago that no hotel would agree to be the site of a gathering of LGBTQ people. In the 1950s, when a group of homosexuals gathered for a meeting, they did so in a private home, with one person assigned to keep watch at the window in case the police arrived. All it took was a call from a suspicious neighbor.

"Have you seen a lot of change?" I'm often asked. The answer is, "Yes, of course," but how do you measure change, and is it permanent? The Hallmark Channel having Gay family holiday movies is obviously an indication of change. When I came out in 1974, I never would have imagined that the words "Gay" and "Hallmark" would appear in the same sentence.

When *Brokeback Mountain* was up against *Crash* in the Oscar category of "Best Picture of the Year," in 2006, Ernest Borgnine, who I used to love watching in the TV program *McHale's Navy,* said about *Brokeback Mountain,* "John Wayne would be rolling in his grave." John Wayne, a name many Americans today wouldn't recognize, stood out in Borgnine's mind as the epitome of true masculinity. True men, apparently, didn't like movies about Gay men falling in love.

In 100 years, no one will recognize the names of most people in the world today, including mine, but the world, I believe, will continue to evolve towards Love, and an awareness of the lives of minority groups will continue to advance across the globe. I've seen such very special things in my life. "Giving" is its own reward, as we know, and if you're lucky enough to witness and participate in change, it changes you.

When I was asked to train the upper-level managers at Toronto Dominion Bank, I urged them to invite me to a meeting of the executive committee to explain in just fifteen minutes what I would be doing in my trainings. I knew from experience that once I started, they'd ask for more than fifteen minutes. After my talk, the committee was very enthused and asked what they could do. I suggested that if one of them opened each workshop with a comment about having had time with me, and about how important the training was, it would help get everyone's attention.

Before we ended, one of the officers asked me how you enable a Gay person to come out. I shared with them the analogy of the Steven Spielberg movie in which Elliot uses Reese's Pieces to coax E.T. out of the shed. I told them they could proactively create openings for people to share, but that Gay people won't come out if they don't trust they'll be okay. The officer went on to say she had a colleague that she knows is Gay, but he never brings it up, even when she shares details about her family life.

I suggested that she take her colleague out for coffee and say, "You know, over the time we've known each other, I've shared a lot about myself, but I don't know much about your home life. I'm wondering if I'm doing something that makes it difficult for you to share." She liked the idea.

There were 800 managers to train, which I did forty at a time, mostly in Toronto, but also across Canada. In one of the later workshops, the officer in question opened the training with an enthusiastic endorsement. On her way out of the room she told me that my suggestion worked perfectly, and that the Gay man in question was a participant in that day's workshop. I said to myself, "I saw him walk in." My Gaydar works almost every time.

Tim, who I guessed was Gay, sat in the front row. I made no more eye contact with him than I did with anyone else. I had two hours, so I didn't need to trim back the presentation. I had, by that time, dropped the guided imagery because I felt it had the same purpose as my story. And my cultural references were dated. Funny how that happens as you age. "Who's Annette Funicello?"

From the activity of having participants assess the work environment at Toronto Dominion Bank, I wasn't surprised to hear from them that the environment at Toronto Dominion Bank was very welcoming to Lesbian, Gay, Bisexual, and Transgender employees, and that if I was their Gay colleague, they thought I should feel comfortable coming out to everyone.

"Here's what doesn't make sense to me," I said. "Using the lowest estimation of 5 percent of the number of Gay people in the population, there ought to be twenty Gay people among the 800 managers taking this class. Correct? Why then, do you think, I've only had two people identify themselves as Gay in the workshop?"

The room got quiet and pensive. "If it's as welcoming as you believe it to be, wouldn't you think more people would feel safe enough to identify themselves as Gay in this training?"

"It must not be as welcoming as we thought," someone suggested.

I told them about Ray and me joining a Unitarian church in Naples, Florida, and how we had pressed the group to designate themselves a "welcoming congregation," something most Unitarian churches had done around the country. "Well, we're already welcoming," was the response. "You're all very nice people," I replied, "the most liberal group in Naples, but you haven't asked us if we feel fully welcome. You must ask Gay people themselves."

"Tell us then," they asked. "Do you feel welcome?"

"Last Sunday, all the new members were called by name to come down the aisle to the front of the church. You brought down all the heterosexuals as couples, but you called Ray and me down as individuals, at different times in the process. We've been together at least as long as many of those other couples have been. We didn't feel as if we were being treated equally."

"We didn't intend to make you feel unwelcome."

"There's a difference between intent and impact. It wasn't your intent, but it was your impact. And that's why you must ask, rather than assume the environment is welcoming. Becoming a 'welcoming congregation' will make it less likely such mistakes are made. It's not homophobia. It's heterosexism, which is a system that values Straight people over Gay people, and assumes that everyone is Straight, or ought to be."

Heads nodded in recognition among the TDB managers. I then shared with them my own story. These were all good people. All the managers had been thoughtfully invested throughout the series of twenty workshops. When I shared with them my experiences of growing up with a secret that I didn't understand and was afraid to share with anyone, their faces reflected their empathy.

At the end of the workshop I said, "That's it. Thank you all for your thoughtful participation." But before they got out of their chairs, their colleague Tim jumped up from his seat in the front row and asked everyone to please stay seated.

"I need to share with you that I'm a Gay man. I've known many of you for years, and you may have wondered about my sexual orientation.

It's very important to me to let you know so that any awkwardness you have felt in the past can be eliminated. Thank you."

Before Tim or anyone else could move, I walked over to him, put my arm around him, and asked him, "Tim, tell me what you're feeling right now?"

"I'm feeling a little scared, but also relieved," he said. "I just want to be able to be myself at work."

I told Tim, "I promise you that you will never forget this moment. Ever. I'm very proud of, and happy for you." And then I said to Tim's colleagues, "Tim just gave you an incredible gift. He decided that he trusted you and was willing to make himself very vulnerable. This is a sacred moment, and I'm grateful to have witnessed it." Tim smiled at me, and then all his colleagues came to the front to shake his hand, pat him on the back, and thank him. It was a beautiful sight. It's what my life's work has been about and what kept me doing the work even when I believed I didn't have the energy to board another plane.

Chapter Twenty-Nine

Say the Words, Then "Thank You"

AFTER YEARS OF CONDUCTING training for many corporations, I got an invitation to speak at the NSA (National Security Agency.) A classmate of mine from high school, Mark Walsh, worked at the NSA and was an "angel" (Straight senior management supporter) of the organization's LGBTQ resource group. When the group said they'd like to have me speak, Mark reached out to me. I was honored, of course, but I said I'd come only if attendance was mandatory for all senior personnel.

It took a while for the NSA to agree to my terms, and I don't recall whether it was mandated or if the head of the agency sent out a note to all senior personnel saying he'd be there and he'd be disappointed not to see them. Prior to my speech, I had lunch with the deputy director, a general, Mark, and Kim Nelson, one of the hardest working, most dedicated Gay employees I've known. She was the driving force behind the invitation. I said to the general prior to my heading into the auditorium, "After my talk, please tell me if what I say could also be said to the Joint Chiefs."

I'd been told that there would be guests in the audience from the CIA and the FBI. If I had received this invitation soon after being fired by *The Michigan Catholic*, I would have been so anxious I wouldn't sleep the night before, and I'd clutch my notes. But, by then I used no notes, and I felt very at home on the stage. I requested a clip-on mic as always so that I could walk around and see the audience. I hated those events in a pitch black auditorium with a spotlight in my face, because I draw my energy, my magic from the faces of audience members. As my sciatica sometimes made it difficult to stand for long periods I began to ask for a stool.

Homosexuality was not an unknown subject at the NSA. The audience knew the story of Alan Turing, the brilliant British codebreaker who was publicly punished for being Gay. At the NSA it's fine to be Gay but you must be out to avoid the possibility of blackmail. The NSA recruits "the best and brightest" employees from elite universities, competing with corporations who promise a safe work environment for LGBTQ people.

The head of the NSA was out of town, so I followed the deputy director into the auditorium and was unprepared to see everyone in the auditorium stand up. ("Hey, can we do that again?") By that time in my career, I had confidently shortened my biographical sketch to my key accomplishments. I was grateful that it was the deputy director who introduced me, and that applause accompanied me to the stage. The members of the NSA audience and I were in resonance. I spotted Kim smiling broadly and proudly up at me.

After speaking about our music, and what vibrations people pick up from us, I talked about the need for heterosexuals to be proactive in their efforts to create an environment in which their LGBTQ colleagues, as well as their family members, would feel included and valued. I reminded them of Elliot and *E.T.*

"Not laughing at anti-Gay humor isn't enough, but it helps. We Gay and Transgender people can't jump into your arms without knowing for sure that you'll catch and hold us. How do we know that you're ready for us to tell you who we are? It's by your Reese's Pieces.

"I'd like you to do two things for me after this presentation," I said. "First, please go back to your group, and say to those who weren't here today that you're coming from a presentation on Lesbian, Gay, Bisexual, and Transgender workplace issues. Use the words and not the acronym as often as you can. Some people think LGBTQ is a sandwich. But if you say the words, someone will take notice.

"And then tonight, when you go home to your families, ask at the dinner table, 'How was your day?' Let everyone share something, and then you say, 'Well, I was at a presentation on Lesbian, Gay, Bisexual, and Transgender issues in the workplace. I learned a lot.' By doing so, you're letting your family know through your music, not just your words, that you're safe to talk to."

A bit later, I asked the audience, "What's the first thing you say when someone tells you that they're Lesbian, Gay, Bisexual, Transgender, or

Queer?" I stayed silent for a few seconds, and then said, "'Thank you for sharing that with me.' Don't say, 'What a waste,' or 'I never would have guessed,' or 'Are you sure?' Say 'Thank you' because of all the people they might have chosen to share this fact about themselves, they chose you."

At the end, when I told them about God asking me, "Did you sing the song I taught you?" I expanded the question to ask each of them. "Are you singing the song God taught you? We're all supposed to be singing the songs together in perfect harmony."

To the surprise of many, and to the delight of Mark and Kim, I got a long, standing ovation. I didn't expect such a gesture of affirmation, and apparently speakers at the NSA don't usually get standing ovations. The deputy director of the NSA came on stage, shook my hand warmly with a big smile, and gave me two NSA medallions, one from him and one from the director. This, I learned later, was a special honor.

The general with whom I had lunch came to the stage to answer my question about whether my presentation was appropriate for the Joint Chiefs. "The whole thing was just great," he said. "We're not ready for the Transgender part" (this was prior to Transgenderism being a topic of discussion in the military) "but otherwise don't change a thing." I never did get invited to address the Joint Chiefs of the Armed Forces, but I'm certain they were presented information, and they had a general in their troops who was enthusiastically an ally.

The next day, I received an e-mail from a senior person in the NSA. He said, "Brian, you changed my life. I did what you suggested we do. I went home last night, and I told my family about you and the great presentation on Lesbian, Gay, Bisexual, and Transgender issues in the workplace. A couple of hours later, my oldest daughter came into the bedroom, and said, 'Dad, we need to talk. I'm a Lesbian.' And I did what you said to do, I said, 'Thank you, honey, for telling me.' Then she burst into tears, and I started crying, and we hugged and hugged. I told her I was going to get one of your books. I can't thank you enough. It wouldn't have happened if I hadn't said the word 'Lesbian' in a positive way."

Almost all my correspondence over these many years is stored in the Cornell Human Sexuality Archives, but Ray saved one card that he handed me several weeks ago. It reads:

"Brian. I can't tell you enough how much it meant to me to be in the audience at the NSA with you speaking to the group, and to me. I've admired and respected your wisdom, strength, and courage for many years, knowing also how much you love and feel for your work. It was a cherished memory for me that I will carry with me forever. You were so wonderful. I was so proud to be there as a member of the family. With much love."

And then, a few years ago, when my heterosexual high school classmate, Mark Walsh, retired from the NSA, he sent me a message saying that being part of the group that brought me in to speak on LGBTQ issues was the highlight of his career.

That affirmation made me very happy. My experience at the NSA was certainly one of my most satisfying. But, so too, was creating ripples of understanding among people in India, Japan, Australia, Singapore, and Hong Kong, especially knowing that it was the first time the rainbow flag had been planted in the workplace of some of those cultures.

I've received awards over the years, but there are no awards on shelves in our home, or pictures of me with famous people. I gave them or threw them all away. I was really touched to get the "Mary Lee Tatum" award from Planned Parenthood Leaders in Education (APPLE) and the "Selisse Berry Award" from Out and Equal. But the one I had the most fun with was the Legacy Award from the Stonewall National Museum & Archives. Carson Kressley flew down to present me with the award. Prior to me walking up to receive it, a video montage was created, starting with me debating on Miami television Anita Bryant Ministry. I heard actual gasps in the audience when they saw this very young, handsome, confident man tell the viewers why he was proud to be Gay. Ray was probably the only person in the room who knew me at age twenty-nine. The others only knew my gray hair.

The Stonewall National Museum told me that I had just five minutes to speak, and I promise you I practiced and practiced trying to squeeze a meaningful message beyond "thank you" into the timeframe. When I was heading toward the stage to receive the award from Carson and have our photo taken, I said to God, "You've got five minutes. Say what you want."

After thanking the board and staff for this honor, I told the audience that if I could break the award into 300 pieces, I'd send each of them home with recognition of how we all have a legacy to be proud of; that none of us have done it on our own. The seismic shift in cultural attitudes toward Lesbian, Gay, Bisexual, Transgender, and Queer people didn't happen just because Brian McNaught got fired for being Gay by *The Michigan Catholic*. Every LGBTQ person who has come out and put a face on the issue, and every ally who has stood up to their colleagues or clergy, are the ones who created the atmosphere in which it made perfect sense for the United States Supreme Court to rule in favor of marriage equality.

I told them the story of the man on the plane so that they might trust the ability of people to change their attitudes, even when those people are Evangelical Christians. And I told them about the question I got from God about singing my song. Receiving that award was a truly scared moment for me because I felt connected soul to soul with everyone in the room. They all stood to applaud at length when I finished after fifteen minutes. I know it was supposed to be five, but who among us has the courage to tell God to quit talking? The next day at a meeting of the Stonewall National Advisory Committee, we were asked to name something we learned the day before. I said that I was shocked by how much one could say in five minutes.

Chapter Thirty

Would You Take a Pill to Make You Straight?

Ray, Brit, and I left the high rise in New York when Ray retired from Lehman, and headed to our new home in San Francisco. Renovated and decorated by our friend, Monty Collins, it was a jewel box and had the most magnificent view of the Palace of Fine Arts. Our neighbors were all Straight, and with time became friends.

Every morning by seven, Ray and I would run through what was then Crissy Field, down to the Golden Gate Bridge, touch it, and head back home. At night, we'd often wander down to the marina and walk out along the breakwater as far as we could. We'd venture out to the Castro to see a live Christmas performance of the Gay Men's Chorus on the stage of the classic Castro Theater, and, of course, we saw *Beach Blanket Babylon*. We loved walking through the rainbow flags that hung on every post down the Castro. It felt very safe, as once did Key West until people yelled "faggots" at us out the window of a passing car. Is there any place that won't happen?

Living in San Francisco was not the experience of mecca that Ray and I had anticipated. We still think it's the most beautiful city and area in the country, but our sense was that there was an accommodation of Gay people because of our large presence; but we were tolerated rather than celebrated. Once Ray and I heard a lineman, up on a telephone pole, talking about the "faggots." Outside of the Castro, many Gay men we met were still cautious about being labeled as Gay. It wasn't that safe and affirming atmosphere we dreamed of. We only stayed three years in what we both think of as one of the most enchanting cities in the world. But we really left because of Brit.

On our trip to the first full summer in Provincetown, we flew from San Francisco to Boston and Brit traveled in cargo. I heard barking through much of the ride but wasn't concerned because Brit wasn't a barker. When we arrived at the Boston airport, I still heard constant barking, and thought, "The owners of that dog need to pick him up." I wandered over to the baggage claim area designated for dogs and saw that it was Brit who had been barking the entire time. Once we got our rental car to drive to P-Town, and Brit had settled down, he slept the entire way. That was his last experience of the cargo hold. For the next two years we drove with him cross-country. If we didn't stop to see any national parks, it would be a solid five-day drive. Otherwise, it was seven.

The best part of the drive each time was listening to the six-part interview Bill Moyers did with Joseph Campbell on *The Power of Myth*. Campbell, who wrote *The Hero with a Thousand Faces*, was the world's leading expert on mythology from culture to culture. He coined the phrase, "Follow your bliss."

Our repeated playing of the interview helped Ray and me make the huge step toward the awareness that every culture throughout history has developed stories with the same goal of understanding the same God. We'd combine the Campbell interview with daily readings from the *Tao te Ching*.

After San Francisco, we moved to Naples, Florida, at the suggestion of a Lesbian couple who said they had scouted the whole Eastern coast of the United States and all of Florida and thought we'd be happy there. We made great friends in Naples, such as Jack and Jean McGlynn with whom we met regularly for game night to play Mexican Train; but finding other like-minded people was a challenge.

There was a Catholic church a couple of blocks away in which I spent Good Fridays and often went to Mass. I loved the charismatic priest and gave him copies of all my books and DVDs to help him educate the congregation. Sadly, a very wealthy Catholic member of the parish got the diocese to remove him because he suspected that the priest was Gay. This is what upsets me most about the workings of many religious institutions. Money ultimately rules the day. I quit going to Mass in Naples.

I recall that when my family lived in Birmingham, Michigan, the pastor of St. Regis had come to the house because Dad had stopped his financial support of the parish. He objected to the pastor condemning from the pulpit the American war in Vietnam. Do power and money rule, or is it love? In response to my father's actions, my brother Tom and I hung our American flag upside down in front of the house to signal dire distress.

Hoping to be surrounded in Naples with people who shared Ray's and my values, we found refuge in the Unitarian Universalist congregation that was a magnet for every spiritually free soul in town. I started a monthly "Gay Movie Night" that was well attended, mostly by Straight Unitarians who wanted to learn more. I shared earlier our successful attempt to get the church to become a welcoming congregation. In Naples, most LGBTQ people who we encountered seemed less free than we did in acknowledging ourselves. I think that is changing.

For much of our relationship, Ray and I have taken advantage of any workshop aimed at our spiritual awaking. We did the Body Electric in Atlanta. Ray got a great deal out of a rebirthing exercise we did in the Bay Area. We also attended a training led by Jack Kornfield in the Spirit Rock Meditation Center. Jack had us fast in the morning and later we were each given one raisin. He told us to hold it in our mouths and to truly taste it. That one raisin was the best I've ever experienced. In Naples we were part of a Buddhist Sangha led by Fred Eppsteiner, a close friend of Thich Nhat Hanh. There, we sat and did a walking meditation through Fred's home. In Provincetown, we had our own weekly gathering of friends for meditation in our second-floor library.

In 2001, on our twenty-fifth anniversary, Ray and I drove to Vermont to get a civil union. At that time, Vermont was the only state that recognized Gay relationships as having legal status. Before the entire US accepted marriage equality, Ontario, Canada was the place to go. So, in 2003, we got married in a simple ceremony in the garden of a Unitarian church in Ottawa, the capitol of Ontario. Immediately afterwards, I contacted the editor of the conservative *Naples Daily News* and asked him to place our banns of marriage with all the heterosexual announcements. Instead, the newspaper did a big feature, with a photo, about our marriage. We were delightfully surprised and grateful.

After five years, we left Naples because no matter how hard we tried it just didn't feel like home. I once wore a "Provincetown" T-shirt to the grocery store and in the produce section, an elegant older woman looked at the T-shirt and said, "I hate Provincetown." I asked her "Why?" She looked me up and down and replied, "I'd rather not say." When we drove across the state to explore Fort Lauderdale, I wore the same T-shirt to a restaurant. All the young, diverse waitstaff walked to our booth and said, "We love P-Town." Both experiences made a big impression,

We bought a property and had a townhouse built in Fort Lauderdale, on SE Tenth Ave. near Las Olas, where we lived for sixteen years. There we hosted several social gatherings for the Stonewall National Museum and Archives (SNMA). In one photo we have around the sofa Fr. John McNeill, Elaine Noble, Robin Tyler, Joel Burns, Norm Kent, and Chuck Wolfe, all names of people who have made significant contributions of soul to our community.

Ray and I got involved with the Stonewall National Museum and Archives because of its mission. We share their commitment to documenting, preserving, and presenting the stories of the struggle of Lesbian, Gay, Bisexual, Transgender, and Queer people in the US and around the world. We want this for our generation and for all those in the future.

Over the many years of our relationship, Ray would find treasured artifacts from our community's history and buy them for me for my birthday, Christmas, Valentine's Day, and on many other occasions. There's a long list of our collected artifacts on my website. Some of our most prized items include a four-page handwritten letter from Susan B. Anthony on Suffrage stationery, and a leather-bound copy of collected works by Walt Whitman in which he crossed out lines of type in three different places and made last minute changes in his own handwriting. Only one hundred copies were printed and ours belonged to his best friend. We donated the priestly robes worn by Bill Johnson, the first openly Gay ordained minister, and a love letter from Hitler's best friend, Ernst Rohm, head of the Brownshirts, to his boyfriend, among hundreds of other items. Our donated items are held in a special collection at the Stonewall Museum.

In 2019 we downsized into a small two-bedroom home in Wilton Manors, a true Gay snow globe in southern Florida, only steps from Fort Lauderdale. Our young grandnephews and grandnieces miss the three-story elevator they loved to ride in the townhouse during their vacation visits. We live on the Middle River in a totally enclosed yard in which we've created a beautiful Zen garden with lots of bamboo, bougainvillea, orchids, wind chimes, bells, fountains, bird feeders, and hanging rainbow-colored glass. Ray and I are more than content to finally have the time just to look with love and gratitude at each other. We hold hands every night before dinner and give thanks for all the people we encountered that day, for those in need, and for the bounty of our lives, conscious of those who are hungry, homeless, and living in fear. We have everything we need. A grateful heart wants for nothing.

Both Ray and I have body ailments that slow us down. My sciatica can act up so badly, that a few times when I was taking our beloved Labradoodle, Lincoln, for a walk, I'd have to stop and stoop from the pain. My voice is lower and softer from the many years of public speaking, and I forget things easily. Yet, recently I did a one-hour Zoom presentation to Dr. Sandy Caron's human sexuality class at the University of Maine. When I finished and got off the iPad, I sought Ray out to tell him how beautifully it went. I didn't get lost in a story as I feared I might, and I felt my soul dancing with the students.

Ray has a bad knee and unceasing pain in his back. He has so much hardware holding his backbone together that he must go through airport security with special handling. But he's happy and has been a source of great joy for me since he first climbed into the red Opel and met me and Jeremy in 1976. We talked recently about how everything would have turned out so differently if he had a boyfriend at the time or if I had never moved from Detroit.

Because Ray took an early retirement from Lehman, he was able to travel with me to all my international speaking engagements. He'd take care of all the details of our travel in the area after my talk, such as going to New Zealand from Australia, or to Vietnam and Cambodia after I spoke in Singapore. We've kayaked through the Galapagos, and slept on its beaches, and the next day flew to Cusco to climb for five days through the Inca trail to Machu Picchu.

We've taken a romantic river cruise through China with other Gay male couples, and an ocean cruise to Alaska. We saw the celebration of Gay Pride in Thailand where the population is so Gay "because of the fertilizer they put on the mango trees." From London we went to Scotland and Wales where we visited the home of the Ladies of Llangollen, Eleanor Butler and Sarah Ponsonby, two upper-class Irish women who escaped in 1780 and lived as a couple for the remainder of their lives, both walking through town in top hats and capes. We financed all our travel with my speaking fees. Our favorite adventure was twelve days in Ghana and a safari in South Africa. My favorite animal is the elephant, and on our return from the last outing of our trip, I asked the Universe for the sight of just one more elephant. I teared up when I spotted one very regal one heading toward our jeep on the dusty road.

Toward the end of my travel, just before COVID, I decided I didn't want to fly six or more hours to give a talk, even if, as often happened, it was a series of talks. I was seventy-one or seventy-two when I told Ray that I didn't think I could make another trip. The travel, even flying in business class, and staying in beautiful hotel suites, was too stressful. I never wasted my time on the plane ride, though. I'd read something about the place I was going or reviewed the notes I had made when my hosts first contacted me. Or, I talked with the person sitting next to me on the plane, and maybe discovered after I told them why I was flying to Hong Kong, that they had a child or grandchild who had come out, or they'd think back about their Uncle Clem who never married but had a housemate for forty years.

Foolishly, about ten years ago, we loaned all our savings to friends who can't pay us back, so we now live on Social Security and some savings, but we are content and so very grateful that we have each other. We can't travel anymore because of physical disabilities and a much tighter budget, but we're completely happy at home together in what is the simple life we sought from the beginning. We now have an Aussiedoodle, named Sebastian, and live next door to a younger Gay male couple, Chris and Andrew, who keep a close eye on us, as do George and Anthony, all guardian angel gifts from the Spirit. We've both recently said that if we died tomorrow, we'd feel we had lived full, happy, and most satisfying lives.

One way that I have stayed involved in our struggle for equality is through my column in the Gay newspaper *Out South Florida*. My column was originally called "Two Guys and a Dog." We've had a dog in most of the years we've been together. Jeremy, the Irish setter, as I've said, is buried in the yard of our former home in Gloucester, Massachusetts, and Brit is buried beneath the pine tree in the back of our former home in Provincetown. Lincoln's ashes sit in a beautiful box waiting to be mixed in with Ray's and mine. He was an amazing service dog who we noticed one morning was sick to his stomach and that afternoon, at age six, we had to put him down because of pancreatic cancer that had spread to his liver. It took us months to get past the shock and pain of that loss. And, now, Sebastian is learning about the glories of life each minute of the day. He's already jumped into the pool twice and into the Middle River once and he's only been with us three and a half days. The column is now called "The Wise Snowy Owl."

Here we are, two Gay altar boys from Irish Catholic Midwestern families of seven, recently celebrating forty-eight years as a couple. A talk show host once asked me, "If I could give you a pill that would make you Straight, would you take it?" I replied that I would have at age six in 1954, and at age thirteen in 1961 when I was afraid of being discovered, but not since then.

"I love my life as a Gay man. It is full of joy, serenity, gratitude, and a sense of completion."

"Do you believe in God?" I'm asked. "Heavens yes," I say. "I've had too many experiences of God in all its forms not to believe. The Spirit owns me."

"What are you most grateful for?" "That's easy," I say. "It's the privilege of living at this time in history and having had the opportunity to positively impact so many lives. I worked very hard to keep the window glass clean so the light could shine through. I'm equally grateful for the storybook relationship I've had with Ray, not without its challenges but always filled with mutual respect, loving kindness, and a commitment to grow. The key to having a happy relationship is open and honest communication, patience, forgiveness, and a good sense of humor, all of which are required for maintaining an ongoing relationship with God."

There is no stopping the evolution of the Universe, and the Universe can't fully evolve until our presence as Gay, Lesbian, Bisexual, and Transgender people is treasured. Each generation of us has been and will take on new challenges to have our presence in the world celebrated.

I know deep in my heart that the Universe, in its ever-evolving manner, brought me forth to help others experience its Love. There is no separating my loving kindness from my being Gay. That is not to say that Straight men can't be and aren't givers of loving kindness, nor does it mean that all Gay men manifest loving kindness, but in my life experience they are inseparable.

It was the fault of the world's slow evolution that I was ever feared or despised. Ignorance prevailed, and people called me and other Gay, Lesbian, Bisexual, and Transgender people horrible names. But as global consciousness continues to evolve, the world will be embarrassed by its behavior toward us. We use the words "Gay Pride" to remind ourselves to keep our heads up high during this unconscious ignorance of who we are and why we're here.

I'm pleased with the books I've written and videos in which I'm featured, especially the first video *On Being Gay*, and the last, *Anyone Can Be an Ally, Speaking Up for an LGBTQ-Inclusive Workplace*. My rhyming children's story, *"What's 'Gay'?" Asked Mae*, was so perfectly illustrated by my good friend, Dave Woodford. Pioneering sex ed filmmaker Mark Schoen turned it into a three-minute animated movie and won the prize for "Best Animated Movie" at the Toronto LGBTQ Movie Festival. Mark, who is Straight, had called me to say, "I read your book to a Gay couple with kids last night. They cried. How about we make a movie?" What makes this movie super special for me is that the voices of the two characters, Mae and her cousin Ray, are those of our grandniece and grandnephew Auden and Easton. (To see the film, go to my website at www.brian-mcnaught.com.)

Coming full circle, it feels good to give Catholic Bishop Tom Gumbleton of Detroit the last word. He wrote before his death, "When you were fired as a *Michigan Catholic* columnist, I regret that I did not object to what happened to you . . . my reaction to you was in the very least insensitive and certainly a cause of pain for you. I regret this very much . . . I continue to admire all you have done to be a voice for the Gay community in the church, and society on the local and international stage. Many are indebted to your commitment, and I am one of them."

Glossary of Terms

It's very understandable for people of all sexual orientations and gender identities to have trouble keeping up with what feels like an ever-changing landscape of terminology on sexual attraction and gender. We know that in today's parlance "Straight" means that we're attracted to people of the other sex. "Cis-gender" refers to those of us who are totally comfortable identifying with the sex we were named at birth. "It's a boy!" "It's a girl."

When I began my process of coming out you were either Gay, Bisexual, or Straight. Additionally, you either liked being your sex or you didn't. Since then, there have been a number of "colors" added to the rainbow community, colors that have been there all along but invisible to the average person. Today, you might see LGBTQQIAA2S+ or some form of those letters and numbers in an acronym. Here are what the letters currently represent.

The "L" is for "Lesbian," females who are attracted emotionally and/or sexually to other females.

The "G" is for "Gay," a term used for males who are emotionally and/or sexually attracted to other males. It can also be used by some to mean all homosexuals, male and female.

The "B" is for "Bisexuals" who have the capacity to be attracted to both males and females, but rarely equally. Bisexuals usually have a "major" and a "minor." Many Bisexuals embrace the terms "Gay" or "Lesbian," because of their desire to affirm that part of themselves that is homosexual. It also affords them easy access to the Gay and Lesbian culture.

The "T" is for "Transgender," an umbrella term that covers transsexuals, cross-dressers, and anyone else who feels that their gender, "man" or "woman," doesn't fit their biological sex, "male" or "female."

The "Q" is for "Queer," a word that for some is an umbrella term for anything other than the norm. It can mean "Gay," "Lesbian," "Bisexual," "Transgender," "Gender Queer," "Sexually Fluid," "Intersex," and "Non-Binary." Because the word "Queer" is experienced with a flinch by many Gay men who hoped never to be called that growing up, and because the word "Queer" doesn't tell us anything specific about the individual, I don't like using it, but also don't want those who identify as "Queer" to feel left out.

The "I" is for "Intersex," individuals whose sex is unclear based on exterior genital features, interior chromosomes, and levels of estrogen and testosterone hormones. However, when asked at birth based solely on the infant's genitals, it is named to be a male or female. If the genitalia is unclear, the name given is Intersex, as opposed to the less acceptable "hermaphrodite."

The "A" is for "Asexual," who are people without sexual interest or drive.

Letters are sometimes added to the acronym, such as another "Q" for people who are "Questioning." You'll also see an extra "A" for "Allies."

2S is for "Two Spirit," individuals who were and are important shamans of Indigenous people.

At the end of the acronym, you may see a "+" sign. That is supposed to take in any group not yet identified with a letter, such as people who identify themselves as "Non-Binary." People who are Non-Binary reject the social construct of male and female gender. They usually prefer the use of the pronoun "they."

I've always made the distinction between "homosexual" and "Gay." A person who tolerates their same-sex attractions is "homosexual" and a person who celebrates their same-sex attractions is "Gay."

My hope is that everyone is happy with what they name themselves and with how they live their lives. I don't use the word "Queer" to identify myself, nor do I put preferred pronouns under my name. The rainbow stickers on our car are the traditional colors that were usually used. That's just me.

In writing this memoir, I wanted to be as inclusive as possible, but from 1982 to 1984 I was the mayor of Boston's liaison to the Gay community. We didn't have acronyms for ourselves back then, but in my mind "Gay" took in all of us.

I don't like using the acronym LGBTQ+ because it allows us not to say the words "Lesbian," "Gay," "Bisexual," "Transgender," and "Queer."

But sometimes, it feels tedious to the reader to repeatedly see all the words in a sentence. A second problem with the acronym LGBTQ+ is that some groups feel left out, such as people who are Intersex. They don't much like having their lives represented by a "+" sign, any more than I did when I was referred to as "other." College and corporate spokespersons used to say, "We're concerned about the discrimination faced by women, people of color, and others."

When I came out to my folks, I didn't tell them that I was LGBT. They would have had no idea what I meant. The word "Gay" is sacred to me because I fought so hard to keep it a secret, so hard to say it, and so hard to have it not just tolerated or accommodated by me and by others but celebrated.

You may wonder why I capitalize the words Gay, Lesbian, Bisexual, Transgender, Queer, and Intersex, among others in our rainbow community. I've also capitalized the word Straight. Why? I initially didn't understand the capitalization of the word Black when referring to an African American. However, there is a color black and the term African American doesn't include a lot of Black people from the Caribbean. It's also a recognition of the unique history and circumstances of being a Black person. I asked a very smart, and wise Black friend of mine, Pam Wilson, about capitalizing the word White, and she agreed that for the same reasons used to capitalize Black, White is more than a color when referring to a person.

I feel that just as the word "gay" can mean "lighthearted and carefree," when referring to a person whose life has been strongly impacted, and in some cases defined by their sexual orientation, the word "Gay" should also be capitalized, and so should the word "Straight."

In this memoir, my use of the word Gay to also represent Lesbians and Bisexuals reflects my age and not my bias. When I came out in 1974 as Gay, the other words weren't commonly used. I think that by now, most Lesbian, Gay, Bisexual, Transgender, and Queer people, along with our Straight allies, know that I've got their back and would do nothing to diminish the significance of their unique souls.

About the Author

Brian McNaught's website is www.brian-mcnaught.com. His e-mail address is brian@brian-mcnaught.com. Many of his books, and nearly all of his DVDs are available for free viewing on the site. The three-minute animated movie, *"What's 'Gay'?" Asked Mae*, based upon his children's book by the same name, can be viewed on his site.

Brian's bimonthly podcast with Hayley Evans, called "Are You Happy Without the Movie?" can be accessed through YouTube or on Facebook. His newspaper column is available on his Facebook site and in *Out South Florida*, available in both print and electronic forms. His site "A Parliament of Snowy Owl Elders" is on Facebook.

www.ingramcontent.com/pod-product-compliance
Lightning Source LLC
Chambersburg PA
CBHW030854170426
43193CB00009BA/612